Looking Both Ways

A Theology for Mid-life

David J. Maitland

John Knox Press
ATLANTA

Library of Congress Cataloging in Publication Data

Maitland, David Johnston, 1922–
  Looking both ways.

  1. Christian life—1960– . 2. Middle age—
Religious life. 3. Theology, Doctrinal—Popular works.
I. Title.
BV4501.2.M3295   1985   248.8'4   84-48514
ISBN 0-8042-1127-2

© copyright John Knox Press 1985
10 9 8 7 6 5 4 3 2 1
Printed in the United States of America
John Knox Press
Atlanta, Georgia 30365

Acknowledgment is made for permission to quote from the following sources:

To St. Martin's Press, Incorporated for lines taken from THE ARTIST BY HIMSELF: Self-Portraits from Youth to Old Age. Edited by Joan Kinneir. Copyright © 1980 by Joan Kinneir. St. Martin's Press, Inc.

To Westerheim Press for use of Bill Holm's poem, "Genealogy," which appeared in the centennial publication, *Happy Birthday, Minneota*. Westerheim Press, Minneota, MN.

To G. P. Putnam's Sons for lines taken from *England Have My Bones*, T. H. White. Copyright 1936 by T. H. White. G. P. Putnam's Sons.

To Harper & Row for eight (8) lines from "A Letter of Recommendation" in AMEN by Yehuda Amichai. Translated from the Hebrew by the author and Ted Hughes. Copyright © 1977 by Yehuda Amichai. Reprinted by permission of Harper & Row, Publishers, Inc.

To Random House, Inc. and Alfred S. Knopf, Inc. for lines taken from *Markings*, Dag Hammarskjöld. Translated by Leif Sjoberg and W. H. Auden. Translation copyright © 1964 by Alfred A. Knopf, Inc., and Faber and Faber, Ltd. Foreword copyright © 1964 by W. H. Auden. Originally published in Swedish as Vägmärken. © Albert Bonniers Förlag AB 1963. Alfred A. Knopf, Inc. And for lines taken from *Invisible Man*, Ralph Ellison. Copyright © 1947, 1948, 1952 by Ralph Ellison. Random House, Inc.

To Harcourt Brace Jovanovich, Inc. for lines taken from"Little Gidding" in FOUR QUARTETS, copyright 1943 by T.S. Eliot; renewed 1971 by Esme Valerie Eliot. Reprinted by permission of Harcourt Brace Jovanovich, Inc. Also for lines taken from "Choruses from 'The Rock'" in COLLECTED POEMS 1909–1962 by T.S. Eliot, copyright 1936 by Harcourt Brace Jovanovich, Inc.; copyright © 1963, 1964 by T.S. Eliot. Reprinted by permission of the publisher.

Preface

A few years ago I published a book which reflected understandings to which I came while struggling with the issues of my middle years. The reaction of readers has been heartening: by their appreciation they provided reassurance that my experience was not unique. Thus, in consequence of seeing their own lives in more positive light, they have reassured me about my own.

The emphasis of that book was primarily on what I had learned from social scientists about the stages through which lives pass. Less attention was paid to theology than I originally intended. As I indicated then, I was doing theology backwards: paying close attention to my actual experience in the hope that this might illumine my understanding of Christian faith. In this I was sufficiently successful to prompt one reviewer to suggest a sequel in which I might try to do theology forwards. The present work attempts that.

Because of who I am, however, the same dialectic is present: it is with the *relationship* of human experience and traditional Christian faith that I am still concerned.

Neither the life cycle nor Christian doctrine is a series of unrelated entities. At any life stage a particular set of tasks determines the configuration of one's total resources. For example, those in the process of proving themselves capable of intimacy have less need of their capacity for solitude than may be required at another time. Relevant resources come, hopefully, to hand; those less relevant to that task are, for the time, marginal. Similarly, to focus upon one doctrinal affirmation means that the other ingredients will be arranged in a configuration determined by their relevance to the item one is seeking to understand.

This dynamic understanding of the similar character of both the cycle of life and of Christian faith indicates why clarifications will be neither easy nor to everyone's satisfaction. Not only are we working with two sets of variables, but with the integral relation-

ship between them. . . . The possibilities for illumination of both
issues in personal maturation and in Christian doctrine are considerable; the dangers are no less real. (David J. Maitland, *Against The
Grain: Coming Through Mid-Life Crisis*, New York: Pilgrim, 1981,
pp. 157–58.)

Only the emphasis has changed, and that probably not enough to satisfy all readers. In an attempt to assure address of issues central to a
classical Christianity, I have concentrated on most of the articles of
"The Apostles' Creed." I have not tried to explicate these primarily in
terms of their original intent; certainly there is little discussion here
of the many historical attempts to understand them. Others have written these books.

What I have attempted is to look at the apostolic affirmations with
an eye informed by the issues of mid-life as these have been experienced in late twentieth-century America. I have done so on two assumptions: (1) that it is necessary to consider any affirmation from
some perspective—in this case my own life development, and (2) that
it is in the attempt to relate such entities that both may be illumined.
Neither experience nor doctrine exist apart; both raise questions for
each other. In the difficult process of trying to look both ways, we may
find a theology for human growth—and limits. Such is my hope.

At least because of its unfamiliarity to some readers, my emphasis
on the need to correlate experience and convictions must be explained. What may seem initially alien is central to the way in which
we shall proceed throughout. As a method of doing theology this is
not unknown in Christian history, but it is different from the way in
which much theology has been written.

For many people it is religious texts which are exclusively authoritative. Depending on one's tradition, the Bible and/or one of the creeds
may be absolute. From such sources instruction for behavior is derived. This is probably the ordinary way in which believers view their
sacred literatures. We should be quite clear about the importance of
such texts for all who profess Christian faith. There is no question here
of abandoning the literature by which the churches have been shaped.
Those who wrote the Bible and fashioned the creeds recorded the ways
in which they believed that the living God had been present to their
experience. That material constitutes one of the foci—historical and
personal experience being the other—with which we shall work
throughout this book.

Theology, however, is not merely a restatement of the biblical nar-
rative. In its original form, which produced a new mode of literature,
it was the attempt of thoughtful writers to bring together the dynamic
legacy of Judaism—the tradition of the God who acts—with the more

static categories of Greek philosophy. Because circumstances and historical sensibilities change, that work must be done in every generation. As Christians we may not simply appropriate unchanged from the past some individual interpreter as exclusively normative. Even the writings of the New Testament have their periods of relatively greater and lesser importance. Everything depends on the realities of any particular period of history or personal circumstances of which believers must make sense. For example, the euphoria of the long-childless couple to whom a child is born will be nurtured by texts which may mean little to those recovering from a family death. Or, a nation in the full flush of arrogant power will need to hear words to which a defeated people might be deaf. Proclamation of God's judgment would be as appropriate in one instance as may be the assurance of compassion in another. There is no way to escape responsibility for doing theology in our own time and from our particular experience.

The reason for this continuing obligation can be simply stated: we are both like and unlike our predecessors in the faith. Like them in that we, too, fall short of the glory of God; unlike them in that some of the causes of our failure are distinctive to life in the late twentieth century. Like them inasmuch as we are in comparable need of reason for hope in adversity; unlike them, perhaps, in the particular causes of our hardness of heart. This is not to argue the utter uniqueness of our experience in this place and time. Shylock reminded his anti-Semitic fellow Venetians of their common humanity.

> "I am a Jew. . . . [Am I not] fed with the same food, hurt with the same weapons, subject to the same diseases, healed by the same means . . . as a Christian is? If you prick us, do we not bleed? if you tickle us, do we not laugh? if you poison us, shall we not die?" (William Shakespeare, *The Merchant of Venice*, III.1.)

At least quantitatively we have much in common with all who have gone before us.

These similarities should not obscure what may be our distinctive temptations and opportunities. Christian proclamation often presumes a complete identity of human experience in all times and places. While it is important to be able to recognize similarities between our own experience and that of all others, it is no less vital to be able to claim those general experiences which are distinctive to men and women of these times. For example, are not the challenges to faith forever different for those who live after such events as the Holocaust and the splitting of the atom? The depths of human depravity have been exposed as never before and the potential for utter self-destruction after 1945 is a reality unknown to all earlier generations.

Beyond that, it is equally crucial to be in touch with and responsive to the experience of our particular lives, especially to where we are in life's stages. This is where we should be most alive to what is happening in and through us. It is in this dimension of our lives that we should be most responsive to God's chastening and renewing presence. That we are not suggests how effectively we have been discouraged from paying attention to our own life-giving or life-denying experience. We may be told as Christians, for example, that we should incorporate suffering in our lives. However, few are likely to do this until they discover in their own experience—perhaps by a surprising awareness of the fragility of all lives or by being helped to acknowledge those losses which are part of mid-life—that to be human is to suffer. Only at this point may the abstractions of much Christian exhortation became concrete and empowering ingredients of an emerging self-understanding.

It is for such simple, but largely neglected, reasons that I find it necessary as a Christian to keep my distinctive, incomplete experience in dialogue with the more universal experiences of believers of other times and places. Our lives are similar but not identical. I am not at liberty to dissolve my uniqueness into the larger experience of others. Because it accounts for more of reality than I may ever be able to appropriate is why I would not remain ignorant of the larger tradition. I am convinced, however, that I will only be able to grow in that direction as I am effectively in touch with the realities of my own, actual experience. For good and ill, I am so limited. That limitation I take to be evidence of my status as a creature of God. The glorious paradox is that it is by assenting to this status, rather than attempting to deny it, that I become able to extend my limits.

By "experience" I refer primarily to the natural fact of aging. I take this process, which has gone on from the moment of our birth, to be the universal means by which we become who we are. Within the life-long passage of time there are identifiable stages with tasks distinctive to each. (Some of these are described in Gail Sheehy's *Passages: Predictable Crises of Adult Life* [New York: Dutton, 1976].) I further assume that there are times during this process when we are particularly sensitive to deeper questions about the meaning of our lives than are accounted for by the roles we perform. The middle years I recognize as one such time when we may be especially teachable. In those years we are often made aware of both our mortality and of the unavoidable transiency of many things we have pursued and valued. Despite its lack of drama, I assume the experience of gradual aging to be a more reliable stimulant to religious reflections than other natural promptings. The stages of a life are both more immediate and less ambivalent than are the "evidences" of God in nature. It is, of course, not necessary that anybody use the experience of these stages as the means for his or her maturation in faith. Because of both inner resistance to change and negative societal attitudes, there is much that discourages such religious usage of life's stages. Finally, I am convinced that we are insufficiently encouraged to pay attention to these mid-life experiences. We prefer to act as though we could, by ignoring them, avoid the need to incorporate into our maturing self-understanding the things they have to tell us about ourselves.

By this effort to be indifferent to our experience of growing older, we diminish what I believe to be God-given means for the nurture of Christian faith. As does the psalmist (cf. Ps. 90:12), I believe that there is something crucial which we must begin to learn from our experience. He beseeches God to teach him to number his days that he may get a wise heart. I suggest that this process requires us to pay loving attention to our experience in order that we may recognize in it the questions which are being raised about the meaning of our gradually unfolding lives. For it is only as we are willing to live with the questions which our experience poses that it is possible for God gradually to make clear to us directions in which answers lie.

This is the key to the method of correlation which we shall use: to bring our actual experience into dialogue with the articles of Christian faith formulated by those who believed that they saw God's presence in their experience which, as we have said, is both like and unlike our own.

It is through such lenses that I have looked at one of the apostolic affirmations of faith. For me it has been deeply instructive to do this. In order that the reader may be familiar with some of my experience, the opening, briefer chapters provide a sketch of the middle years. First, a reminder of the largely unavoidable losses of mid-life and of our reluctance to acknowledge them. Second, a more autobiographical chapter in which, by a review of my relationships with the three women most important in my life, we may appreciate the need for self-love with reference to the conflicts which persist in lives. With this overview of human experience I proceed to an examination of the major articles of "The Apostles' Creed" in the hope of finding there a theology for human development and limits. As always, the double task is to discover how these creedal articles illumine our experience as late twentieth-century persons and how the questions generated by such experiences may cast light—or shadows—upon the convictions of those who fashioned the Creed. The work is endlessly dialogical. Given my personal history and my understanding of God's dynamic and creative presence in the lives of men and women of all times and places it could not be otherwise. Hopefully, some light will be shed as we proceed upon the important issues of self-love and self-denial which are the focus of the concluding chapter.

Some acknowledgments are necessary and may be interesting to the reader. Much of what follows was written during a sabbatical partly spent in Oxford, England. Several persons there and one institution were particularly encouraging: Peter Spicer, since retired from Oxford University Press; Professor Marjorie Reeves of St. Anne's College; Tony Tucker of the counseling staff of Oxford Polytechnic; Caryl Micklem, minister of St. Columba's Presbyterian Church; Dr. Harold Harley, physician and neighbor; Bill and Anne Williams, dear friends; John and Barbara Winfrey, American academicians on leave. While I wish to acknowledge their friendly interest, I am quick to exclude them from responsibility for anything that appears here. The same must be said of Principal Donald Sykes of Mansfield College. As always, he and Marta provided a warm welcome to a place where, some years ago, I directed summer study programs for North Americans.

It is perilous to express appreciation to specific people, some of whom may be surprised to discover their importance to the work of a temporary, resident alien. More serious is the possibility of overlooking somebody no less important. During any period of residence abroad there are many people who, by their manner, provide important reassurances: these include landlords, shopkeepers, delivery people, groundskeepers, and public transportation staff. By gracious acceptance of our presence in their noble city, they enabled me to get on with this work.

Closer to home there are two friends to whom I would express special appreciation: Professors James B. Nelson of the United Theological Seminary of the Twin Cities and Bruce B. Roberts, Chair of the Psychology Department, St. Olaf College. Both have read portions of the manuscript and made constructive suggestions for its improvement. For willingness to take time for this from very busy schedules, I thank them. Belatedly, I would acknowledge Carol Bly's extended and helpful comments to an earlier draft of this essay. Always a stimulating conversationalist and speaker, she encouraged me to pursue an understanding of Christian life informed by psychology.

There are two professional acquaintances to whom I wish also to express appreciation for support and counsel. Were we ever able to spend time together, both The Reverend Richard Swanson and Dr. John G. Gibbs could probably become personal friends. "Swanie," who was for years the able Chaplain of Augustana College, Rock Island, invited me to deliver lectures to the Annual Pastors' Conference of the Illinois Synod, The Lutheran Church in America. Some of the material is here incorporated. Having responded favorably to an earlier book, John

Gibbs has thoughtfully encouraged me to prepare the present manuscript. I am indebted to both men.

At the John Knox Press I am indebted to two persons who improved my original manuscript: Patricia Steinbrook and Joan Crawford. As Supervising Editor Ms. Crawford combines competence, persuasive prodding, and a delightful Carolina/Georgia accent. I am especially grateful for her help.

While I hope that she knows how much I value her and our life together, I would not fail to indicate that Betsy was my almost constant companion during eight glorious and productive months in the States and Europe. As I said in a report upon returning home:

> The rich variety of experience—setting up apartments, making and keeping travel plans, meeting friends at many points along the way and getting acquainted with new people, making the myriad choices which inhere in such a schedule—enhanced my relationship with my wife. This had much to do with the fact that we were largely in control of all of our time and were in general agreement as to how we wanted to spend it.

For her nurturing and stimulating companionship through several of life's stages, I am deeply and permanently grateful.

David J. Maitland

Contents

This book is dedicated to all those friends and organizations—churches, colleges, clubs, media, etc.—who, in response to an earlier publication, have challenged me to clarifications of which I was once incapable. As has been true all of my life, though now more readily acknowledged, I get by with a lot of help from others! To all of you, only some of whom know who they are, my sincere thanks.

It is dedicated also to those who fashioned an early apostolic creed and who, in succeeding generations, have tried to incorporate its affirmations in their lives.

I believe in God the Father Almighty, Maker of heaven and earth;

And in Jesus Christ His only Son our Lord; who was conceived by the Holy Ghost, born of the Virgin Mary, suffered under Pontius Pilate, was crucified, dead, and buried; He descended into hell; the third day He rose again from the dead; He ascended into heaven, and sitteth on the right hand of God the Father Almighty; from thence He shall come to judge the quick and the dead.

I believe in the Holy Ghost; the holy Catholic Church; the communion of saints; the forgiveness of sins; the resurrection of the body; and the life everlasting. Amen.

I. Mid-life's Cluster of Losses

I have had many opportunities to talk about mid-life and to learn from the experiences of others. Two things are immediately clear: (1) the variety of ways in which people come to their middle years and (2) the subtle common threads which characterize these experiences. Thus is preserved both the distinctiveness of each life and the reassuring commonality of lives. My experience is never identical with anybody else's, but there is enough similarity to assure that I have not lost my humanity in middle age. We may have strayed from the path in a dark forest but, despite fears to the contrary, we are not hopelessly and forever lost.

One of the clues to finding our way again lies in acknowledging the reality of the losses which occur unavoidably in life's middle years. This will not be as easy as it sounds since the acknowledgment implies the need for *internal* changes which, initially and feeling alone, we will be tempted to resist. Gradually, and as we discover that others share our perplexities, the resistance may diminish. After we have acquainted ourselves with some of these losses, as we shall shortly, we shall suggest reasons for our initial denial of them. By these discussions I hope that it will be possible for the reader to admit the inevitability of, and begin to see the gains latent in, the God-given trauma of mid-life.

At points it will be necessary to restate some basic matters. For example, following our identification here of life's losses and our reluctance to acknowledge them, we shall review some of the understandings of Erik H. Erikson with which I began to find my way out of the dark forest. These are, I believe, congenial to the work of Christian faith. The chapter will conclude with a reminder of the transiency of the visions by which our lives have, to this time, been empowered.

But first, let me say that more often than not the onset of mid-life is *not* very dramatic. I say this both because it is true for most people and because media hype is not interested in ordinary experience. Like most of the inflated programming to which we are overexposed, interviewers are looking for the extreme responses to something currently deemed newsworthy. Such reactions—the spouse who walks out of what appeared to be a model family, the executive who abandons a position envied by many, dramatic changes of lifestyle—interest me minimally.

This is, in part, because such has not been my experience nor is it true for most people. I remain with my first and only wife, enjoy good relations with our grown children, and am well into the third decade of a job which has not lost all of its appeal. Thus, I probably have little to say to those in whose dramatic changes the media are apparently exclusively interested. In their preoccupation with the abnormal, I sense the pathos—if not the evil—of media which are obliged to come up daily with something new.

While it is true that extreme symptoms of change are more easily recognized than those which are more subtly depleting one's energies—like an unrecognized ailment—I am put off by media preoccupation with only extreme evidences of mid-life traumas. As a society we are little helped by such reporting. The subtle ways in which we are reminded in mid-life that things are unavoidably changing are more widespread than are more dramatic behaviors. We need to be able to recognize that gradual changes are also serious and deserve respect if we are to be helped to come to terms with them. They are opportunities for growth rather than material for headlines or two-minute media analysis. It is only *gradually* that we are able to admit that, without anything being dramatically different, we sense change occurring. One of the important reasons why many experience alarm in their middle years is that they have little control over what is happening.

It should not surprise us, given the gradualness of the onset and the painful growth expected of us, that denial is our first reaction to mid-life. It is bewildering and the evidences may be minimal. We tend to hope that, like the haze which gradually replaces clear skies and may be the harbinger of a storm, it will miss us. The rain will fall elsewhere—maybe. Let us admit that, initially, we are likely to deny any danger. It is hypochondriacal to be preoccupied with possibly ominous symptoms.

For most of us, however, the storm finds its way to our lives. But though the picnic may have to be postponed, farm and garden will quickly be renewed by the rain. So, I believe, it can be for us in mid-life *if* we acknowledge that disturbances are already at work in our lives. These tremors are, I believe, from God. Like the plants and flowers, we may be renewed by the storm.

Those who will have the most trouble acknowledging the presence of tremors are those who have been for decades most self-neglectful. Not so strangely once one thinks upon it, these will also be the men and women in the helping professions or those, like some parents, whose focus has largely been on others' well-being. It is at least ironic that those who have long given themselves to others, who have recognized external needs and responded consistently to them, often have the greatest difficulty taking their own needs seriously. It may be part of the price to be paid by those who have overdone self-denial. It could be tragic, for *the* issue of mid-life is this: how do I wish to spend the balance of my life? This is no exhortation to selfishness. Rather, because of the passing of largely externally prompted agenda of one's earlier years, people unavoidably reach a stage where it is difficult to avoid self-acquaintance. God help those who, at that point, continue to live either as though they had no wishes or that their wishes are valueless. We do not become indifferent to others' needs by acknowledging our own; we become able to help others appropriately as we realize how needfully like them we are.

Three convictions underlie this chapter: (1) that the middle decades are for *everybody* times of great change, (2) that the gains latent in these traumas are largely undervalued, and (3) that those who have overdone self-denial have probably cared more faithfully for others than for themselves.

Such persons at mid-life get a double whammy: they both share the human predicament and either are not allowed or cannot allow themselves to acknowledge that they, too, are plagued. That these issues may be part of God's pedagogy is my more important and elusive conviction. We avoid them at our peril.

The onset of mid-life's unavoidable changes forces many such persons to begin to face the consequences of extended self-neglect. Especially as we are required then to come to terms with the question of our *long-term* usefulness, we may discover that we have been poor stewards of whatever gifts God has provided us. The issue at mid-life is not whether or not we have been energetic and winsome during our early adulthood. Most probably have been so. Rather, as energies naturally diminish, the question is whether or not we are sufficiently acquainted with ourselves and able to deepen that self-understanding in order that we may continue to mature as persons and, thereby, become ever more useful in our later years. There is no way in which we should try to live in our fifties as in our twenties. We are not the people we were then. Fundamental to our stewardship is the ability to pay attention, as we have often failed to do, to our own needs and real potential.

It will be on the basis of both Scripture and social science observations about the needs of people in the caring professions that I shall argue for the need and rightness of paying such attention to ourselves.

The text is in Jesus' summary of the Law:

"You shall love the Lord your God with all your heart, with all your soul, and with all your mind. This is the great and first commandment. And a second is like it, You shall love your neighbor as yourself. On these two commandments depend all the law and the prophets." (Matt. 22:37–40.)

There is biblical warrant for some kind of self-caring. We postpone consideration of that until later. Before we can attend to possible resolutions, we must first identify and *feel* the issues. Answers before questions are of little enduring value.

The relevant understanding from social science is equally pithy; ". . . human nature being what it is, the man who pours out his . . . energy in confirming others will need more and not less confirmation of himself. . . . This makes the [caring person] unusually dependent on the confirmation he can get from friends and family, and especially from colleagues . . ." (Leslie H. Farber, *Ways of the Will: Essays Toward a Psychology and Psychopathology of Will*, New York: Harper & Row, 1968, p. 173). This assertion exposes the fundaments of our self-neglect. We have not taken seriously the depleting consequences of our self-denial. We have either presumed that our resources for self-confirmation were endless or, when it was available—and probably not often enough—we have tried to let the approval of others substitute for rather than being the basis of the more difficult work of renewal. At mid-life it is our self-image which is up for review!

Thank God for mid-life! It aggravates the chafing which we have long tried to ignore. It is something like going to the doctor with a minor complaint. The doctor often says either that the situation has to worsen before a diagnosis is possible—or that the symptoms may go away. I am convinced that, as Christians, we must not just let the mid-life symptoms disappear. There is no way back to our earlier years. It is our soul that is at stake: we are being invited by God to move beyond preoccupation with self-image to the search for self-knowledge!

In no sense is this task obligatory. Most people actually refuse it, often apparently with impunity. Dr. William A. Nolen is but one who assures us that, ". . . the crisis will pass." (Cf. "Male Menopause: Myth or Mid-Life Reality?" *Reader's Digest*, June 1981, in which he describes five simple things to do and to avoid during the time of turbulence.)

To do nothing *is* a way to survive. To do nothing, however, may be to miss the last major opportunity to discover what or who it is for which our hearts are endlessly restless. In the process of stepping back from reliance on our self-images, we will begin to discover some of our own exciting and frightening depths. In these depths, which are only partly subject to our direct control, we encounter evidences of the presence of that God whom we profess to see in Jesus as the Christ. Hidden deep within each of us, long concealed by cultural and even religious attitudes is the potential self to which God would endlessly give life. The potential for growth never ends, nor does our need for it. If we are to be ever more fully men and women of God, we may never be content with last week's or last year's good work. As we accumulate experience we should become ever more life-giving vehicles of the gracious God whom we profess to serve. As we become more vulnerable to life, to developments within ourselves which time occasions, as we allow God to confirm those things about ourselves which we have long tried to conceal, we will become ever more adequate confirmers of others. That there is a price for such growth will be no surprise.

As always, that there might be resurrections there must be prior deaths. This is *the* momentous faith issue at mid-life. Without immediately rejecting anything of our past, all of which is being shaken by the unavoidable losses at mid-life, we are invited to review the self-images by which we have controlled our experience to date. To accept the invitation is agonizing for all. In this death, however, all is not loss—though it may seem to be initially. If we persist, we will discover that there are false burdens to relinquish—obligations arising from the inauthenticity of our prevailing self-image.

Let's now recall some of the ways in which all lives are disturbed during the middle years. After recollecting the cluster of unavoidable losses, we shall think about why we resist acknowledging our condition. Finally, I want to say some things about the Christian faith for those on the mid-life plateau.

A Cluster of Losses

On a trip to New England a couple of years ago, I saw several signs which I want to use as introductions to each major section of this chapter. The first was on the Molly Stark Highway east of Bennington, Vermont. On a particularly steep descent stood the following sign: "Runaway Truck Escape Route." Part way down the hill was a diversionary road for vehicles whose brakes failed. That sign seemed to characterize the mid-life experience: the sense of being out of control. I was reminded of a line in the great Black musical, Green Pastures. As he saw valuables floating by in the flood, Noah exclaimed, "Everything that was nailed down has come loose!" For good reasons, that's often how a person feels in the middle years. One is unavoidably subject to a cluster of losses. Some of these are obvious; others less so.

Among those losses which are clear and undeniable are the following, not necessarily in the order in which experienced: the loss of one's youthfulness, the death of parents, the maturation of one's children, the loss of friends—and often less obvious—work disenchantment. Let us look briefly at each of these.

By various evidences—the loss and/or graying of one's hair, diminished energy, slower recuperation from illness—it begins to become apparent that one is no longer young. Often accompanying these evidences is an increasing existential awareness of one's own mortality. That which we long knew intellectually—that someday we, too, would die—no longer seems as remote as formerly. This awareness of one's finitude is often furthered by the deaths of parents. Not only is this usually a grievous loss, but it catapults one into the unfamiliar role of being a family elder. Further, during the middle years one's children mature. No matter how much one has desired their increasing independence, one loses the privilege of being the parent of children who needed us more than they do in adolescence/early adulthood. Often this loss leaves parents uncertain about what it is that, in their unfamiliar freedom, they now want to do with their lives. As the result of years of living with *deferred* gratification—the needs of children often having taken priority over all else—such parents may not only *not* know what they really want, they may even be unsure that they have a *right* to do whatever they like.

In addition to these unavoidable family-related losses, one often loses—either by death or by the mobility of society—old and trusted friends. This was a particularly poignant loss during my own middle years. The fact that it took me almost a decade to acknowledge the reality of my deprivation suggests how willfully blind we can be to the importance of significant relationships. For most of us, there are ordinarily only a few true friends. In close friendships, which are not to be confused with the much wider range of acquaintances which most of us have, we are free to share significant facts about ourselves. The absence of such persons is not a loss which we may ignore with impunity. There are periods of lives when friendships are more easily established. They probably do not come as easily at fifty as at half that age. On this score, there is some ancient Jewish wisdom:

> Do not forsake an old friend,
> For a new one is not equal to him.
> A new friend is new wine.
> When it grows old, you will enjoy drinking it. (Ben Sirach, quoted in E. Beier, ed., *Wit and Wisdom of Israel*, Mt. Vernon, NY: Peter Pauper Press, 1968, p. 41.)

In addition to these reasonably evident losses, there are at least three which are more subtle: (1) the loss of absolute certainty, (2) the loss of a sense of one's invulnerability, and (3) the loss of naiveté about one's single-mindedness.

The certainties of my youth and early-adulthood—the ease with which I once saw things as good or bad—have been modified by experience. Learning about the varied ways by which people put their lives together, each of which has at least some validity, has made me much less judgmental than I once was. While I am not suggesting the loss of all one's power of discrimination, the passage of time reminds one of the uneven resources with which persons cope with their lives. Behavior which some achieve with ease may remain permanently beyond the grasp of others; tasks at which many fail, others handle almost without thought. We are not equal in abilities. Increasingly, I am convinced that what matters is not the distance which anybody covers in his or her life but the general direction in which lives move. Whether or not this is part of aging's wisdom—or just resignation—it is a far cry from where I once was.

Less discussable may be the loss of one's sense of invulnerability. Over the course of their lives most people experience either external caprice and/or their internal inadequacies. Couples who marry rarely anticipate the possibility of giving birth to retarded or handicapped children. Never are we prepared for the accident of illness which strikes down somebody close to us. From the outside and utterly beyond our control, we encounter life's unavoidable riskiness. I listened recently to some of the recordings of the English cellist, Jacqueline DuPré. Almost overnight her exceptional artistry was taken away by a progressively debilitating disease. Each of us knows comparable stories of people who took lifelong invulnerability for granted.

Often it is by internal events, for which we could have no foreknowledge, that we are made undeniably aware of our inner inadequacies. Few who take their first drink face the possibility that alcohol may be for them addictive. While we all have many illustrations of such susceptibility, I was struck recently on learning that Jinx Falkenburg and Sterling Hayden, jet-set persons of talent, are arrested alcoholics (TV Week, 26 December 1982–1 January 1983). Hear Hayden's report of his very gradual awareness of his problem. "I didn't have a drink until I was 22 years old, and I didn't have a hangover until 1965. The last five or six years have been real bad . . . I was able to withstand the punishment but I can't anymore."

No more willingly recognized is the propensity which some of us have for addiction to work. Many seem to believe that by something approaching total involvement in their job they can avoid loss of invulnerability. In the course of time even this may become a perilous refuge.

Shortly before last Christmas, a fellow minister of the United Church in Minnesota committed suicide. As you may imagine, the contributing factors were complex and largely unknown to those to whom he was closest. (That he was not really close to anybody may have been the most ominous of these factors.) Unfortunately, his attempted death by incineration— to assure insurance for his family—was not successful. He survived for a few days the fire which he ignited.

Had I not read his son's reactions, it would be quite inappropriate to rehearse these grisly facts about a 47 year-old, work-compulsive colleague. The son's reflections about his father's attempted total involvement in his work are, however, central to the story.

> He was just a very, very intense man who spent so many years helping other people that he didn't know how to get help for himself. . . . [A typical day often meant that his family saw little of him. . . .] He would usually spend most of his day at the office at the church, come home, eat supper, and go to a meeting at night. The way my mom puts it, she spent a lot of years of her life sharing him with other people.
>
> My dad is a church healer. He'd go to a parish that needed help, stay for five to seven years, and then move on. It was time that he was moving again, had it not been for my mom's illness.

The conference minister described him as an "appreciative and devoted and hardworking, able pastor . . . who . . . did not approach us or consult us about some possible help . . . that's very consistent with who he is" (*Minneapolis Star and Tribune*, 17 December 1982).

Finally, among the more subtle losses of the middle-years is the erosion of illusions about one's single-mindedness. In time, and with the help of others—who are our true friends—we may come to recognize that there are enduring conflicts within each of us. Whereas these often surface as conflicts between us and others, about which I shall have much more to say in the following chapter, the fact is that the ambivalences are *within* ourselves. If purity of heart is to will one thing, which exhortation I find dangerously misleading, we are among the impure. Inasmuch as we once assumed utter dedication to our primary commitments, mid-life may be a time when we lose that illusion. Whatever else it may trigger, mid-life involves a loss of innocence about life as unchanging. It is the undeniable dynamic character of lives which we must learn to affirm or die.

The significance of these, and perhaps many other losses of mid-life, is that they erode the bases of our identity. In those early years we gathered together aspects of our lives in ways that were comfortable and to which significant others could assent. What we often failed to recognize was that there was more to us than was taken account of in our self-perception and in the image which we projected to the world. It is as though during mid-life, long-neglected aspects of our being—parts of ourselves at variance with our image—were asserting themselves for overdue attention.

Therefore, I look upon mid-life as the invitation/summons to fashion an identity appropriate to "life's afternoon." No longer young, the temptation is to try to live according to the morning's agenda. Perhaps overstating, C. G. Jung put it graphically:

> Thoroughly unprepared we take this step into the afternoon of life ...[on] the false presupposition that our truths and ideals will serve us as hitherto. But we cannot live the afternoon of life according to the programme of life's morning—for what ... in the morning was true will at evening have become a lie. (C. G. Jung, "The Stages of Life," *Modern Man in Search of a Soul*, New York: Harcourt, Brace & World, Inc., 1933, pp. 124–25.)

There are, of course, continuities between life's morning and afternoon. It is one's *attitudes* towards many of life's basics—food, sex, work aspirations—which are subject to significant change in the middle years. Clearly, this is a time of life fraught with peril and potential. How one responds to these losses is both vital to future well-being and is the issue with which Christian faith must enable us to cope. We are dealing with the years in which, more clearly than most, our heart's restlessness is almost undeniable. That God may be our immediate troubler as well as our ultimate peace is precisely the issue which we may ultimately come to see. That is my thesis.

The problem to which we may now turn is that we may be less than keen to undertake the work of life's "afternoon." Having become adept at the "morning's" agenda, we will be tempted to stay with what we know how to do well. It will be difficult to do otherwise for at least two reasons: society both honors competence and is little interested in the fact of aging. To take on the afternoon's agenda will imperil our competence, perhaps even our reputations. We shall have to acknowledge some uncertainty! This will require strong motivation as we learn to defy societal expectations.

Resisting Mid-life Instruction

The second of the signs which I saw on that New England trip was not by the roadside. Approaching the educational wing of the church of my childhood, I saw an old poster. It was a lovely photograph of two giraffes on Africa's Serengeti Plain: an adult standing as erect as only that animal can and a recently born calf struggling to get to its feet. Very poignant and universal. It was the added text that troubled me: "All of Life Is Learning." Especially in the context of the photograph the text is misleading. In the genes of the baby giraffe—i.e., in what we call the creation—were "instructions" about standing. The ability to stand and to move quickly is crucial to its survival. This is but one of the many learnings which our instincts teach us. We did not have to be taught to suck or to swallow or to yawn.

The assurance that all life is learning is both true and deceptive. By suggesting that all learning is analogous to that of the giraffe's ability to get to its feet, the text hides the fact that there are learnings which are not instinctive. There is pedagogy which we actively resist! This would appear to be true of what may be God's tutelage during life's mid-years. Unable to see the positive possibilities in the cluster of losses we have just listed, we often resist the considerable cost of some new things to be learned. That gains may accompany some of the losses is not easily seen.

While I want shortly to suggest what may be some of the sources of our resistance to such learning, let me first read a statement written about 150 years ago by a renowned Japanese painter, Hokusai:

> "From the age of six I have had a mania for sketching the forms of things. From about the age of fifty I published many designs but of all I produced prior to the age of seventy there is nothing very remarkable. At the age of seventy-three I finally came to understand a little of the true structures of nature, animals, grasses, woods, birds, fishes, and insects. Therefore, at eighty I shall gradually have made progress, at ninety I shall have penetrated the mystery of all things; at one hundred I shall have become truly marvelous, and at one hundred and ten, to me, each dot, each line, all shall possess a life of its own." (Joan Kinneir, ed., "One Hundred Views of Mount Fuji," *The Artist by Himself: Self-Portrait Drawings from Youth to Old Age*, New York: St. Martin's, 1980, pp. 223–24.)

To what extent do we readily recognize the truth of Hokusai's assertions? If true, are they true for everybody? If so, equally? If they are equally true for everybody, what are the consequent "assignments" for us at our present life stage? What should we be learning in order that, when we reach a century-plus, ". . . each dot, each line, all shall possess a life of its own"?

I assume that we do not immediately find Hokusai congenial; and not just because we do not expect to live that long! One of the reasons for this is that we have been led to believe that life and knowledge of life is essentially cumulative. We have been led to assume that there are only *gains* to be enjoyed by the industrious and the disciplined. Ours is an arithmetic sense of the learning process. We would build onto instinctual learning an adding machine model: learning is a matter of endlessly accumulating information. Rarely do we acknowledge either the turbulent transformation inherent in education or our inner resistance to acquiring certain learnings.

In a biography of the seventeenth-century painter, Nicholas

Poussin, there are some fascinating observations about aging painters.

> ... great artists develop in the last years of their lives a sublime style, symptomatically different from that of their youth and maturity. The works in the late ... styles of Titian, Rubens, Rembrandt, and others display in form and idea a deepened, broadened imagination that compensates for the natural uncertainty of vision caused by the decay of the artist's physical powers. Aged artists seem to strive in their late works for totality of impression, and are less concerned with delineating details. Their works are frequently filled with a new, moving lyricism that is a revival of their youthful style, but in a different ... tone that contrasts with the clear, more vigorous narration or action expressed in their mature work. (W. Friedlaender, *Poussin*, London: The Warburg Institute, 1966, p. 82.)

The issue may lie at an ancient and deep level of disagreement about the nature of knowledge. It could be another manifestation of the Athens/Jerusalem conflict. Put too simply, for the Greeks true knowledge is like passive seeing. In knowing something one acknowledges the essential properties of the thing in itself. Knower and known are related only in that the one contemplates the other. By contrast, for the Hebrew prophets, in addition to acknowledging the thing to be known, knowledge has a movement of will and even of emotion. The whole self is involved, and affected, by knowing. Knowledge gained is a function of what one wants to know as much as of what is "out there" to be known. Hebraically, ignorance of important matters can involve guilt because one's will may have obscured the truth. The fault is not in one's brain, but in one's heart: often what one does not *want* to see controls what one *can* see. As you recognize, this issue was central to Jesus' conflicts with his Jewish adversaries.

Less readily seen is the importance of these distinguishable kinds of knowledge for our own middle years. While it is difficult enough to be more Hebraic than Greek in our knowledge of anything external to ourselves, the task is compounded at mid-life. It is not a matter of knowing lots of facts, of being familiar with varieties of theories about human development—

though these *may* be helpful. I emphasize only the possibility that knowledge about the dynamics of human development may be helpful. The tasks of self-acquaintance in the middle years are not different in kind from those encountered earlier or later. However, at least because of the number of unavoidable losses and their centrality to one's matured self-understanding, the difference in degree from other times of change almost amounts to a difference in kind. Every therapist knows the difficulty of working with intellectuals who tend to assume that knowledge about something is all that is needed. Usually such persons fail to recognize the crucial difference between the existential knowledge called for especially at mid-life and knowledge which may be adequate to the classroom. The task of the middle years is to embrace as good and intrinsic to our present identity the cluster of losses which we share with all persons, to admit kinship in frailty with all humankind. At best we will be wounded healers and our power to heal will be in direct ratio with our ability to acknowledge our wounds. (Cf. Henri J. M. Nouwen, *The Wounded Healer: Ministry in Contemporary Society*, New York: Doubleday, 1972.)

I suspect that Henri Nouwen's characterization of ministry may be more familiar than congenial. The society of which we are products does not highly value vulnerability. Being in control, being sufficiently remote as to be unhurtable, becoming successful by being able to manipulate and to avoid manipulation, being strong: these are more the aspirations which have been bred into us. Caring is for many an affliction to be avoided rather than a virtue to be sought. Rarely is the price of the desire for invulnerability as clearly identified as it was in a mother's recent letter to a newspaper. She wrote a fortnight after her youngest son, a varsity football player at the University of Minnesota, had committed suicide. Hear the words by which she characterizes the environment in which he grew up. I assume that it has wider applicability than to the Johnson family of Minneapolis.

> ... We are not always strong [nor] perfect; Eric was no exception. ... His determination helped him to become a fine athlete.

But he was also hungry for affection and recognition, afraid and lonely.

His friends and even those of us in his family admired the first set of qualities and were at times ignorant of his sensitivity. Eric himself did his best to hide it. He was ashamed of being human, and we must feel partly responsible for this. For all of us have created an environment where strength is greatly admired and vulnerability is judged a limitation. We don't acknowledge it in ourselves and don't see it in others.

Achievements do not fully represent us. How terrible that those of us who are looked up to as examples and guides cannot step down, drop a role and ask for help, fearing that this step is a fall. By admiring people for their achievements and seeing only their power, we rarely know and understand them. We may achieve, but achievement fades or passes and we are all left with the tender, suffering core, which we may hide and run from or choose to expose. And in exposure, we reach our fullest humanity. (Diane Cassone Johnson, *The Minneapolis Tribune*, 25 June 1983.)

Mrs. Johnson began her letter with feelings which I trust we readily recognize: ". . . I grieve for his loss and wish he were here so I could tell him. I also feel that there was something more I could have done so he would be here now and we could benefit from his living. But he is not, and we are. We are left to transform our lives from his death." I suspect that many of us wish that, had it been our son who took his life, we might have written so revealingly and with such perception.

Our role as Christians in these middle years is inherently difficult: many want us to be towers of strength when we may be almost overwhelmed by our weaknesses. Further, we must overcome decades of basically Greek thinking—in which we remained at a safe distance from the objects known—because the thing to be known is no longer "out there." It is now my losses which increasingly define me, *my* aging which indicates that there is a new agenda to which I must respond. It is no longer life's morning. It is at least the afternoon, and we move toward evening.

By this language of Carl Jung, I would emphasize the positive, God-given potential in our middle and later years. Inasmuch as we affirm God's goodness, it cannot be for naught, certainly not for punishment, that we grow older. According to the psalmist, we have the promise of getting wise hearts—if we number our days aright. Our tendency to think otherwise indicates how ill we are served by a society which values only youthfulness, or, as I believe, the ability to produce and to consume. Such views caused me to see that, in the middle years, we must learn to live against the grain of assumptions which function as Paul the Apostle's principalities and powers. For is it not these structures, these unexaminable societal attitudes, these family environments "where strength is greatly admired and vulnerability is judged a limitation," by which we have been shaped and misshaped? Might mid-life just be God's traumatic gift to recall us by calling us to become ourselves? So I believe.

The struggle at mid-life is that titanic—and that filled with potential for good. To be sustained in such effort we will need a compelling vision of God. Nothing less will enable us to resist societal powers which urge conformity.

Old and New Visions of Empowerment

The third of the signs noted on the trip was at the approach to Cape Cod. Long familiar with its natural beauty—e.g., beaches, dunes, grasses, birds, fish, and wild fruits—I was not prepared for the following welcome on an oversized billboard: ENJOY THE BEACH WITH A COIN DETECTOR!

People claim to enjoy such search for treasure. But is this anything other than an electronic version of the ancient desire to strike it rich? I cannot escape feeling that this suggestion as to how to enjoy Cape Cod—or any place of natural beauty—represents a lack of appreciation for treasures which nourish. The coin detector symbolizes the pathos of the modern mentality: roughly equivalent to shining deer or detonating fish. People who so approach life desperately need a more adequate vision—of themselves, their neighbor, and of nature. Rarely is the need for God so blatantly declared.

The very qualities which are so functional in morning's agenda contribute to the onset of mid-life and are, ultimately, lethal in the life of faith.

In pursuit of success one concentrates both on limited aspects of one's wholeness, shalom, and on proving oneself better than one's competitors. Only parts of the self are functional to the tasks by which one undertakes to prove oneself. This concentration yields a certain role identity which, because very partial, contributes to the crisis of mid-life. If we are lucky, two things eventually become apparent: (1) that there is more to us than is taken account of by either work or family roles, or by the combination and (2) that adult life is more susceptible to unavoidable losses than we earlier realized. About these losses we shall not say more.

The very qualities, once functional but gradually undermined during one's middle years, are also lethal for faith. Long before they challenged our adult identities, they precluded the possibility of meaningful faith by alienating one from one's real self. This was accomplished both by the self-distancing pretenses involved and by the substitution of achievement/roles/successes for honest self-presentation. Often, without realizing it, we have been in bondage to our alienation from ourselves. Recently I heard about a man who, after a long and troubled first marrige, remarried only to find himself plagued by a continuing sense of failure in intimate relationships. Very deservingly self-confident in his public roles, he found himself repeating destructive behavior in his private life. Thus, in addition to the futility of attempted justification by works, we must see the deeper, religiously more serious, concealment of our largely unacknowledged real self. Failing this we come to confuse who we really are with our meritorious self, which is always less deserving of approval than we let on or than others realize. We pretend that our "best self" is all there is to us. The more determined one is to maintain this partial self-presentation, the tighter and less nourishing the bondage. The agenda of life's morning is, at mid-life, something to be relinquished. That we rarely know how to let go is suggested by the commonplace extreme reactions of either self-destructiveness or the ever greater determination to force the morning's agenda to continue to work.

There seem to be at least two liberating realities which the pursuer of success cannot acknowledge: (1) there is more to me than meets the eye and (2) ". . . by the grace of God I am what I am . . ." (1 Cor. 15:10). With reference to the losses of the middle years, we have two needs: (1) to be able to admit that there is more to me than my roles have allowed and (2) to be able to assent to the largely determined aspects of who, and whose— both genetically/historically and ultimately, I really am. Such assent to the basic realities of my life *is* Christian faith, which is neither a resigned nor a despairing acceptance of God's grace. Once this is acknowledged there is nothing more to prove or to fake; there is but love to show.

This assertion—that it is the mark of Christian faith to assent to the givenness of one's life—may be unfamiliar. At the best it may be but my language which is different; at the worst I may be wrong. My point is that at all times, but especially in mid-life's teachability, we must be able to recognize that there is more to us than is self-made. And those layers of our lives which are other than self-made may be more important than whatever of ourselves we have consciously fashioned. Note, please, my Freudian assumption about the greater importance of one's earlier years for self-understanding. Not all students of human development agree with me; and some contemporary autobiographers—Norman Mailer in *Armies of the Night* (New York: New American Library, Signal, 1971)—reject my assumption outright. One episode, Mailer insists, may be the revealing paradigm of a life, the means of self-discovery and self-disclosure. He is indifferent to continuity; I am not. The givens of our lives are, in my understanding, the keys to our story. They are affirmed in Christian faith when we recognize their source as gracious.

The point is that we have been empowered to reach mid-life by a "vision" which is gradually becoming obsolete. Evidence of a society's viability lies in its ability to motivate youth to appropriate effort. Key to such motivation is a vision of how both society and self will be served as one acquires prescribed skills, experience, and reputation. To be so motivated requires a believable appeal—a vision of the rewards of hard work and of luck—to galvanize young adults to the necessary effort. Among the qualities which the vision must sustain is the ability to believe in the worth of deferred gratification. We accept the assurance that, at some later time—after one is certified—there *will be* rewards.

While the person may be quite secular, such visions function for him/her as a religious faith. The vision assures the believer in several ways: (1) that the society needs the skills which the believer is acquiring, (2) that present merits, especially those requiring the greatest effort, will be appropriately rewarded, and (3) that the vision-inspired success will be both applauded by others and will be a source of personal fulfillment. For many privileged people the vision proves for a long time to be empoweringly true: they assent to the tasks and find themselves rewarded. (We do not consider here what happens to the disadvantaged who may never even have encountered the vision.)

We need to note at this point that the vision fails to mention several things which gradually become increasingly important. First, the unavoidable losses which herald mid-life's onset. Second, the long-neglected—in most cases since adolescence—aspects of the self which seek belated recognition. Many of these will be intrinsic to the self which takes shape during life's afternoon. Third, a set of tasks—*the* new agenda—with which we must deal sometime after the "noon hour." While there are many ways to speak of these tasks, and there are undoubtedly more than I shall mention, let me list four associated with the names of some of the noted theoreticians of mid-life: mortality (Elliott Jaques), internality (Carl Jung), contradictions (Daniel Levinson), generativity (Erik Erikson). (Since the publications of Elliott Jaques may be less familiar than those of Jung, Levinson, and Erickson, the reader may value reference to his important essay, "Death and the Mid-life Crisis," *International Journal of Psychoanalysis*, vol. 46, October 1965.)

For reasons largely rooted in the peculiarities of our society, we resist these tasks. Were we the products of other cultures some of these tasks would appear more congenial. In earlier times—in ancient Rome, or even a century ago on the American frontier, when people built their own coffins when death seemed imminent—mortality was less denied. Even today, in such professions as the military, the possibility of sudden death is more affirmed than by our death-denying society. Similarly, were we Asian children we would attach greater importance to the fashioning of our internal lives. External achievements would bear less of a burden for providing life's meaning. And within nonapocalyptic Judaism there are resources for undertaking Erikson's generative concern for future generations. At the moment the questions, What kind of future do you want for your children? and How do you work to achieve it? are as meaningful as a sincere How are you today?

If we are to overcome the built-in societal resistances to such tasks, we need a vision more compelling than the pursuit of success which has motivated us till now. We need a vision which will free us to set aside, or at least to minimize, the instrumental concerns which have long preoccupied us. We need a vision which will help us to assent to the tasks of life's afternoon, which will enable us to see the struggle with internal chaos as the key to the possible fulfilling agenda of life's afternoon. We need a vision which will reacquaint us with the real self from which we have long been alienated. We need to move beyond the pursuit of success to the search for fulfillment. We need the Christian vision of God.

What we need at mid-life the gospel has always assured us that we have: a God who accepts us just as we are. The assurance is simple and absolute: "While we were yet sinners Christ died for us" (Rom. 5:8). All that is required of us is acknowledgment of our condition and acceptance of God's unqualified love.

So simple—and so elusive—until the experience of the middle years may help us to recognize our sin as the refusal to be ourselves. Much has been written about sin in quite different terms than these. There is no necessary disagreement in differing statements. My point is that sinful behavior always results from either over- or undervaluing some aspect of God's creation. In this instance we have undervalued those aspects of ourselves irrelevant to the pursuit of success. Sin follows. All the time that we were supposedly thinking about nobody but ourselves, we have been busy thinking about anything but ourselves. This is the legacy of the pursuit of success. This is why it is *spiritually* lethal: it has caused us to act, and eventually to assume, that there was nothing more to us than could be seen in our roles. Thank God for the middle years in which we may discover *by experience* the inadequacy of the partial self which pretended that was all there was!

By encountering a cluster of unavoidable losses, we may let go of the pretense of self-reliance based upon a too limited self-acquaintance. This will not be easily accomplished; we have lived too long within our limited selves. But, by God's grace—as in fruit which seeks to ripen in the sunshine—there is that within us which desires acknowledgment. There is the yearning for wholeness: "more of me" wishes to be embraced, to be brought forth for the good yet to be accomplished. However, unlike the ripening fruit, which will mature as the sun shines, the inner yearning for shalom does not assure that benediction. The struggle will be intense because there is a death involved, and we do not readily die. It will be possible only as the vision of God's unqualified love for us in our broken particularity becomes more compelling than the vision which seemed to satisfy during life's "morning." It will be possible only to the extent that we can recognize the fraudulence of many of the assumptions by which we have lived thus far. For complex reasons we will resist that recognition despite God's attempted tutelage at mid-life, despite the yearnings, until we are seized by the realization of the folly of our efforts to justify ourselves.

In a society which believes that to know the good is to do it, the temptation is to assume that we act on our knowledge. Unfortunately, when that knowledge calls for internal change, willingness is less likely than when knowledge is applicable to an external situation. We are at the heart of the matter. Nobody knows just how personal knowledge—the inadequacy of the morning's agenda for life's afternoon—will be used. We all have our ways of ignoring information that we don't know how to integrate into our present life. The persistence of discrimination based on sex, age, race, religion, etc., indicates the depth of resistance to accurate information. The person in mid-life will ordinarily cling to past attitudes and behaviors for as long as they are meaningful, however minimally. Many maintain these patterns long after they are demonstrably false. The yearning for a better life—for greater wholeness, to be able to discard some of one's pretenses—will not in itself move us beyond familiar patterns toward a more integrated life. Such is the powerful inertia of the prevailing vision by which adult lives are shaped. The yearnings may evince the residual presence of the *imago dei* within every person; the residue alone is too meagre, however, to overcome long-established, societally-rewarded habit.

At that point we will either despair or we will be grasped by the simple, overwhelming realization of God's love: we could not have lived other than we have and we need not continue to try to do so. "By the grace of God I am what I am." It may well be that we cannot avoid despair, at least despair of our ability to save ourselves. Whether we will emerge from that despair, or how it will happen, is also God's matter.

With that realization everything has been made new! A new vision has replaced that which long empowered us. With the acknowledgment that *all* is by God's grace, we escape the bondage to the self-justifying efforts of our partial selves. We are liberated from our culturally imposed, self-accepted understanding of who we are and who we may become. We have been freed to love: ourselves because we know ourselves unqualifiedly loved; the neighbors because they are our kin comparably given life by the grace of God.

Some may feel that I have overestimated our instructability at mid-life. That is possible. For some, God's pedagogy comes dramatically—and often painfully. For others, the leadings are gradual and cumulative. Neither method is assuredly instructive for all. What I am trying to show is that the middle years are times of unavoidable opportunity. Things, which challenge the assumptions that society provides as the basis for meaningful effort, happen universally in lives during these years. Self-justification is not the only motivation for intentional effort. We are not self-justifying. In this we have been misled. The basis for responsible life in the world is other than we have been told: we act not to prove something but to demonstrate that all important matters have long been proven. We act in love because we have been loved. There is no other way for it to happen.

II. | Embracing Conflict

In the previous chapter we suggested some of the unavoidable changes which make mid-life traumatic for many. We saw also some reasons why, at least initially, people incline to deny the reality of such changes. Rarely is it possible to recognize the benefits which may inhere in the cluster of losses requiring modifications in self-understanding and in ways of relating to others. By emphasizing these losses we implied that the conflicts of these years were primarily internal.

In my experience this has often been the case. I was being called to growth which I was reluctant to affirm. It would be seriously misleading, however, to leave it there. While many of the tensions are inward, they are in part caused by our changing relationships with people significant to us. In the context of three such relationships important to me, I want now to show that these relationships contribute both to the onset of some of mid-life's troubles and to their resolution. The latter is one of the pleasant instructions of the middle years: we are not isolated entities—pool balls with only external contacts—who both cause and must resolve our exclusively *inner* conflict.

Our problems at mid-life, and their resolution, arise from conflicts which are unavoidable between us and all those who matter to us. Such conflicts may seem especially threatening because of the instability of this particular stage of life. The fear is warranted. However, it is important to note that it is this very instability which potentially makes us both more instructable and capable of constructive change. Nothing is assured, however, beyond the fact that it is an era in which all have the opportunity to move beyond the pretenses which have characterized their adulthood. That the often frightening opportunity for such growth may be central to God's pedagogy during the middle years is my unfamiliar thesis.

We start by acknowledging that religious groups often fail to give permission to acknowledge the contradictions within lives. Thus, rather than enabling people to work at and with their highly imperfect resources, they often create an atmosphere of pretense. Is this why churches are more like the theater—worlds of pretend—than places where the truth is spoken in love?

But, since God is to be worshiped in spirit and in truth, it strikes me that persons are notoriously disserved by what appears to be our exclusive emphasis on presenting only one's "best self" in church. It may be good that we are able to dress up and put on our faces for public worship, since that is part of what we are; it is monstrous if only that is allowed. So much of what I increasingly believe to be God-given reality is "out-of-bounds" to most religious people's understanding. The impression is that it is only their best sides that may come to church. Is this why so many lives seem to be on "hold"?

Of course, those who cannot tolerate their actual lives— either because they are too destructive or even self-destructive—are encouraged to "seek help." The rest, who may be no less conflict-ridden, are assumed to be only what they present themselves to be. The insistence that parishioners be only their "best selves" undermines the very search which brings many people into our congregations. The amazing thing is that, even while ill-served, so many continue to come in hope. The tragedy may be that they become reconciled to, even comfortable with, the deceptive pretense which we often nurture.

Assuming that conflict is at the heart of our lives, I want to take a quite different tack. Rather than necessarily indicating the absence of love, conflict is the God-given reality with which faith may enable us to deal lovingly. To the point of death there are undeveloped resources which we may learn to use. The catch-22 is that this latent energy, this potential for doing some good, is enmeshed in both inner and outer conflicts; and that we are averse to conflict. There is wisdom in our aversion: conflict is always fatiguing and often destructive. It is, however, such a central reality in our experience that, despite the dangers involved, we must find ways of assenting to the conflicts in our lives and in our relationships. It is with the *actualities* of our lives that we must begin. Until we do so *as an expression of our faith*, we will be playing games that—because they are predicated on self-hatred—preclude the possibility of change. For such hatred of ourselves is the wish to be other than one is; the refusal to do what good one can with what one has and is. As one of the seven cardinal sins, self-hatred represents a rejection of one's life as from God. Pandora's box must be opened and it is by faith that we are gradually able to release these energies.

It is to the conflicts in our society, and especially those deep within our selves, that we must learn to be open. Such conflicts *are* the God-given opportunities for Christian maturation. How we choose to deal with the universal agenda will determine the extent of our need for growth in faith. I trust that we understand each other clearly: the fact of conflict does not necessarily mean absence of love. It is an all too common assumption that love and conflict are mutually exclusive. (How we sustain such an attitude, which contradicts so much of our actual experience, is a good topic for some other occasion.) It is crucial to recognize that love is but one of several ways in which we may deal with life's unavoidable conflicts. Both chronic avoidance and violence are unacceptable alternative responses.

Since these conflicts are legion, I want to mention a few which I have experienced in my relations with the *women* most important in my life. The topic is broad enough to enable all of us to recognize the reality of our experience. It will be specific as I report and reflect on aspects of my own life—as a child, spouse, and parent. It is appropriate to speak of these conflicts for at least two reasons: (1) they have considerably determined who I am—to what I am sensitive and insensitive and (2) every one of you has had at least one of the roles I will mention: parent, spouse, child. Thus, we shall be dealing with much of my experience and some of yours. We *have* some common ground.

Following discussion of these relationships—with my mother, wife, and daughter—I shall speak about ways of dealing with such unavoidable conflicts, and, finally, about how I understand God's presence in this process of acknowledging and possibly resolving deep conflicts.

Several Illustrative Conflicts

In presenting aspects of several significant relationships, I want two things to be clear. First, these women helped to evoke development which need not otherwise have occurred. Had I been born to another mother or married a different wife, I would be a somewhat different person. Had our daughter arrived earlier or later, I would have been a somewhat different parent. Who each of us becomes, what we make of our God-given potential is largely the result of the life-giving—or life-withholding—qualities of those persons to whom we are closest at crucial times in our lives. Since no human is fully life-giving, we are all partly able and partly handicapped. Like Jacob, who is the unacknowledged, universal patron saint, we all limp. In even the best of relationships only certain aspects of the self may be developed.

Second, as I discuss these relationships I shall use some of Erik Erikson's categories to characterize the growth which is potential at particular life stages. Thus, we shall be working with specific material from one person's experience and interpreting it with the theories of another. While I have found Erikson useful in understanding my own life, the emphasis will be on particular experience rather than on the generalizations of developmental theory. Too rigorously applied, the neatness of theory obscures the turbulence of actual lives.

It is with our turmoils, which we are always tempted to

conceal, that Christian faith enables us to deal. How belief illumines and empowers the believer is not, however, our immediate concern. We reach too soon for faith if it is our hope thereby to avoid the conflicts inherent in lives. It is with some of these that I want to start.

One thing we all have in common: we were born to our mothers. In Erikson's understanding, the mother's initial and fundamental task is to instill in the child a greater sense of trust for life than mistrust. This is communicated to infants by the life-giving potential of the mothering person.

To understand my mother (and father), you should visualize an immigrant couple, small of stature and no longer young, stepping from the boat which had brought them from Glasgow to the land of opportunity. The woman was pregnant with the only child she was to bear. It was in the home that they created that I was to learn of the world's basic trustworthiness, and in consequence, to be more trusting than suspicious of my own perceptions. From some combination of their disappointments and the lures of the larger society, I became the bearer of their unfulfilled hopes for success. Decades passed before I began to be aware that there were flaws in the American dream.

The point is not that the dream is inherently wrong; rather, that it takes time to realize that success and fulfillment are not equitable. Whether or not one is successful is not a matter which the individual may assert; only significant others may so judge. On the other hand, whether or not one is fulfilled is not a matter which others are capable of determining; only from within is such a judgment possible.

Let's go back to my parents—John and Jean—to expose a basic conflict between them which endured to the end of their lives and of which I am the bearer. John was primarily social in his understanding of reality; Jean primarily personal. The product of a Scottish industrial city, and very much influenced by the trades union movement, John saw evil in class structures— to which organized religion gave its distinctive support. Jean, whose attitudes had been shaped by a devout father and evangelical sectarianism, emphasized the perfecting of individual lives. My father was primarily committed to improving the well-being of the working class; my mother, though she would never have put it this way, sought to escape the confinements of poverty by self-improvement. (Cf. Robert Crichton, *The Camerons* [New York: Alfred A. Knopf, 1972], for a novel illustrating a similar conflict.)

This conflict lives on in me and was the basis for an exciting realization a few years ago about what it meant to "honor one's mother and father." In my instance, the particulars are different from your own experience. I honor them to the extent that I refuse to destroy the tensions between their respective outlooks, which they were themselves never able to resolve! That this leaves me somewhat schizophrenic is, I now believe, to experience the human condition.

That we remain more the children of the past than we dared admit when younger, has been powerfully suggested in a Minnesotan's poem.

I

When she went to Iceland at sixty
to see her father's farm
the relatives looked down at the bony knuckles
the veins popping up
and said—see—
she has the Josephson hands
even after a hundred years.

II

In his own house
there were no attacks
on Franklin Roosevelt,
and when the Republican uncle
made fun of FDR,
he would bellow grandly:
"You crooked son of a bitch!'
See, they would say:
that insufferable Gislason arrogance.

III

Now when I bellow at parties or look down at my own hands—
knuckles growing, and veins

rising as I age—I think
how can I live
with all these dead people inside me!
I will have to eat like a grizzly bear
before the winter denning
to feed them all
dragging whole carcasses
miles across the tundra
inside my body. (Bill Holm, "Genealogy," *Happy Birthday, Minneota*, Minneota, MN: Westerheim Press, p. 97.)

With some emerging identity, I was able to move into those relationships which Erikson characterizes as the capacity for intimacy. While sexual intimacy is not essential to what he means by this stage of development, physical relations are often part of the experience of giving oneself to another. In this regard two important facts need to be stressed: (1) it is only on the basis of an adequately developed sense of personal identity that one is *able* to enter into intimate relationships with others— the ability to copulate should not be equated with the capacity for intimacy and (2) genuinely intimate relationships involve the identity-derived willingness to commit one's *imperfect* self to an *imperfect* other. This is in sharpest contrast with all romantic notions about love which presuppose an ideal relationship. When identity is diffused, one prefers the safety of distance to intimacy's risks. Such a person, yearning for a romantically faultless relationship in which mistakes are impossible, becomes only increasingly self-isolated.

Fortunately, almost forty years ago, I met a young woman who was willing to risk me as I was her. We have had a good life together. It would be profoundly misleading, however, if I were to give the impression that ours has been a problem-free marriage. We have often hurt each other. Could it have been otherwise as the daughter of a proper, upper New York State family and the ambitious son of immigrant parents learned to negotiate basic issues? The particular points at which we stumbled and struggled are distinctively ours; marital conflicts, however, I take to be universal.

Perhaps one illustration of an issue with which we have

been grappling for some years will illustrate how such conflicts both endure, though partially resolved, and emerge in new guise as time passes. We do not agree about the balance between activity and rest which should characterize our lives. We both tend to hyperactivity. During decades of child-raising and career-establishing, such busyness was both unavoidable and functional. Probably we will never escape the pattern completely.

Some years ago I was reminded of the heart's fundamental rhythm of activity and rest. For as long as we live that vital muscle works and stops to refresh itself. Whatever its rate, it is both working and resting. Because it is so basic and because I was looking for such a model, that rhythm is the pattern for the life I desire. Busyness, which I once thought utterly necessary to my sense of well-being, is no longer as attractive to me. Betsy and I are not on the same timetable on this matter. While it is an issue about which we talk occasionally, more important is our decreasing discomfort with our dissimilarity. That we have ineradicable reasons for the different pace at which we wish to live illustrates why every enduring, important relationship has endlessly to be renegotiated.

As Erik Erikson understood the basic life tasks, the ability to enter intimate relations with others leads to the next question of adulthood: will one have a generative concern for, or a stagnating relationship to, the world's future? Generativity is an attitude which does not necessarily involve the biological act of parenting. The alternative is not necessarily the refusal to have children but an indifference to either the young or to their future.

The presence of a primarily generative attitude does not solve all problems for those who become parents. This, I am sure, comes as no surprise! When I became a parent for the first time over thirty years ago, I was ecstatic: my wife had had a comparatively easy pregnancy and delivery; we had a healthy daughter. All had gone according to the book. The point, however, is that I knew next to nothing about how to be a father. I knew only what my own father had been for me.

Several realizations gradually emerged over the years. One of these parental learnings is that you cannot give what you lack. To put that less negatively, parents rarely know what they are really conveying to children. At the worst this accounts for the often deserved cliché, "What you *are* speaks so loudly that I can't hear what you *say!*" It is our behavior over time, and the underlying covert attitudes, from which children learn. (That we are often less than fully aware of the contents of our statements is clear in this observation of a contemporary artist: "It is very intriguing to hear the interpretation of my work by others, especially as the meaning or symbolism sometimes seen in it is completely nonexistent for me, consciously at any rate" [Kinneir, ed., "M. C. Escher," *The Artist by Himself*, p. 151]. Positively—and very simply—the parental lesson which I finally learned was that I could only be the father that I was capable of being. This meant that there were only *some* things which I was able to pass on to our children.

The most recent of the conflicts at which our daughter and I have been working came initially as a surprise. In a public talk I had indicated that it was my primary desire as a parent in this society to encourage our children in all possible ways to claim their independence as adults. That is, I was more interested in the development of their wings than with the nurture of their roots. As you may already have guessed, there were many reasons why I preferred the ability to fly over the cultivation of origins! (I suspect that, in part through correspondence with our daughter and other maturing experiences, if I were to be a parent at my present age, I would probably attach more importance to the continuity of family than I did thirty years ago.) Our daughter feels that I overdid the "flying" and that I have much to learn about the *inter*dependence of lives. It might be helpful to quote from the extended correspondence that we have had.

> . . . You both are very lucky to be happy with each other, to have health and money, fulfilling work and lots of free time, friends, and a supportive environment. Self-sufficiency and success are linked in our society, both as self-sufficiency leads to success and success

provides the means for further self-sufficiency. [This puts you] in the envied but dangerous position of not having to ask anyone for anything.

Luckily, circumstances have forced me to see some of the arrogance of that position. I do believe there is something to the notion that poverty teaches humility, and I am really grateful for the lesson because I have also been learning that there is a joy in being grateful and in receiving/accepting gifts and help from other people. Needing a ride, needing someone to talk to, needing to borrow money, needing to be cheered up, no longer seems a humiliating indication of my lack of inner resources, but rather needs are occasions for asking and being terribly grateful, to you and to my friends. These interactions bind us together. And knowing how it feels to need things adds to pleasure in giving too.

You recognize the indictment. It is a wonderful—if painful—opportunity for the immigrant son who had to become independent if he was to fulfill some of his parents' aspirations to learn from those parents' granddaughter. The only question is about my willingness to grow.

In this rehearsal of my relationships with my mother, wife, and daughter, I have tried to illustrate some of the potentially instructive conflicts which have been part of my life. I assume that they are not completely unfamiliar. All of us have to work with the tensions between the desires for success and for fulfillment, the need to balance the impetus to activity and the desire for rest, the challenge of an interdependence which adequately takes account of our yearnings for both independence and dependence. Such conflicts are never resolved with finality.

In addition, it is most important that we recognize why this is impossible: there is truth on both sides of what we often perceive as mutually exclusive polarities. Because of my involvement with other lives, I cannot be wholly indifferent to their appraisals of my efforts; but in self-respect I cannot be absolutely dependent upon others' judgment as to whether I am a success or failure. Nor may I with greater ease settle either for an utterly active or a completely inactive life anymore than I can destroy the tension between my need to be dependent and independent. I experience both the possibility of growth and some real limitations. It will not do to try to destroy the God-given energy which is inherent in the tension between them. They represent the human condition with which, I believe, it is our privilege as children of God to grapple.

Before considering some of the few things I have learned about dealing with enduring conflict, it is important to emphasize that such issues are never fully resolvable. Clearly, it will not do for them to be constantly and deeply alienating people from each other, to be sources of daily domestic strife. Everybody is capable of some improvement in even the most conflicted relationship.

There is, however, a world of difference between some amelioration of a situation and its perfect resolution. We need to be able to feel better as the result of some small improvement in a relationship; unfortunately, that is not true of our society. We have been misled to assume that problems should not endure; there should be some remedy which will cause them to disappear. With reference to the kinds of tensions I have described, this is a hopeless expectation. As I shall suggest momentarily, the reason for this is that the sources of the conflict are as much *within* each person as they are between us and others. This is simply the nature of our lives and there is no point in assuming that the fundamentals of our makeup can be changed. As Erikson makes clear in his discussion of the polarities at each stage of human development—from the initial tension between trust and mistrust to the final conflict between a sense of integrity about one's life and the reasons for despair—the basic ingredients endure because they are true and functional. It is not a matter of destroying one in order that the other may prevail. Like the environment of wild flowers or of certain plants and insects, the relationship is symbiotic. One may work to emphasize the positive pole in any tension without scorning or seeking to eliminate its complementary. This is, for many of us, a difficult but crucial understanding to acquire.

That our lives are so constituted is not in itself evidence of human sinfulness. Sin, of course, often exploits such a highly fluid situation. The point, however, as we shall see in a later chapter, is that sin's method is to obscure the inherent ambivalences of which we've been speaking. Thus, in Christian circles, we are usually encouraged to be persons of faith as though doubt were somehow expungable. The reality is that it is no more possible to be a completely trusting than a wholly mistrusting person. That is the God-given reality which the person of faith seeks to affirm rather than to conceal.

Procedures for Conflict Resolution

It is with such representative tensions in mind that we may now consider some positive procedures in conflict resolution. Given our culturally influenced tendency to prefer to emphasize *either* our growth potential or our limits, this is not an easy process.

The first step is to be able to affirm the inevitability of conflict in all significant relations. This is clearly acknowledged in the language of marriage vows: couples take each other "for better, for worse." However, it is a rare bride and groom who believe that there will be a "worse." We are not a society which affirms that possibility. Such is our preference for simplicity that we are largely incapable of recognizing that better and worse are inseparable from each other. If there is the possibility for the one, the other is an inevitable concomitant.

The result of our blindness about the universality of tensions in all significant relations, which we wrongly identify as representing the absence of love, is that we are not encouraged to develop skills in the "marital arts." Conflict goes on but is often so oblique and subtle as to undermine the relationship rather than to mature it. The causes of such conflicts are always specific to particular lives. The consequences, however, of inability to deal with issues as they inevitably arise are uniform: either trauma or progressive hopelessness. Recently I saw an excellent production of Henrik Ibsen's play, *A Doll's House.* Written over a century ago, it is a powerful description of the violence to which a woman was led by a too long suppressed acquiescence in a dependent domestic relationship. An unacceptable alternative to such violence is the diminished hope of a person who submits over a long period of time to another's "authority." As those who write about "date rape" suggest, it is never too early to begin to face up to the reality of conflict. The problem is, as with young women on a date, that it is very difficult to know clearly one's own mind and feelings soon enough—and to have the courage to risk disagreement. That is, the intimacy which one allows on a date will depend upon the adequacy of one's understood identity. Something similar is needed in the lives of married persons if they are to take with equal seriousness both the "better" and the "worse." (Karen Barrett, "Date Rape," *Ms.*, September 1982. Cf. also Linda Pastan, "Because," *The Five Stages of Grief: Poems by Linda Pastan* [New York: W. W. Norton, 1978].)

Another thing that I belatedly learned is that timing is crucial. In the desire to get at and resolve significant differences, there are better and worse occasions on which to begin. It is now spectacularly clear to me that one does not launch such discussion in the hours before a dinner party! Nor before breakfast! After many years Betsy and I discovered, to avoid frustrations building up to a point where it became impossible to deal with them, the desirability of a time—often as frequently as once a week—when we scheduled serious conversation. Spontaneity is inadequate to sustain an important relationship. For more than a decade we have simply committed ourselves, in the midst of often extremely busy lives, to having some specific time exclusively for each other each day. It does not have to be a lot of time; it *has* to be regular.

I have talked about the process of resolving conflicts only in terms of the relationship between two (or more) parties. That aspect of conflict resolution is vital. Nothing that I am about to say is to detract from the importance of both acknowledging the inevitability of conflict and of mutually acceptable times for exploration.

When the process is working properly, when neither party is defending a stance thoughtlessly or utterly resisting self-exploration, both find that they have *interior* work to do. Rarely is the conflict ever just between the parties. To the extent that one takes the external evidences of conflict seriously, the thoughtful person begins to recognize that there are internal tasks. (In Erikson's terms this involves reacquaintance with the always partially inadequate way in which the polarities of prior life stages were resolved. For example, a heavy dose of mistrust early in life contributes either to paranoia or to cumulative lack of confidence in one's own perceptions and judgments—or both. Or, the issues of adolescence may have been resolved either in a prematurely clear sense of identity which omitted significant but latent aspects of the self, or by too sweeping an identity diffusion.)

This is the fundamental and trying work of self-acquaintance. Willingness to sustain such effort may be variously motivated: by the importance attached to the conflicted relationship and by recognition of one's contribution to the conflict, as well as by what I believe to be our God-given desire better to understand our own lives. Ignorance about one's self, often seemingly urged on Christians, is no more justified than is self-rejection. Self-hatred represents apostasy rather than the desire to honor God which I believe we do by being true to the nature which God has given us. That our lives are revealed to us primarily through our relationships with significant others is one of the facts which had gradually become clear to me. That this discovery is often made possible by painful conflict is one of the ironies of which we need not be ashamed. Increasingly I am convinced that growth would not otherwise occur.

Two things need to be said about the demanding work of self-acquaintance. First, it requires more solitude than is taken by most people and more than is approved in our society. Without such time apart, however, the work will not be done. For several of my middle years I found it necessary and helpful to keep a daily journal. Not only was this useful as a device for keeping track of my time, it is simply more difficult to be dishonest with oneself *in writing.* Some self-deception persists, of course, but it is harder to lie in writing than it is in solitary reflection or in the heat of conflict. Some of the new material gradually becomes the matter of one's prayer. Again, even putting ourselves consciously into God's presence does not instantly make us completely honest about ourselves and the relationships in which we are involved. Rather, it is an act to which believers are drawn as they recognize both that it is one's very being which is at stake in the important conflicts of our lives; and, inasmuch as that is the truth about us, nothing other may appropriately be brought to God at such a time.

Second, none of this is recommended as a panacea. The process of growth is never easy or painless. Perhaps most important is the recognition that the ambivalences which both empower and plague our lives probably persist to the end. I can think of no better illustration of the reality of inner ambivalence than that which T. H. White described in a book written fifty years ago and recently republished:

> [En route to shoot rabbits, I] . . . saw a heron almost at once. He was standing in green fields and attracted my eye as he got up: a great sweeping bird trailing a sweeping shadow behind him. I marked him down in a little brook, and wondered whether I could get up to him. Herons are reasonably cunning, so I thought it would be good sport to try. I kept telling myself that I was not going to shoot at him, as he was a beautiful bird, useless to me and doing no harm to anything I valued. *Another part of me said it would like to shoot a heron.* . . . I had marked him down farther off than he actually was, and suddenly here he was bustling out of the ditch by my right hand in a great flurry. I shot him mercilessly. . . . He came down flump, in a crumpling parachute of blue-grey feathers, and I was miserable at once. (T. H. White, *England Have My Bones*, New York: Putnam, 1982, p. 28 [italics added].

This is more graphic than our experience often is and the context may be unfamiliar. That we continue both to want and not want something is a central part of the experience with which we are trying now to come to terms.

Wherein Is God's Presence?

Throughout this I have emphasized the inevitability of conflict—both between people and within each of us. We both want and do not want to shoot the heron.

Earlier generations seem to have it simpler: they thought it possible to have an utterly clear mind about all important matters. Here is how Charles Darwin's granddaughter described Edwardian England:

> Neither had [any of my uncles] any idea of the complications of psychology. They found it difficult to conceive of a mixture of motives; or of a man who says one thing and means another; or of a person who is sometimes honest and sometimes dishonest; because they were so completely single-hearted themselves. (Gwen Raverat, *Period Piece*, London: Faber & Faber Ltd., 1960, p. 189.)

One or both of two things may account for the discrepancy between their time and ours: either they suppressed their ambivalences better than we or the world of "certainties" which supported their single-mindedness has been overturned. In no way is this more obvious than in the difference between the confidence they had for the future and our uncertainty as to whether or not there will be one. Just one sentence from a most important recent book records the dramatic discontinuity between then and now.

> [In imagining extinction] we are left only with the ghostlike future generations who, metaphorically speaking, have been waiting through all past time to enter into life but have been turned back by us. (Jonathan Schell, *The Fate of the Earth*, New York: Alfred A. Knopf, 1982, p. 144.)

More immediately, note how much has changed when confidence in the rightness of one's particular views becomes an awareness of the variety of world views. The Edwardian single-mindedness was bought by ignoring diverse reality of which we must take account. This obligation is both burden and liberation. As we are open to each other's differences, we are helped to acknowledge inner contradictions which they denied. While we may hanker for the firmness of a more parochial world, that is no longer an option for us. Thomas Wolfe was right: "You can't go home again!" For that we must learn to thank God.

In both public and private life our task is to take our conflicted experience with the seriousness it deserves. There is danger in this statement. Since we are but mortal creatures, there are at least two temptations: (1) to overburden our real but modest resources and/or (2) to attach unwarranted importance to aspects of our experience. Perhaps two simple illustrations will suggest their peril. During the worship service last fall I was made aware of three elderly women immediately in front of me. The minister had exhorted us to come alive to the excitement of the onset of autumn and the beginning of a new academic year. (Schools are big in Northfield!) It struck me that this was also a reminder that winter was not so far off, which might be a source of distress rather than exhilaration for the elderly. We do not all have the same resources for responding to reality. What one person may handle with ease taxes to their limits the resources of others. It will not do to lay the same burden on all.

Because the opportunities are so sweeping, it is more difficult to illustrate the temptation to attach unwarranted importance to our experience. (Cf. William French, "Auden's Moral Comedy . . . ," *The Christian Century*, 24 February 1982: "Perhaps through laughter we can, for the very first time, come to see ourselves as we are. The central irony of the moral life is that simply by not taking ourselves so seriously, we may become more serious moral agents and more serious Christians.") It is easier to see others succumbing to the temptation than to observe oneself yielding. For example, students, especially freshmen, are constantly inclined to inflate tomorrow's quiz out of recognition. All other reality can be temporarily obscured by exclusive concentration on today's homework. Only another person, sensitive to different considerations, may view as excessive the preoccupation with such a tiny slice of reality. The work of faith is to enable us to lose ourselves in immediate details while being able to return to and care for the larger picture.

In this context how helpful is Heschel's assertion that history is the record of God's experience? (Abraham J. Heschel, *The Prophets*, New York: Harper & Row, 1962, p. 172.) No greater enlargement of the human picture is imaginable than that prophetic faith which Jews and Chritians affirm. The question which we must ask, however, is this: does such an understanding of God's presence enable us better to work with the often conflicted experience of our lives? May we assume that it is possible to translate God's presence from the larger canvas of history, with which the prophets were concerned, to the minutia of daily experience in our families and congregations? May we attach proper importance to the daily events which often seem trivial in the light of the earthshaking news with which the media endlessly confront us? (Is media-reporting the only criterion of what is important? To what extent do the media *make* events?) The tension inherent in these questions is undeniable. It will not go away, though we all find ways temporarily of resolving it.

The larger movements within the world are the background of all that we have said. I focus, however, on our daily lives. It may be the essence of presumption, or of ignorance, but I am persuaded that the events of our often humdrum existence are also the record of God's experience. Whatever more it is, the big picture is at least a composite of myriad small ones. As the prophets were utterly specific about evidences of societal faithlessness—selling the needy for a pair of shoes (Amos 2:6)—so must it be with us. It is in the particulars of our love for God, neighbor, and self that we manifest our belief in God's presence—or absence.

I believe that the weakened element in this triadic summary of the law is the commandment to self-love. All of us are strong and regular in our exhortation to love God and neighbor. We are probably less consistent encouragers of love for self. I appreciate our hesitance; we are unsure about the demons we may release. Better, we suspect, not to risk.

My conviction, however, is that the weakening of any one of these ingredients of our love life—self, God, or other—unavoidably distorts the others. Only as I take seriously as from God the unavoidable conflicts within myself—the tension between my potential for growth and my present limitations—am I able to take with the seriousness they deserve the tensions between me and my neighbor, and between God and myself. The commandment to self-love is not license for self-satisfaction or indifference. Exactly the opposite. As we learn to take ourselves seriously, the resultant honesty is the source of both humility and a sense of kinship with all other beings. Rather than encouraging smugness, the love of self yields amazement that, by God's grace, there is some good of which even I am capable. Here are the roots of gratitude.

In self-love I am not enamoured by my limitless potential; I discern both my capacity for doing harm and my limited but real opportunities for good. In self-love I am not superior to my neighbors; in them I recognize aspirations and limitations akin to my own. In self-love I am not defiant to God and confident of my deserts; I am thankful for the particular, partial endowment with which I may undertake my life as a child of God.

The great danger of any emphasis on self-love is that it will further the privatization of lives which is probably the present alternative to Christian life and community. Wrongly understood, such "love" supports the desire to withdraw from all demanding connections. Erikson sees the adolescent failure to establish a credible identity as the cause of the inability to undertake the risks of intimacy. False self-love distances us from others.

It is because I take these dangers seriously that I emphasize the importance of self-love. It will not do simply to exhort love for the neighbor nor to thunder God's commands. These appeals are appropriate but, in themselves, insufficient. They do not build upon our actual experience. Because they are theory, with all its beautiful neatness, they lack the angularity and tensions of actual lives. As such the appeal to love my neighbor may seem addressed to somebody other than me. Love of others and of God cannot long be sustained without encouragement to love my damaged self. A wise observation was implied in a question asked by an ancient Jew. "How can a man be merciful to others who is merciless to himself?" (Abraham Hasdai in E. Beier, ed., *Wit and Wisdom of Israel*, p. 32.)

By self-love I may begin to take my limitations seriously and to desire to do *some* good even with my brokenness. Permission to acknowledge my actual condition as to who I now am and what I actually have to work with—the assurance that I am accepted—seems to me the neglected biblical key to the life of love for which we are created. It is by assenting to this assurance, which is *the* essence of faith, that the believer may begin to make something good—often more than imagined—with what one has. The abandonment of pretense is the beginning of growth. It will not do to urge self-denial before the vital and painful work of self-acquaintance has begun. Who I am, and what I have to work with, I must first accept as from God.

The risks of this corrective emphasis may be greater than I realize. Are they greater than exclusive emphasis on either neighbor love or love for God? The peril and the promise lie in the dynamic triad which is at the heart of the faith we profess: God-neighbor-self. For as long as we maintain that faith, we cannot escape the perilous work of assigning appropriate importance in changing circumstances to these never easily balanced obligations.

The unacceptable alternative is to refuse this assignment: to pretend that conflict is absent from our lives, that we can avoid using power. I am too much the Niebuhrian for this, though I am often so tempted. The awesome solution lies in the faith-derived ability to affirm both the unavoidability of action *and* of the endless need for our deeds to be informed by love. Martin Buber puts it thus:

> We cannot avoid using power, cannot escape the compulsion to afflict the world. So let us, cautious in diction and mighty in contradiction, love powerfully. (Rollo May, *Power and Innocence*, New York: W. W. Norton, 1972, p. 241.)

Consider, finally, the benefit from the three relationships about which I spoke earlier: greater truthfulness about my own life. It is by the honesty of self-love that I acknowledge without resentment the immigrant couple who were my parents. From John and Jean, genetically and in our family life, I was partially equipped to live as their son—and more. They did not provide totally; no parent does—as I now better understand. In self-love I accept their particular, conflicted legacy and the capacity for trusting my perceptions of the world. I know that these perceptions are partial but not thereby worthless.

It is by the honesty of self-love that I acknowledge without resentment the particular woman with whom I covenanted years ago. We have been less good to each other than we might have been, and as we yet hope to be, but we have learned to be more accepting of each other's limitations. In this acceptance we find the motivation to yet make something of the conflicting legacies which we brought to our marriage. We have both built upon and grown beyond our families of origin. Having risked intimacy without disaster, we find ourselves more caring than indifferent about the future of humankind. I have been less than the perfect husband; her patience with my limitations has kept me from being as destructive as I might have become.

It is by the honesty of self-love that I admit being the father I have been to our children. I have not been all that they needed. I both regret my limitations and am resigned to what has been. I wish that I might have been more adequate, and may yet become, but I now realize that I was not obliged to be God for them. It would be nice if anon they felt for me as does a contemporary Israeli poet for his father:

> I remember my father waking me up
> for early prayer. He did it caressing
> my forehead, not tearing the blanket away.
>
> Since then I love him even more.
> And because of this
> let him be woken up
> gently and with love
> on the Day of Resurrection. (Yehuda Amichai, "Letter of Recommendation," *Amen*, New York: Harper & Row, 1977, p. 66.)

These acknowledgments do not come easily. Some of them I could not have made ten years ago. A decade hence I expect to be more accurate about such conflicts and, hopefully, more contrite about my continuing contributions to them. The rate of change in lives is more like those in geology than in engineering. If it comes at all, it is very gradual. For those imprisoned in the assumption that instant solutions alone matter, this will be unacceptable. Those who appreciate how long our "wires" have been badly twisted will realize that even a very little change is all that is needed to rekindle hope. In time, as with a minor adjustment of a ship's heading, one reaches a quite different destination. Too rapid a change in the direction of one's life is as destabilizing in the home as at sea, and no less difficult to sustain. Modest change is not just all that is possible; it is all that matters!

Whether or not change comes depends upon the depths of one's self-love and the resultant honesty about one's limited but real potential for compassion and devotion. It is such honesty which frees one to imagine new ways of relating to neighbor and God. We will be endlessly conflicted but need not be locked into old ways. Isn't this the paradox of freedom: that it becomes possible only as we acknowledge our bondage? The enemy of change is willful ignorance about oneself—self-rejection—and the resultant life of pretense. Neither God nor neighbor can penetrate that shield. One can only believe with Shakespeare that, "Who covers faults, at last shame them derides" (King Lear, I.1.280.). So spoke Cordelia to her sisters who were not bothered by the falsity of promises to their father. Their greed-inspired misrepresentations are expressions of self-hatred rather than self-love.

That it is hate pretending to be love is not long concealed—as Lear quickly discovers to his sadness. Such change as occurs is not in either Goneril or Regan. Self-deceived, they proceed unhaltingly to disaster, taking many with them. Their father undergoes change via the madness he dreaded. Belatedly, Lear recognizes both his fatal pride which had demanded the words Cordelia could not speak and the fact that he had failed to look behind the flattery of the self-serving sisters.

Not all change extracts such a price; this is theater. But there is no change which is cost-free. As much faith is required to assent to change as to assent to one's limits. Let Shakespeare

have the final word: "Nothing almost sees miracles/But misery."
(*King Lear*, II.2.160–62.)

On the basis of the brief review in these opening chapters
of some of the features and tasks of the middle years, we turn
directly to the articles of The Apostles' Creed. These worlds
may seem incommensurate; certainly they will not be glibly
connected. At the least there is a great distance between lives
of the late twentieth century, introspectively illumined by social science, and those of the early Christian centuries. Any
bridge we may build will be fragile at best.

But is there any alternative to attempting such a construc-
tion for those of us who both live today and profess allegiance
to a historic Christianity? This work will be somewhat easier
as we see clearly some similarities between the material of
these introductory chapters and the New Testament. In our discussion of the cluster of losses which characterize mid-life, we
implied what may now be made explicit: such losses constitute
the death of the self rather than merely its diminishment. In
the unavoidable losses of the middle years, men and women
are challenged at the depths of their being. Gradually all of the
roles by which lives are held together—often with pleasure,
always with more pretended well-being than is warranted—are
removed. This is a time of radical crisis, a storm in which the
ship may well founder. It is not a season for cosmetic changes,
not a brief era in an otherwise sound life. For the first time since
coming of age, and possibly for the last, in these losses the
persons in mid-life crises experience the death of all that they
have taken for life. While there are many ways to obscure the
consequences of such losses, and many who would so blind
themselves, these diversions are not the way to the new life
which God promises. Because they involve concealment and
self-deception, they assure that these promises will always
elude us. In the losses of the middle years, as in losses at all
transitional stages of life, the route to renewal—to resurrection—is by recognizing and embracing the reality of one's loss.
Never again will we be the selves we previously were. But we
may become something new and no less valuable. Such are the

experiences underlying Chapter I which may enable us to consider anew a patristic creed.

In the issues central to the second chapter, we have a no less direct connection with the Gospels. There we tried to indicate that conflicts endure in all lives. They are completely expungable neither from our relationships with others nor from our inner life. As was true of Jesus, our lives have authority only to the extent that we recognize the conflicts which we experience. For such was the human source of Jesus' authority: both that he was not blind to the conflicts within—the pattern is uniform from the wilderness temptations to the prayers at Gethsemane and Golgotha—and that he engendered conflict in others. Not many struggled as desperately as did Saul of Tarsus to suppress it; more are like the disciples who hoped that Jesus would keep the conflicts to himself. Since many church members stand in this avoiding tradition of the disciples, in consequence of which Christianity is so insipid, it is imperative that we recognize this true key to Jesus' authority.

It is by his acknowledgment of inner conflicts that we are freed to recognize, rather than to conceal, our own. In this we experience—as did the authors of The Apostles' Creed—the truth which enables us to get about God's business as our vocation. His is indeed a strange and glorious authority: it frees us from the burdens of pretense for works of love.

III. Growth and Limits: God's "Curriculum"/ Human Truancy

The basic human need is for an understanding of life which will guard against two primary sources of despair: (1) perfectionism, with its assumption that one must be error-free and (2) resignation, which assumes that nothing can be other than it now is. Since both of these antithetical extremes have often wrongly been equated with Christianity, it is our immediate task to indicate why such identifications are inaccurate.

That both perfectionism and resignation are inadequate protection against despair may be illustrated in many ways. Since mid-life is a time when men and women are often caught between the claims of both their children and their parents, it might be useful to illustrate two sets of attitudes toward the care of the aged. The first involves a couple in their sixties who have recently had to put an aged parent into a nursing home. This decision was reached after fifteen years in which they had willingly cared for the progressively ailing nonagenarian in their own home. Finally, after frequently pondering the need for action, they decided that the care needed was beyond their ability and the aged mother was institutionalized. She never complained about the action. Unable to accept the fact of their limitation, the couple continues to be self-recriminating.

The other behavioral extreme was depicted by the children of an aged father. With believable reasons and rationalizations, they were prepared to abandon the old man to society's care. Nothing could or need be done beyond the simple matter of signing a few papers. They intended to visit regularly, but they did not. They were resigned to their inability to do anything constructive for a father whom they had various reasons to dislike.

Whereas the couple of the first illustration experienced despair from their inability to affirm their limitations, the children of the second illustration despaired that anything could ever be better in their relationship with their father. Whereas the former felt that nothing they might do would be right, the latter were willing to settle for anything. Without suggesting that the care of aging, and often ailing, parents is a matter easily resolved, or that there is any one procedure which fits all situations, I find neither perfectionism nor resignation adequate to the realities of this or of many other circumstances regularly encountered.

God's Gracious Initiative

It is for this reason that I want to begin our discussion about the relationship of Christian faith to the life cycle by considering the need to be able to embrace limitations without capitulating to them. I shall do this by taking account of two articles from The Apostles' Creed—the affirmations about God and about the forgiveness of sin. Having indicated in the previous chapter that this linking of items from the Creed would characterize our procedure throughout, I trust that the reasons for coordinating discussion of God and forgiveness will gradually make sense.

All writing about or discussion of God is both distorted and dependent upon referents within human experience. No statement about reality which transcends human experience can ever be assuredly accurate; all statements about such reality are metaphors from human experience. Thus, when the Creed affirms belief in "God, the Father Almighty, Maker of heaven and earth," it is clearly dependent on several human experiences. While it is not germane to our present purposes to emphasize the unavoidable distortions, it is necessary to note both the inadequacy of the single parent reference and the fact that, in Christian understanding, to the omnipotence must be conjoined the utter mercy of God. Power without compassion is intimidating. And it must be clear that all language about God is by analogy from human experience: statements about God are not only from family and court but from all instances of *making* things. Excepting the limitation inherent in reference to a single parental analogy, I intend no quarrel with the Creed's language. It is conditioned, but even if it were infinitely enlarged, it could not be otherwise. What we know is our experience, from which words are always one step removed, and it is these experience-derived words which we must use if we are to speak usefully of that which transcends our experience. In his first letter to the church at Corinth, Paul stated clearly reasons why words spoken with one's (experience-informed) mind are to be preferred to the ecstatic utterances which may accompany direct experience of the transcendent.

Our task, then, acknowledging these limitations, is to speak of God's relationship to human life. That is, we must indicate how Christians understand three matters: (1) the meaning of the divine initiative, (2) the fact that something is awry in human experience, and (3) the nature of God's response to human truancy.

Belief in God's gracious initiative is at the heart of Judaism and Christianity, and Islam. The distinctive character of all Jewish sacred writing and of the New Testament is reflected in the stories about the origin of the natural world told at the beginning of the Hebrew Bible. That this literature is also part of canonical Christian Scripture indicates that the early church understood itself in the tradition of those called into being and given their identity and mission by divine initiative. A couplet from colonial New England captures cryptically the amazement of those who so believe:

How odd of God
to choose the Jews.

Both the natural world and the events of human history are seen, for example by the psalmists, as evidence of the beneficence and reliability of God's initiative. Nowhere in literature is adverse human experience more clearly presented than in the book of Job and in the historical events of the crucifixion. But, before looking more closely at some of the forces which have thwarted the divine will, I must make clear how God's initiative may be seen in the opportunities of the life cycle.

It is my conviction that, in the stages through which men and women may move from birth to death, we have the most familiar "evidence" of both God's grace and human truancy. Unfortunately, for reasons arising from long religious indifference to the tutelage inherent in the life stages and contemporary preoccupation with both biblical literalism and the more esoteric religious experience, few are able to recognize in their own daily experience the presence of divine initiative. As we shall suggest in greater detail in the next chapter, that the familiar has become quite unfamiliar results both in alienation from oneself and the inability to be nourished by biblical imagery. The persuasiveness of the central metaphors of the Bible which point to the divine initiative is directly determined by the intensity and vividness by which the metaphors are confirmed by one's inner experience. Such a ritual as the Jewish Seder rightly stresses the importance of combining a rehearsal of important past events with the imaginative identification with the people to whom the events occurred and occur. You Are There was the title of an early television series which, like many history books, suggested that the past is not really lost. In Jewish and Christian practice, it is crucial for the believer to have been there by being able to confirm in one's own experience the importance and meaning of significant stories and past events. The fall is not an event which can be placed and dated. It is in faith an "event" which one either "knows" or does not know from one's inner experience.

For many people the stages of life are an end in themselves. For the person of faith this is not so. The various stages through which one may pass provide the experiences with which it becomes possible to confirm inwardly the biblical images which point to the divine initiative. Progress through the life stages is not optional for the Christian. What one may perceive and assent to on the basis of one's experience as a child is adequate for children. While the perceptions and fears of one's childhood endure for a lifetime and are an important source of nurture, they are not alone adequate. To those experiences much should be added as one grows older. Paul's opinion that we must "give up childish ways" (1 Cor. 13:11) may be inaccurate, but he did understand that accumulated experience takes us beyond the limitations of childhood.

Each of the potential stages of human life has the function of putting us in touch with ever more of reality: our own feelings and thoughts and the analogous experiences of others. It is by the ever deepening and broadening appreciation of the variety of human experience that we are equipped to internalize the "evidences" in nature and history of the divine initiative. To refuse to move beyond some comfortable adjustment to a particular life stage not only impoverishes one's own life but inhibits one's ability to relate to others. It also means that one's understanding of God is condemned to remain static. Thus, when one's faith remains stuck at a grade-school level, one's life is developmentally arrested.

Contrary to popular attitudes, it is not the function of faith to insulate us against encounter with reality. Faith is but one of two basic responses—fantasy is the other—to experiences not yet integrated into one's self-understanding and one's ways of relating to the world. Always the challenge is to be able to acknowledge the reality of ever more of whatever one encounters.

Each of the life stages confronts one with the possibility of new experiences. While few experiences are utterly unprecedented—e.g., adolescent sexuality has its sensual precursors and even death follows on many smaller but grievous losses—many experiences are sufficiently intense or far-reaching in ramifications as to be anticipated as novel. How one receives or enters into such experience and how one is able to incorporate it into one's self-understanding and ways of dealing with the world is crucial. The way of faith, equipped by prior experience, seeks to limit the power of the experience by incorporating it into an understanding of reality which is informed by a sense of the divine initiative underlying all things. Nothing is beyond God's grace. The way of fantasy, to which imagination is forced when no limitations are available, creates specters. The life of faith, informed by prior integration of the life-stages experience, is, thus, a way to limit the power of fantasy.

The "fact" of God's gracious initiatives is either inwardly recognized and results in its grateful embrace, or nature and history are simply arenas for human activity to be justified as best one can. While this puts the issue perhaps too sharply, obscuring both the infidelity of those who act contrary to what they profess to "see" and the reverence of some who cannot "see," I shall stay with the rough distinction between those who have vision and those lacking it. Otherwise, the difficulty of my somewhat unfamiliar thesis might be hopelessly complicated. For I am contending that it is in the ordinary (scheduled) progress through the stages of life that we have the most familiar evidence of the divine initiative. In these stages, and in the relationships which are inherent in them, we have the God-given means for calling forth from each life the maturation of which all are varyingly capable. This is what I am calling God's "curriculum": the syllabus from which we are ordinarily to learn how to be ever more appropriately in touch with ourselves, ever more fully related to other life. I do not assume that all can or should develop identically; there are genetic differences, time and place of birth, etc. The point is that in the opportunities of life between the cradle and the grave we have the means by which to evoke vast potential for creativity, usefulness, and enjoyment. That this does not occur is either explained or obscured, depending on what one "sees," because of sin. Something—indeed, a great deal—has gone wrong. Before attempting to discuss that, I must stress the intentional, temporary impreciseness of what I mean by the work of the life stages.

There are many social scientists who are able to identify in considerable detail the progress that people should be making as they proceed from one stage of life to the next. I am indebted to them. It may just be that somebody will have to work carefully at their specific clarifications, to demonstrate how a theological approach illumines and/or is illumined by close attention to the details of human development.

For the moment, however, my task is different. I am saying that, whatever the particular "assignment" of any stage of life—and these probably vary depending on the assumptions which inform the work of different researchers—there are two largely ignored theological convictions: (1) human beings are called to grow over the course of their lives (this capability being an important evidence of grace) and (2) such development is often aborted by both corporate and personal sin. In order to get to our discussion of the latter, it is crucial that we see it as a factor of the former. Despite the social injury which results from it, sin is not primarily a sociological category. It is an inherently theological term to identify the misuse or distortion of that which was intended for good by the divine initiative. In this instance the "Maker of heaven and earth" has so fashioned human lives, both as individuals and corporately, that they are capable of endless, dynamic growth. For reasons to which we shall shortly turn, this process is often arrested and/or distorted. That the intent of the gift is thwarted must not obscure the source of the gift. It is for this reason, in our discussion of the life cycle, that we must link the Creed's affirmation about God and the forgiveness of sin. It is in the light of God's "curriculum" that we may and must talk about human truancy. Whatever may be the cultural distortions of the life tasks, and they are probably as numerous as they will be endless, in the instruction which is latent between birth and death we have God's "natural" means of bringing us to God by bringing us to ourselves. Thus, social developments, which make it impossible for lives to mature as they should, are to be resisted because they deny people access to instruction which is crucial to their developing well-being. It is vital, for example, that youth be in touch with age not only for the use they may be to the aging but in order that the young may be put in touch with the aging one within themselves. Not to be so in touch is to be alienated from part of oneself.

Likewise, means must be found to free people from the debilitating effects of personal acquiescence to distorting social attitudes about the life stages. Prior to any experience of the forgiveness of sin, which is for Christians the means sought, it will be necessary to acknowledge the extent to which one has so acquiesced. That distorted attitudes are widespread in the society is no excuse for one's complicity in these attitudes. Not only do such attitudes underlie much social injustice, as the women's movement has made clear, but they make it impossible for men and women to be in touch with complementary sexual components which are within each person. Thus, for one's own development and for the sake of avoiding further injury to others, it is imperative to be able to acknowledge one's accountability for the perpetuation of attitudes, and behaviors, both personal and institutionalized, which one did not originate. We may now begin to see the truth of the ancient order of events: judgment before mercy. To be capable of being freed by forgiveness, one must be able to acknowledge the societal bondage which has resulted from prior blindness to and violation of God's grace.

Human Truancy: What Is Awry?

Something is radically wrong. Wherever one looks the story is much the same: people of high and low estate manifesting behavior which is rooted in some aberration of normal human development. A few years ago the English press was filled with court cases involving both Scotland's senior peer of the realm, convicted of various escapades with preadolescent and adolescent girls, and the former head of the Liberal Party, accused of conspiring to murder an acknowledged homosexual who claims to have been his lover. The stories are newsworthy less because of the uniqueness of the behavior than for the positions both men occupy. The bizarre behavior seems less important than that *public* figures are accused of it.

That something is radically wrong is less flamboyantly but more powerfully suggested in these portions from the review of Bernard Malamud's recent novel.

> *Dubin's Lives* gives us . . . the terrible sense of human frustration, of time hanging heavy and no way forward . . . the sense that . . . there is no possibility of radical change or blinding illumination—and yet that something in us genuinely longs for such change, for a glimpse of what we essentially are, what our life ultimately means. (Gabriel Josipovici, *The Listener*, 7 June 1979.)

On the assumption that one of America's most perceptive novelists is reflecting what are often unrecognized longings in people whose careers will not be marred by public accusation and court trial, we have evidence of deep dissatisfaction. Much of this dissatisfaction arises from aberrant understandings of the nature of the life cycle.

Having established the need to discuss together the Christian understandings of God and human life and having indicated why and how the stages of life may be viewed as one important evidence of what is meant by divine grace, we are now equipped to consider how it might be that things have gone so badly awry. Badly distorted are those sequential stages through which men and women may be put in touch with themselves, thereby creating the conditions for people to be more appropriately and completely in touch with each other. The evidence is endless. Children are hurried out of their childhood by parents anxious to see to it that they are equipped to compete successfully in an endlessly competitive world; adolescents are burdened with the expectations that they will more than compensate for the failures and inadequacies of parental lives; youths, no longer sexually repressed, are neglected by a permissive society which often seems uninterested in helping them integrate their awakened sexuality into an adequate self-understanding and to appreciate the inherently interpersonal nature of human sexual relations; older persons are ignored, often ghettoized, as though isolating them from the rest of society could conceal the fact of human mortality; adults are so busy and so out of touch with their own experience that they are incapable of intelligent opinion about a film or about the adequacy of the "news" reporting of the news magazines; adults also have little capacity for nurturing intimacy (see the divorce statistics); men and women, and perhaps children also, are terrorized at the prospect of spending any significant amount of time without the media diversions by which life is kept at arm's length; singles, especially women, are viewed as objects of both disdain and exploitation. The distortions are legion.

Let me suggest two attitudes which may help us understand why progress through life's stages goes awry: (1) the preference for the part to the whole and (2) the intolerance for ambivalence. These take myriad forms and are sins by which the divine grace is obscured and then rejected. These attitudes must be recognized and acknowledged if there is to be renewing forgiveness.

The preference for a part of anything, or anyone, is first to be seen in attitudes toward the life cycle itself. Probably all societies have preferred some single stage of life over all the others, suggesting that happiness or wisdom or some other form of fulfillment is to be found only there. Since Lao Tzu was eighty years old at birth and since his wisdom was assumedly the fruit of his years, it may be said that Taoism venerates age above the earlier life stages. The permissiveness of the Trobrianders with infants and small children suggests that for them the earliest years are best. Ponce de León's search for the fountain of youth would appear to appeal to many modern westerners, though I believe that America's preference is for something we have called "adulthood." For us it is the evidence of "adult" power (ability to produce and consume) to which we hasten youth and from which the elderly are excluded to their shame. It simply seems to be the case that the particular dynamic of every society is the result of an idolatrous preference for one of the stages of ordinary human development over all the others.

At its worst this tendency forces all other life stages, with their distinctive needs and potentialities, to justify themselves in terms of the characteristics of the "normative" stages. The aversion which many Americans feel to the fact of aging (and death), and their impatience with the "unproductive" indecisiveness of many young people, reveals the inclination to invest one stage of life with absoluteness.

From this ubiquitous effort to prefer the part to the whole follows alienation: from oneself and from others. At no time are we nothing but one of the life stages. As we have said, there are at different times of life appropriate configurations for the self's many components. It would be ordinarily inappropriate, for example, for the adolescent to configure his or her resources in the manner of an aged person. It is to the young person's peril, however, to obscure too completely the fact of the aged one within. Within each of us at all times, from birth and infancy onwards, there is potential for growing old which we must learn to welcome. On the other hand, utter preoccupation with aging and death—even for the dying—alienates one from prior configurations and their continuing resources. The inner adolescent or young adult has not abandoned the elderly, although youthful preoccupations and fears—always only partly resolved—may rightly be more marginal in age than was once appropriate.

Not only are we alienated from inherent resources of the self, but by acquiescing in this cultural preference for a particular life stage, adherents are largely cut off from reciprocal relations with those at less valued stages. There may be necessary, instrumental relationships—the occasional visits to the nursing home, the check sent to the child away from home—but the possibility for mutual relationship has been largely eliminated. The potentials for delight, instruction, empathy, etc., which inhere in all reciprocity were abandoned when the creed of the inherent superiority of one stage of life over all others was embraced. Notice also the anguish experienced by cultists of "adulthood" upon discovering that time is moving them out of the dominant circle. The moves made to conceal this would be humorous but for the fanaticism of the conviction that a part is preferable to the whole. The fact that the elitism is based upon a misreading of the life stages does not diminish the impoverishment felt by those who no longer belong to the elite.

A "disease," which we might call the pathology of the "best self," often accompanies the idolatry of the preference for the part. Perhaps a simple illustration will begin to suggest what I mean by this "best self" pathology. Who has not found her or himself blaming others for having triggered feelings for which we refuse to accept responsibility? My wife may say some innocent thing—a reminder that it's but half an hour before dinner guests are scheduled to arrive—only to encounter a reaction of accusatory anger from me. She is to blame I feel, and sometimes say, for provoking a reaction which I am unwilling to own. My procrastination about getting dressed, or helping with preparations, probably conceals (but not from my wife?) at least my mixed feelings or downright unwillingness to proceed with plans to which I agreed. This attempt to put the blame elsewhere rather than where it belongs suggests that I am out of touch with my real feelings. Rather than expose and explode the myth of my "best self," I project the blame onto the often surprised other. Those familiar with the story of the Garden of Eden will recognize in Adam's response to questioning—"the woman whom thou gavest to be with me . . ." (Gen. 3:12)—an early version of this tendency. Every effort to deny the negative particulars of our particular life is a manifestation of this pathology. That it arises from the attempt to let a "best" part of ourselves be the whole of us is what we need to see clearly.

This preference for a part or parts of our lives has one additional feature to be identified. I refer to our neglect of the inner events of our lives. For reasons partly suggested above, we are a society exceptionally preoccupied with externals. At the worst this takes the form of exclusive interest in appearances. As long as things look right, everything must be alright. However, appearances can be deceiving.

One way to get at our often total preoccupation with externals lies in correcting the mistaken belief that, apparently because physical maturation is largely completed by late adolescence, little of significance is occurring within the lives of men and women during the first adult decades. While it is true that most of people's time and energies during these years are directed to external matters—acquiring career skills and status, establishing a family and raising children—it is grievously wrong to assume that lives can be so thoroughly externalized. To the extent that one succeeds in this effort, the price will be paid in eventual emptiness and resentment and/or in an explosive rejection of all the externals which seemed to identify the person. The emptiness is more to be feared than the explosion. Persons who feel emptied and who are finding no way to get back in touch with themselves may become resigned to the life of appearances—the blue-rinse syndrome—and to an increased inability to relate to others in anything approaching a *personal* way. The exploders, on the other hand, will surprise many—and probably hurt some—but they may be trying to get back in touch with nourishing sources from which largely externalized lives have isolated them. Those troubled ones will not substitute for the whole the external aspects of life.

A classic case might be the dutiful wife and mother—a comparable scenario might easily be done for husbands of comparable disposition—who for years assumed most of the domestic responsibility, always allowing major decisions to be the husband's responsibilty. It should be noted that there is an important self-serving ingredient in the willingness to let another make the decisions: the passive party is thereby free of all responsibility for the outcome of any particular choice. At the worst the nondecider is able to undermine in a passively aggressive way even the good plans of the decider. To everybody's surprise, the good woman or man, often in conjunction with the offer of love from another source, simply walks away from the family. It is easy to condemn such behavior—probably none do it better than the person who walks away—but the point needs to be stressed that it may well be the action of somebody desperately determined to get (back?) in touch with a long neglected need for inner development. The curse of roles, which externalize lives, becomes unbearable.

The obvious but largely unacknowledged cause of the universal alienation from oneself is the fact that few persons want access to more than part of what we are. The mark of a friendship—a growing relationship as distinguished from an acquaintance—is that it encourages ever more inclusive disclosure. The willingness of another to know more about us without taking advantage of that knowledge is *the* great gift one person can give to another. Even the closest of friendships falls short of the total acceptance which we desire. A recent newspaper article provides illustration. Some of the friends of a young woman who was dying of cancer were unable to continue to befriend her. The old ways of being her friend became impossible and they were unable to adopt new ways. The young woman wisely recognized the reality of some friends' inability to embrace the new fact of her imminent death and urged only that those who backed off acknowledge the fact of their limitations.

The consequence of this selective acceptance of parts of each other is that we are able to assent to only selected parts of ourselves. This is the source of our over-worked "best" selves and of the fatigue we experience because of the energy required to suppress our "unacceptable" parts. If we are unlucky, we succeed in this effort to pretend. That even long-neglected aspects of ourselves may seek to be acknowledged will disturb all who have acknowledged only their "best" selves. The fact is that it is new life to which the now disturbing person aspires.

The point to be stressed is that much has been going on in the inner life of men and women in their twenties and thirties. That comparatively few apparent physical changes usually occur during these years—though even this can be overstressed—should not conceal the changes which might occur over the decades before one's fortieth birthday. Jack Benny's ability to make us laugh at his endless insistence that he was but thirty-nine was based upon a shrewd understanding of America's fears. The tragedy is that the humor rarely enabled people to exorcise these fears and to begin to honor the inner processes which have never ceased to work despite our refusal to acknowledge them.

We appear to assume that once a young man or woman settles on a mate and/or career everything is settled. Without minimizing the importance of such decisions, which are at least evidences of one's abilities to set some limits and to invest oneself in ordinarily manageable tasks, they do not represent the end of one's growth. Exactly the opposite is the case. While the experiences of marriage and career enable one to draw upon resources acquired in prior experience, they also generate endless opportunities for growth. This becomes obvious in the demands of work where skills relevant to holding a position may have to be acquired: night school classes, job training, etc. Improved abilities and accumulated experience are usually the evidences of growth which account for promotions and job satisfaction. Not only are these not the necessary conditions of inner change, they may serve as substitutes for, or concealments of the lack of, inner development appropriate to the early middle years.

A similar analysis might be made for those who allow the external demands of the home to determine their role-defined lives. Nobody brings formally acquired skills to being a spouse or a parent. At the outset of such relationship we have what we are and that is enough to get a couple launched. All sorts of skills need to be acquired: learning to make and live with (or without) a budget, learning household maintenance, learning how to handle an infant and eventually older children, and becoming less clumsy as a lover. The tendency is to let these tasks progressively provide one's identity. One could come to believe that adequacy in the performance of one's necessary and chosen tasks fully accounts for all of the person, as though the performance of inherently exhausting tasks exhaustively identifies the person.

This is not the case. While the very activities of work and home, to say nothing of public responsibilities, demand the acquisition of skills for the performance of external tasks, they also endlessly generate basic questions: about the adequacy of one's self-understanding, about one's capacity for interpersonal relations, about balancing the often conflicting claims of work and family, about the relationship of personal pleasure and public responsibility. How much time and energy ought the young parent and conscientious school teacher have for a political campaign—or for cultivating the relationship with one's spouse? How one decides these matters may not endlessly be settled with the insights and convictions that one had as a bachelor or a newlywed. Nor may they be endlessly settled by always giving priority to one of the elements contending for one's attention. To make a clear decision requires the elevation of one factor to supremacy, but if it is always the same factor which determines—the claims of one's work or of the family—then a part is being substituted for the conflicting claims of the whole. One is thereby refusing, postponing, or making progressively difficult the opportunities for inner growth appropriate to that stage of life. One is settling for a static and temporarily more secure, rather than a dynamic and immediately more turbulent, way of being oneself. The trouble with such a "decision" is that its consequences are not apparent soon enough.

The results of the neglect of one's inner growth, especially of those ambivalences which are inherent in all lives, begin to surface only as the appeals of the externalized life begin to decline. The seven-year itch is a popular way of alluding to a diminution of interest and satisfactions which is not confined to romantic relationships. To the extent that they have functioned so as to inhibit rather than to enhance one's inner life, all externalized activities—work, family, leisure, church-going—are subject to the "itch." Because they have served to disconnect rather than to connect us more accurately and more completely to our true selves, they become boring. Many people are endlessly in search of something interesting to do, a little excitement. The search is usually fruitless. Neither the expensive camera, with full attachments, nor the recreation vehicle, complete with well-stocked bar, can meet the need for self-acquaintance. Temporarily they may divert us from that need, but God help us—and all those with whom we are involved—if one or more of the many diversions available manage to divert us permanently from the growth to which the seven-year itch calls us.

The trouble is that it is not easy for those who have long been disconnected from themselves to reconnect. In no way is this task analogous, as my language may misleadingly suggest, to reactivating the services at a summer cottage after the winter shutdown. Long-established habits which have excluded or ignored attention to oneself—thinking of oneself, or allowing others to identify us, wholly in terms of roles performed—are not quickly shed. We are talking about the deep ruts in which people, who have for twenty or more years acted as though there were nothing more to them than others could see, find themselves. The fundamental effect of such a life is that *the* means by which we relate to ourselves and to the world have atrophied. How far gone these feelings are will be the result of some combination of their original strength and the extent of their neglect. It is valueless to urge a person to develop some new interests. Such widely given advice misses the point: interests are not to be willed. They arise spontaneously in those who are reasonably in touch with their own inner life, for these are people equipped to relate to the world outside themselves. This is precisely the desire of a maturing inner life: not to be progressively self-preoccupied but to be able to give to and receive from the world outside of the self. These are the marks of a maturing religious faith which is able to confirm from self-understanding the central images of the Bible. It makes a world of difference whether or not the world we inhabit is created or a matter of chance. No less important is whether we see our lives after the cyclical model of ancient Egypt, with the predictability of annual renewal by the Nile's flooding; or, after the manner of Abraham, called forth from familiarity into the uncertainties and excitement of pilgrimage. It makes a world of difference whether we are able to affirm meaningfully in our

self-understanding a normative death and rebirth, the inseparability of gains *and* losses. It is the work of a nurtured inner life
so to equip us.

Basically, the preference for a part rather than the whole of
anything or anyone is an attempt to seize and maintain control
of one's life and environment. The need to be able to set limits,
and thereby to control a situation, is unavoidable. Few tasks—
the painting of a house or the writing of a book—are so simple
that they can be understood and accomplished as a whole. It is
by one word at a time, one sentence after another, chapter by
chapter, that I do this writing or, analogously, paint my house.
In many areas of life always, and in almost all areas at times,
one controls by limiting the elements with which one will deal.
This self-evident specialization is the key to much of America's
prosperity. It is also the source of some horrendous social injustice and environmental problems. It is one thing for industry
to insist on, and to assist with, good oral hygiene. It is quite
another so to employ this criterion that unemployed minority
people must have sound teeth before they can be hired. That's
a catch-22! It is one thing, for example, for the Corps of Engi-
neers to propose to make arid land arable by diverting the natural bed of a river for the sake of irrigation. It is quite another
to ignore or to downplay the effects of such changes upon the
immediate flora and fauna and on the human lives and communities downstream of the old flow. In many important areas
of modern work, of which engineering may be the best illustration, jobs are most expeditiously accomplished by a variety of
task limitations; and efficiency is profitable.

From the theological perspective, two things must be said.
First, that expedition is *not* the determinative consideration
when it comes to the humanization of lives. Second, while task
limitation has some function near the center of religious life—
it is usually possible and desirable to distinguish between
prayer and play—such preoccupation with the part rather than
with the whole of lives is antithetic to Christianity. Control of
one's life and environment is not Christianity's purpose. Ultimately, with one's identity derived from assent to the divine

initiative, the Christian is free to set necessary limits, to address oneself to parts of things, because it is the whole, complex, inconsistent self which has been identified and affirmed by God's grace.

God is concerned with the whole of our lives, and it is only as we assent to that totality, however broken and distorted, that we may be able to perceive the divine initiative. Our continuous progress through the stages of the life cycle is urged for this reason and for the consequent capacity to empathize with lives both less and more privileged than our own. Each stage holds the potential for putting persons more completely in touch with themselves, ever more acessible to and ready for rapport with others, ever more open to the evidences of God's grace amidst both accomplishment and failure. Every preference for the part rather than the whole both obscures the real human condition and blinds us to the God-given ambivalences in which the divine initiative may be seen.

I turn now to the second, and related, reason why embrace of the life cycle is refused: aversion to ambivalence. This may prove to be the source of the truant preference for the part to the whole.

To make our way into this issue it is necessary to call attention to a central characteristic of Erikson's understanding of the stages of normal human development. He insists that a polar tension exists at each stage. Thus, for example, the infant grapples with the lures of both trust and mistrust, the adolescent primarily with the tension between identity formulation and identity diffusion, the person in mid-life with the conflicting claims of generativity and stagnation, the older person with the possibilities of both integrity in and despair/disgust for one's life. Such tensions are the material of human experience; the way in which these issues are resolved determines maturation or regression. Clearly, it is the positive pole which must predominate if growth is to occur. To the degree that this happens the person is equipped to move on to the next of life's tasks. As we emphasized then, however, and probably cannot overstress, the positive pole must only become dominant. It is *not* a matter of obliterating or utterly extinguishing the other pole. My recent examples—mistrust, identity diffusion, stagnation, and despair—continue to have their functions in the total life of persons. For them to predominate is perilous, but it is no less perilous to be unable to continue to embrace them as subordinate resources. The need for some mistrust in a world which is not fully trustworthy must be obvious. Also obvious is the adolescent's need for some uncertainty about a viable, provisional identity. That generative adults know the threat of stagnation and that there is always reason for some feelings of self-disgust makes it unnecessary to deny their reality. It is not fatal to acknowledge the persistence of these negative traits. It could be fatal to further life development to have to deny them; it would be fatal to one's Christian maturation if denial prevails. On the human side nothing is more integral to one's relationship to the divine initiative than the capacity for truthfulness. As in the analogy of human friendships, it is not just our presentable selves which seek the assurance of acceptability. About the presentable there is little difficulty. What we desire is to be able to present ourselves truthfully both to our friends and to God. Anything less than this is pretense which gives a questionable, temporary reward.

The source of the pretense in which all engage to varying degrees is an aversion to ambivalence. While the following illustrations are in no way exhaustive, the reader will be able to see in each its relationship to Erikson's understanding of the polar tensions at each life stage.

The ongoing tension between continuity and change is an unavoidable source of stress in all lives. (By stress I do not mean something inherently undesirable. While there may be times when it is to be avoided, more often stress is evidence of a potential for growth with which we are struggling. As such we avoid it to our peril, as psychiatric reaction to the widespread use of tranquilizers indicates.) It is the case that, since time is the context within which we live, there is an inherent tension between the claims of the past and the lure of the future. Obviously, this reality is equally true in institutional and personal life. At the public level labels—conservative and lib-eral—have been fashioned to characterize those more inclined to continue the tradition of the past and those more disposed to change. In one major branch of Christendom the tension is between those who revere icons and the iconoclasts; in the west the conflict has been between the bearers of tradition—from *traditio*, that which has been handed on from the past about the gospel—and those more open to the leading of the Spirit. (An excellent introduction to these issues will be found in a book by the Welsh theologian, Daniel T. Jenkins, *Tradition, Freedom, and the Spirit* [Philadelphia: Westminster, 1951].) Since one must live in the present, however adverse that may be, there is no way to avoid the often conflicting claims of both the past and the future. Yet all of us at times, and some people with surprising consistency, seek to deny the validity of one or the other of these components. Among those whose consist-ency always surprises me are extremists who cannot wait to be rid of the past and those who cling to it tenaciously. On my understanding of the divine initiative revealed in Scripture and witnessed to in the life of the church, it is most often those partial to continuity who need challenging. Since much public preference for tradition often arises in defense of personal priv-ilege, appeals for change are not readily heard by the privi-leged.

These tensions which are so central to and obvious in public life are no less critical in individual lives. At the personal level, which is our primary focus, and with particular reference to the claims of the life stages, the issues may be less obvious but they are no less important. The successful resolution of the polar tensions at any stage of life takes such time and energy that there is the temptation to call an end to the struggles. I would not deny that an exhausted person deserves a rest nor that successful arrival at a particular stage does not give one the right to enjoy the privileges of the achievement. However, as we have emphasized, *the* point of satisfactorily negotiating one of the stages is that one is now equipped to move on to the next. Fortunately, it is not just a matter of exhortation. The challenge of each next stage both functions as a lure and represents the opportunity to begin to use recently acquired skills. It is misleading to describe the process thus as a series of insulated stages. Lives unfold less systematically and more confusedly than my description suggests. We are often not ready for growth at the time the demand for it arrives. In those instances *we do what we can with what we have.* In personal development, it is only possible to initiate change on the basis of capabilities derived from the past. The adolescent may proceed into responsible intimacy only when equipped with an adequately fashioned sense of identity. To offer to share one's inner life and to invite that of another before one has paid the price involved in overcoming the forces making for identity diffusion will result in a demand for "payment" of which one is incapable. It is that simple. Similarly, it is only as one has positively resolved the generativity/stagnation issue that she or he is able to address the question of the integrity of (or despair about) one's life with some hope.

The refusal of gradual change, which I perceive to be the tendency of contemporary life, can be partly explained in terms of the very limited progress which people make through the early life stages. To what extent the widespread appeal of esoteric forms of so-called Christianity and the lure the Eastern religions are to be seen as responses to offers of dramatic change I am not certain. I strongly suspect, however, this to be the case: that those who already despair of the possibility of gradual and costly change but still yearn for a glimpse of what life essentially means, embrace the proferred panacea. Trapped in intolerable continuity and incapable of slow change, they opt for radical discontinuity.

The evidence is widespread: our aversion to ambivalence, by which the life stages are marked, is nowhere more clearly seen than in our inability to sustain the potentially creative tensions between continuity and change. As it is always the center which is politically vulnerable, it is always the present which is abandoned in personal life for some form of the past or the future. Unwilling to pay the high cost of reworking badly fashioned earlier development, either nostalgia for an ill-remembered past or yearnings for a future which "has got to get better—somehow!" seem preferable to the present. This is not the route to become more fiercely alive but rather an endlessly tempting diversion: either the abandonment of all hope of improvement, or, equally disastrous, the naive expectation of some instant and total transformation of all previous fumblings, ineptitude, and denials. Only a society trapped in both ignorance about the slow, demanding process of human development and in the assumption that there is a pill for every ill could be tempted by such illusions. There are no panaceas for progress through the life cycle. However, there are grounds for appropriate hope for improvement. The gift of the Holy Spirit is less a matter of being issued completely new equipment than of learning how to enjoy and to make better present use of whatever resources one actually has. Those who have been led to believe that there is some alternative to this realism have been deceived not only by their inability to value their particular endowments—but by a technological society which has an instant solution for many problems. To these deceptions must be added the possibly deeper ignorance about the inseparability of gains and losses over the entire course of the life stages. It is to this second aspect of our aversion to ambivalence that we may now turn.

In no way is the embrace of the stages of ordinary human development made more difficult than by our assumption that there are only cumulative gains. Despite evidence from all areas of human experience, modern Americans seem determined to deny the inseparability of gains and losses. It is almost as though it were a matter of national pride or self-understanding that there should be no losses. Just how it was that Richard Nixon "explained" the withdrawal from Vietnam I never fathomed, but it clearly involved the effort to honor/exploit the American aversion to the inherent ambivalence of gains and losses. He had to acknowledge the widely desired gain of returning troops home, but the concomitant (or prior) loss had to be obscured.

As important as are the tortured rationalizations to which this aversion leads is the fact that it leaves no place for the grieving which is appropriate to each life-stage accomplishment. Since gains alone are valued—actually, only they are acknowledged—there is an important sense in which we not only preclude the possibility of grieving but dampen the likelihood of celebration. Where only gains are expected it is difficult to generate the feeling appropriate to genuine celebration. This helps one to understand better the hollowness of so much of our public and personal occasions. They are attempts to engender enthusiasm for much less than the full story. As simple an occasion as a birthday cannot be genuinely honored if the exclusive emphasis is on what has been added by the passage of twelve months. Clearly, that is the primary note to be sounded, but there is a proper place for acknowledging the losses which accompany every such gain. The arrival of one's thirteenth birthday, however intensely desired, should not be allowed to obscure the loss inherent in becoming a teenager; nor should the arrival of one's twentieth obscure the sadness inseparable from the passing of adolescence. That this is not the primary emphasis of such celebration should not conceal the fact that, in order to grasp something new, one has had to let go of something else of value.

Perhaps our inability to affirm the universality of both gains and losses, especially when coupled with our passion for gain, makes our effort to deal with circumstances of real loss so unrewarding. It is a rare funeral or memorial service in which the cause for rejoicing and gratitude is effectively heard. When this occurs it is usually the case that the achievements of the deceased have been sufficiently outstanding that review of them seems to be required. The sole exception known to me was the recent funeral of a retarded woman who had died at age sixty. Well known in the church she attended, and not burdened with the society-wide expectation of cumulative gains, it was possible for people to give thanks for the childlike warmth of this person. The problem is that most people neither achieve exceptionally nor are they retarded. Their lives are marked by modest gains and comparable losses but always hardened by the success-inspired expectations of nothing but gains. Under such common circumstances it is unnaturally difficult both to grieve the loss and to celebrate the gains of the life ended. Our expectations of gain not only minimize the fact of loss, they also obscure the costly reality of most people's struggle for even modest gains: the alcoholic's inconclusive struggle with booze, the promiscuous person's inconclusive struggle for a modicum of faithfulness, the self-denigrating person's inconclusive struggle for self-respect, the suspicious person's efforts to learn to trust. I appreciate that there is widespread uncertainty about any life beyond death, but this is a complicating, secondary factor. The real culprit is the prior inability to embrace the unavoidable fact of the concommitant gains and losses which characterize human experience. Our capacity for both celebration and grief is made shallow thereby: we cannot well give or receive praise, we can grieve but little and will not allow others to grieve for or with us.

There are two crucial reasons why we need to be able to move beyond our aversion to the ambivalence of gains and losses. First, as most people's experience shows, the possibility of loss is at least as real as the hope for gain. We must be equipped to embrace this limiting reality when it occurs. (Of the many things which have been written recently by those in mid-life who have learned of their imminent death, attention should be called to a poignant booklet by Bradford Smith, *Dear Gift of Life: A Man's Encounter with Death* [Wallingford, PA: Pendle Hill Pubns., 1965].) Some may argue that to be aware of the possibility of losing, as in competitive sport, lessens the likelihood of victory. I doubt this. In all events, it is irrelevant in other areas of human life, especially that of the life stages. When it comes to the deep assumptions which either assist or hinder people's efforts to embrace the life cycle tasks, some societies seem to equip their citizens better than does our own. In addition to the familiar verdicts of guilty or acquitted, Scottish law, for example, includes a decision of "not proven." This might well be adoptable into our own court options but for the fact that we have a sharp win/lose mentality. "Not proven" would be a verdict much more applicable to most people's progress through the life stages. While British games are as physically competitive as comparable American sports, I have noted with interest their willingness to allow a soccer game to conclude as a tie. It is apparently not necessary either for the national psyche nor for the ranking of teams that each game be settled as either a victory or a defeat. On a given afternoon, or over the course of a given life, an ambivalent draw may be the best result possible. For such an eventuality we need to be better equipped than the win or lose mentality allows.

Second, and more directly to our purpose, the inseparability of gains and losses in life-cycle progress must be affirmed. Ignoring for now the actual failures which people experience, it is unavoidably the case that an element of loss attaches to each success. If it is true that each life stage holds its own potential rewards, it is inevitable that the achievement involves the loss of earlier ways of being identified. A good example is the seventeen-year-old who finds his or her own sense of self increasingly confirmed by significant others and enjoys that achieved identity. The late adolescent is no longer merely the child of a particular family. Please note that I am not arguing for avoiding the possibility of loss by avoiding growth. I stress the importance of recognizing that loss is inseparable from growth and that provision must be made for the grief which accompanies it. We are not stronger for denying grief's reality; rather, we are forced to conceal the fact and are progressively incapable of empathic identification with those who are free to acknowledge both their gains and losses. The gain achieved by the alcoholic whose drinking is arrested, whose independence and self-respect are thereby enhanced, should not be used to deny him or her grieving access to the loss of dependency which has also resulted. Students leaving home for the first time are taking an important, risky step for which they need to be praised. The homesickness which many experience acutely, and all to lesser degree, need not be denied for the sake of applauding the movement away. On the parental side the joy appropriate to the maturation of one's children often involves (at least temporarily) as much of a sense of loss as of pride of achievement. A friend is currently struggling to bring under more effective restraint his great ambition to achieve. He does so in part because of the destructiveness of this ambition to an earlier marriage, some of the symptoms of which he senses in relationship to his second wife. Should he prevail in this struggle the gain will be something to celebrate, but it would be naive to deny the loss he will experience by bringing his work into sounder relationship to his family life.

How one understands this matter of the inseparability of gains and losses will have a profound effect upon his or her ability to affirm and be nourished by a leading image of the Hebrew Bible and the central theme of the New Testament. Whether or not one will be able to perceive the divine initiative in the experiences of his or her life depends to a considerable extent on one's ability to embrace the ambivalence of gains and losses. Blindness to the unavoidable reality of loss results in the inability to treat the losses in one's own life with the seriousness they deserve. Parents who have failed to recognize and come to terms with their own losses not only impoverish their own lives; it is difficult to imagine them assisting their children through similar experiences. It is more likely that their patterns of denial and concealment will become those of their children. We reproduce our own kind. To the extent that either the possibility of failure or the reality of losses must be denied, there is potential experience on which such a person cannot yet draw in relating both to others and to experiences reported in the Bible. The latter may seem inconsequential while one's energies are high. There usually comes a point, however, when one experiences some de-illusionment with both the emphasis on cumulative gains and the particular goals to which one has aspired. At such a time one may need, as was not possible earlier, to acknowledge some of life's ambivalences. The problem is that such acknowledgment is more easily recognized than embodied. More often than not upon seeing the mid-life consequences of having lived as one has, the person who relaxes a firm grip on the exclusive importance of cumulative gains does an about face into an understanding of his or her life as unrelieved loss. Some of those consequences may be a career which rewards less as it pays more, children who seem unimpressed by the achievements to which one has attached great importance, a spouse from whom one feels "inexplicably" remote, and, possibly, a string of transient liaisons which, at best, inform one's fantasies on those nights when sleep is elusive. The alternative to a widely espoused single-mindedness is not the embrace of ambivalence, not the ability to search meaningfully among cruciform symbol-systems, but despair. The truant does not go unpunished. (Two important modern novels—Joseph Heller, *Something Happened* [New York: Alfred A. Knopf, 1974], and John Fowles, *Daniel Martin* [Boston, MA: Little Brown, 1977]—explore many of these realities from the male perspective in often helpful ways. Capable of affection only for his son who seems able to fulfill some of his own unfulfilled hopes, something significant for the protagonist finally happens in Heller's long novel. Fowles lets us into the life of a man apparently incapable of sustaining any relationships and capable of entering liaisons only with women his daughter's age.)

Many other illustrations might be presented in support of the thesis that one of the major sources of uncertainty about the importance of struggling with the demands of the life stages is aversion to those ambivalences which lie at the heart of human experience. The unresolvable issue of individual isolation and the possibility of meaningful relations with others would be one such. In my experience the tension is not resolvable: individual isolation persists. But the persistence of an ineradicable solitude does not preclude the possibility of mutually rewarding relationships. Indeed, relationships are only possible when the parties entering into them have and retain a degree of autonomy. The extreme temptations are either to absolutize the isolation or to seek to obliterate it by allowing oneself to be absorbed into some larger, undifferentiated group. In both cases the tension between self and others, which is intrinsic to the work of the life stages, has been abandoned. We see comparable tensions, and similarly truant refusals of them, in the uncertainties inherent in the relationship between security and risk, fear and courage, the presence of both sexes within each man and woman.

In the most general terms the moral dimension underlying all these issues is the enduring tension between what is and what ought to be. Again we shall see, as we noted in the illustrations with which this chapter began, that the tendency is either to settle for what is or for the perfectionism which always finds what is unacceptable. Both of these extremes provide a poor basis for engaging the claims of the life stages as God's gracious curriculum.

Is Decisiveness Undermined?

Before concluding this chapter it seems necessary to address the suspicion that my understandings result in indecisiveness. I have stressed the importance of embracing both the whole rather than any of its many parts and the tensions which complicate but may enhance human experience. Does encouragement to embrace life's contingencies effectively undermine the capacity for decision making?

In at least one sense that suspicion is right. A certain kind of decision making—in fact, a certain model of leadership—takes pride in the ability to make quick decisions. I do not doubt either that there are situations in which it is necessary to act quickly or that people vary in the speed with which they are able to size up a situation. Circumstances occasionally call for speedy action; however, to try to treat all circumstances under the same imperative would be a mistake. There should be time, or people should be willing to take time—as the Quakers always do—to allow all of the factors relevant to the issue at hand to be identified. All matters of policy should clearly so be reached. That some people size up a situation, or many of its salient factors, faster than do others may be a fact, but that fact is no reason why the right to make decisions should regularly be accorded such persons. It was not accidental, nor is it irrelevant to the present discussion, that the Founding Fathers devised a system of checks and balances at the heart of our particular form of government. Those quick to see many of the issues have the opportunity to persuade those who may be slower and who may have a different perspective on the issues. The premium is *not* on the speed with which decisions can be made but with a process by which all possibly relevant factors may be identified and weighed according to the best wisdom and the interests of the participants and their constituencies. Almost any other system would be faster; few assure the opportunity for more of the relevant interests to be expressed.

In personal life and relationships the issues are not significantly different. Those who prefer the part to the whole, who destroy the tensions inherent in life's ambivalences, will always arrive at decisions sooner than others. The point to stress, however, is that they are able to do so because they are in touch with fewer of the possibly relevant issues. The same skill which cuts through issues of industrial expansion by ignoring environmental issues or the impact of the proposed change on the life of the neighborhood is able to expedite family decision making with the same eventual costs. Those of whom account is not taken become either passive or active resisters of the decision to be implemented.

What we need to be clear about is that the real issue is not between decisiveness and indecisiveness. Attention to life-cycle issues does not contribute to the latter. *The* issue is between two sources of decisiveness: one of which is informed by as few as possible of the relevant factors, the other of which takes account of as many of these factors as possible. The first is predicated on the importance of speed, authority, and efficiency; the other is less anxious about time and more committed to the likelihood of enlisting the cooperation of all those affected by including their perceptions and concerns in the decision-making process.

The older I get the more I find myself sympathetic with those who bring experience to any discussion. By experience I mean evidence of being in touch with the ambivalences which inhere in each of the life stages. Whatever their age, such people are in touch with the aged one which is within them. Any decision affecting older people would be informed by an appreciation of the fact that they are making arrangements for those in many ways like themselves. I suppose that the qualities I find myself admiring, which clearly do not involve indecisiveness, are to be seen in competent justices—people not quick to condemn and who are familiar with the ambivalences in their own lives. Such persons are not alienated from those judged guilty. By such people the web of life, which clearly includes better and less well-woven sections, is maintained.

The Forgiveness of Sin

We have reached that point where, having completed our discussions of the life stages as God's ordinary curriculum for the maturation of human lives and of some of the main sources of human truancy, we must inquire about the meaning of the Creed's affirmation of the forgiveness of sins. While some of the discussion will anticipate material to be developed more fully in the next chapter, we must at least be clear about what the sin is which is forgiven and how it is accomplished. It is hardly sufficient simply to insist with the roadside sign that Christ died for your sins. That approach has all the appeal of the World War I poster, extended forefinger and all, "Uncle Sam wants you"! Many of those who were sure that Uncle long ago recruited most of us would also say of the roadside sign, "He shouldn't have bothered."

The fundamental Christian assertion, of course, is that God did bother. Equally important in the present context is that God did so for reasons analogous to the experience of those who have proceeded well through the life stages: without equating with us, which would obscure a continuing distinction, God identified with our plight. It is dangerous to pretend to talk too knowingly about such matters. What do I or any person really know about the divine mind? It is safer, with the installers of roadsigns, simply to repeat pithy texts. The landscape which we have been exploring does not allow that option. Despite our ignorance, and with a proper sense of awe, we must attempt to speak about the *gift* of the life stages, human abuse of the gift, and the means employed to restore it. In doing this we are assuming that, however abused the gift has been and however distorting the consequences of that abuse, a degree of kinship persists between the designer and the recipients of the stages of life. However truant we may have been in neglect and misuse of the pedagogical opportunities of the various life stages, nobody thoroughly obliterates the instruction or misses all of the joy of God's curriculum. Analogous to the pleasure which some find in learning for its own sake is the occasional joy of being able to act one's age, to be oneself without pretense, whether that involves a rare expression of anger or of tenderness. In my judgment, nobody is so far "gone" as to be permanently beyond all of the tutelage and all of the simple and nourishing pleasure of being oneself. No matter how limited one's progress through the life stages may have been, no matter how truant, some vestige of the capacity for enjoyment and for being instructed by one's experience persists. The God-given desire for more appropriate ways of relating to self, to others, and to the natural world is unextinguishable. This is the endless, positive attribute of the curriculum which we receive at birth. This is a great gift from a gracious giver.

Negative prompting comes as a consequence of human truancy. The life of pretense may be universal, but there is little evidence that such a life satisfies. In its very nature it cannot: it violates the condition of human well-being which is to know that one's accurate self-assessment is acceptable to all significant others. Progress through the life cycle becomes a religious pilgrimage when one realizes one's utter acceptability to the most significant Other. This is the forgiveness of sins.

The mistake made by many at this point is to assume that this means that God does not mind about sin and/or that now everything that has been wrong will instantly come right. There may be an immediate and renewable euphoria upon realizing that one is at this moment accepted. This is the beginning of a bittersweet process, not its end. Actually the recovery of life's bittersweetness is the gift for those for whom previous experience was progressively embittering. It is the recovery of a proper task for God-given life.

Familiarity with the Gospels determines the ease with which one embraces the tasks of this new start on life. That God has identified with the human plight, that the initiative often only barely discernible in the life cycle has been reinitiated in the life and work of Jesus Christ is the central Christian assertion. Central to it is the insistence that, "In Christ God was reconciling the world to himself" (2 Cor. 5:19). This is to refute every (gnostic) effort to deny the reality of the incarnation. However unfamiliar the language may be the thrust of the claim is crucial: in order to begin the process of setting aright the consequences of repeated human truancy, God has in Jesus as the Messiah *become one with* the truants. The gracious giver of the curriculum has become one with the rebellious pupils in order that they might be freed to learn and to enjoy.

The question to which such students rightly want an answer and which good teachers endlessly ask of themselves, is this: how integral is the material to the person? They want to know whether or not the assignments are diversionary work laid on by the person with authority or if the world is really seen in a different light once the material is mastered. They want to know the extent to which the teacher has internalized his subject; they want evidences of the animation which results from the learning demanded of them. They want to know why and how it matters to enroll in the God-given curriculum of the life stages.

In one form or another this is the question rightly asked of Jesus: why does what you teach matter? It is the question which may lead to the recognition of Jesus as the normative teacher. Ultimately, as for all teachers, there is a price to be paid. Beyond the popular classroom lecture and Galilean homilies by the lakeside, there is the question of how the teacher acts when her or his lessons generate conflict. What is one willing to pay for his or her informed convictions? The Christian answer is that the teacher and the teaching are one. In order to teach as persuasively as is humanly possible, one must not compromise the humanity. After the admirable parables came Golgotha. The Teacher not only talks, not only asks leading questions, he teaches finally and consummately by insisting that the most adverse, the most potentially embittering and alienating experience, lacks the power to destroy his identity in God. This ability to embrace the starkest limitation—undesired and undeserved death—reveals normative humanity. This is the new humanity in whom truants may begin to learn to relinquish unrewarding ways. This is the length to which he was able to go to make unmistakably clear the indestructibility of the divine initiative. It is not necessary, because it is not possible, for truants first to become model pupils. They may never be that. What truants need to learn is that, just as they stand, they are accepted. To sweeten their own lives may lie outside their capability; what is no longer necessary is the self-deception, pretense, and guilt.

This is the glorious paradox: to be able to reconnect the broken pieces of their lives it is first necessary to admit their inability to do so. Progress through the life cycle is not just a matter of having the correct information. We may not assume that, having the facts, we will then have the will. The problem is that the will is impotent to embrace the limitations of human lives. To be willing to make something, however little, with one's very limited resources eludes most people. From this inability arises one of two basic patterns of denial: (1) denial either of the reality of one's limitation, which leads to the perfectionist's despair or (2) denial of the fact of one's limited but real ability to make a difference, which makes for resignation. The truth is that human beings cannot begin to move toward what ought to be without first embracing what is. It is either the effort to conceal one's actual limitations or the inability to see the potential inherent in one's limitations. In a Christian understanding we are given back the ability to embrace our life's actualities without the need for the self-deceptions of either perfectionism or resignation. Truth-grounded lives are empowered to make something, however modest, with what they have. It is the work of the Teacher to draw forth (*educare*) what lies within the pupil. More than that is impossible, but the task is to discover the excitement, the profound satisfaction, of learning with such a teacher. To embrace one's limitations and to begin to discover what can be made of them is not resignation but the beginning of release from its hopelessness. This is what matters.

The mark of such lives is gratitude for having been put back in touch with themselves, having been freed to allow others access and to desire relationship with them, by the gracious God who fully identified with the truants without becoming truant.

It would be profoundly misleading to conclude thus. The struggle to become grateful has only begun; its completion will take at least all of one's years. We must learn to shed—one bit at a time—all of the deceptions and pretense of our truancy. Few of these will yield easily or permanently. Only one, small but vital, step has been taken: we are assured that we will not be abandoned, that what we are *is* the beginning of what we may become. There neither is nor need be any other place at which to begin. It is a modest change, but I am convinced of its sufficiency for the imperfect pupils of God's curriculum. It is the alternative to resignation and the corrective for perfectionism.

IV. | *Jesus Christ: Faith's Struggle with Fantasy*

We began the last chapter by recognizing that there are two common sources of despair: perfectionism, which overrates ordinary human ability, and resignation, which does the opposite. The task is to find an approach to life which both assures greater accuracy about the human potential and enables one to embrace it. That is, we seek an understanding of human experience which affirms both the glory and the repugnance of the ordinary; and it is my belief that the key to such affirmation is to be found in the person and work of Jesus Christ. Those Christians who object to such a suggestion have not paid enough attention to the appropriate articles of The Apostles' Creed.

With the exception of the emphasis on his unique conception and virgin birth, the Creed's affirmations about Jesus as the Messiah provide the basis for this chapter's discussion. It is not that these excepted articles are extrinsic to Christian faith; rather, that they illumine less than the other items the relationship we are pursuing between the divine initiative and the claims of the life stages. Neither immaculately conceived nor born of virgins, ordinary people *can* understand that Jesus suffered, was crucified, dead, and buried. In the insistences that he descended into hell and rose from the grave, that he returns to judge the living and the dead, we have ancient convictions which cast light on modern dilemmas. These articles enable one to make an important clarification between the nature and function of faith and fantasy. I am convinced that whereas it is by faith that the work of the life stages is affirmable, fantasy is the attempted route to life transcendence. It is by faith that the glory and repugnance of the stages of life are embraceable; fantasy forever seeks escape from imperfection. Faith finds adequate nourishment in the ordinary; fantasy's tastes are for something richer.

In this context there are two antithetical misunderstandings common to those outside of the church, and espoused by some within it: (1) that fantasy yearnings are the source and hallmark of Christian belief and (2) that affirmation of life's ordinariness lies within human capability. Both of these views reflect miscalculations of the power of human will. Those who prefer fantasy to ordinariness underestimate the ability of the will, when informed by an adequate vision, to energize and to provide rewarding experience of ordinary life. The others are blind to the impotence of the ordinary will to embrace contradiction and suffering. The former despair of finding an adequate vision of the ordinary to empower the will to accomplish its difficult work; the latter are ignorant of the need for a sustaining vision to maintain the will's ability to work with life's ambivalences.

Perhaps an illustration from a great piece of literature will make clear why I shall pursue the discussion of Christology in terms of the tension between faith and fantasy. In *Doctor Faustus* Christopher Marlowe depicts a man unsatisfiable by any ordinary experience or achievement. An exceptionally accomplished academician, he identified the goals of all professions as "paltry." Crucial to our understanding of life as pilgrimage is the reason for Faust's scorn for the merely human. Prior to making his contract with Lucifer, he asked this revealing question: "Shall I make the spirits . . . resolve me of all ambiguities?" (I.1.76.) Here is the meaning of unfaith: the inability to find in the contingencies of everyday life evidence of God's active presence. Ultimately, sin is the refusal to see in the "paltriness" of everyday matters the ingredients of human pilgrimage. If, as I believe, the satanic is experienced as the result of socially generated hopes which are unrealizable, then *Doctor Faustus* represents the satanic today. Subject to inflated expectations, i.e., unable to enjoy one's particular limitations, one experiences frustrations that lead either to violence, apathy, or fantasy. It is only by faith in God's trustworthiness that we can begin to recognize the potential for growth in ordinary demands and opportunities.

Lacking such faith, we are like Faustus—damned because the "reality" to which we flee is a figment of our imagination. Lacking such faith, we are, like him, incapable of caring about the modest, ordinary good we might do for our neighbor. Like Faustus, only I inhabit the world of my fantasy; cut off from the City of God by unfaith I thereby isolate myself from the City of Man. Self-isolated, I am unable to help or to be helped by another. That is damnation.

Jesus' Temptations: Their Inescapability

It is not by accident that the Synoptic Gospels report the temptations as prologue to Jesus' public ministry. His work could only begin after he had grappled successfully with the fantasies induced by the circumstances into which he had been born. It is always the devil's work, as Marlowe indicates, to suggest ways by which to transcend the paltry hopelessness of the situation in which one finds oneself. Certainly the historical circumstances of a Jewish boy born during the reign of the Roman Emperor Augustus when Quirinius was governor of Syria (Luke 2:1–3) were such as to feed every conceivable fantasy. During the three centuries between the successful Maccabean Revolt and the final, desperate revolution led by Bar Kokba, into the very middle of which period Jesus was born, Judaism spawned innumerable faith and fantasy inspired reactions. Before turning to discussion of the latter, we should note that there are few more noble witnesses to the power of faith in God than the mass suicide of almost a thousand Jews who occupied the fortress at Masada for several years in defiance of the besieging Roman legions.

> My loyal followers, long ago we resolved neither to serve the Romans nor anyone else but only God. . . . Now the time has come

that bids us prove our determination by our deeds. . . . Hitherto we have never submitted to slavery, even when it brought no danger with it: we must not choose slavery now . . . for we were the first of all to revolt, and shall be the last to break off the struggle. And I think it is God who has given us this privilege, that we can die nobly and as free men, unlike others who were unexpectedly defeated. In our case it is evident that day-break will end our resistance, but we are free to choose an honorable death with our loved ones. This our enemies cannot prevent . . . nor can we defeat them in battle. (From El'azar's Oration, 73 C.E., in M. Livneh and Z. Meshel, *Masada*, Tel Aviv: National Parks Authority, n.d.)

The passion for freedom from the effects of occupying troops and officialdom produced, at its best, just such defiance.

Probably it is true that in every country forcibly occupied and regulated by a foreign power, the reactions of the citizenry range from ignominy to nobility. Certainly that was the case in the Judaism of Jesus' day: from the collaboration of the Sadducees and tax collectors to the withdrawal of the Essenes and to the guerilla warfare of the Zealots which led several times to open revolution. So adverse had this Zealot-inspired experience been that, at the Council of Jamnia in the late first century A.D., the assembled Jewish leaders pronounced anathemas not only on the nascent Christians but also on the Zealots. No more revolution! So they might resolve, but forty years later Bar Kokba led a revolution which lasted for three years. While it came within an ace of succeeding, with the brutal crushing of it Palestinian Judaism was ended. It must have been a bewildering assignment for any Roman commandant or legionaire. One can well imagine the reaction to being posted to Palestine: "Oh no! Anywhere but there!"

The point we emphasize is that it was no less bewildering to Jesus. With which of the many parties which sought to recruit young Jews should one ally? One could not affiliate with all, despite the fact that each claimed to be *the* form of a true Judaism under the circumstances. But how could one tell? With all claiming to be the expression of God's will for such times, and with the claims being largely mutually exclusive, how should one affiliate? Did covenant faithfulness call for accommodation to the Romans and the enlightened Hellenism they brought? Or ascetic isolation in the desert? Or resistance to the death? Or was quiet anonymity possible?

For a right understanding of the New Testament and for our pursuit of the relationship between the divine initiative and the claims of the life stages, it is vital that we not obscure the reality of Jesus' uncertainty about these contending matters. Some people are inclined to assume that, "because he was divine," he had instant answers to such questions. The evidence in the Gospels suggest just the opposite: the temptations, the many references to his need for prayer, and that endlessly disturbing cry from the cross: "My God, my God, why hast thou forsaken me?" (Matt. 27:46). The phrases from the Creed—that he suffered under Pilate and was executed—also stress his complete humanity. (No modern film better depicts the restless, "suffering" Jesus than *The Gospel According to St. Matthew* by the Italian Marxist, Pier Paolo Pasolini.) He was not above it all, inspired throughout by assuredly right answers to the hard questions of his day; he was *not* pretending to struggle. To go this route of an endlessly irenic, always illumined and illuminating, untroubled Jesus is possible only by ignoring the evidence from the Gospels and the testimony of the Creed. It is the route taken by the first-century gnostics and all their ancient and modern sympathizers.

Orthodox Christology has always insisted on the two natures of Christ: his full humanity and full divinity. While there have been many efforts to explain the relationship of these "parts," it properly remains a mystery at the heart of Christian faith.

I have no desire to dissolve that central mystery. I do, however, find it necessary to call attention to the persistent tendency to curtail Jesus' humanity. In such a secularized age as the present, many may suspect that it is his divinity which is imperiled. I find otherwise. Since humankind has no direct knowledge of divinity, it is relatively easy, especially for the devout, to feel that it only honors Jesus to emphasize that side of his nature at the expense, if necessary, of his humanity. Since we have some knowledge of what it means to be human, and are often not pleased by what we know, it is comparably easy to play down Jesus' humanity. To make "too much" of that humanity may seem degrading.

The tradition insists on the full humanity and full divinity of Jesus as the Christ. In the following discussion I stress the fullness of his humanity with the conviction that it is only as the reality of his incarnation is seen that the glory of his divinity may be grasped. A right understanding of the humanity is crucial to an affirmation of the divinity. We will not thereby have explained the mystery of the two natures. At best two clarifications will be achieved: (1) of a misunderstanding often arising from pious desire to elevate Jesus at the expense of his humanity and (2) of the radical relationship at the heart of the Pauline gospel: that, as by one man (*Adham*) sin destroyed life's wholeness, so by another man is that wholeness restored (Rom. 5). Jesus' real but distinctive *humanity* is the reality to which all Christian writers respond. Our purpose is to try to clarify this part of the two-natures affirmation. The mystery persists, but there is less inaccuracy about the fullness of his humanity.

The distinctive feature of Judaism and Christianity is the belief in the divine initiative: God acts in human events. Revelation is primarily neither a matter of truth(s) grasped by the intellect nor of moral ideals to which to aspire. Rather, God's initiative is mediated through deeds and events to which the believer responds affirmatively. By affirming the meaningfulness of the reported events of Jesus' work, the Christian is given a new identity: faith yields a new relationship to the ongoing realities of one's life. In place of the defensive and distorted ways of dealing with these realities, one "sees" and can begin to affirm the wholeness which is inherent in them. New intellectual and moral undertakings arise from such affirmation.

Thus, the believer sees the divine initiative in the struggles of Jesus' *humanity*. The possibility for such a new vision of self and others requires that Jesus be fully identified with humankind. Pretended identification will not do. It is how he dealt with temptations such as those to which we are subject which is the key to the believer's ability to begin to deal with them in a new way.

That Jesus "suffered" under Pilate clarifies the issue decisively: he was subject to the limitations of ordinary human life. While I would not minimize the physical pain of death by crucifixion, we must see that the suffering inherent in the incarnation arises from the prior acceptance of human limitations. Total wisdom, endless serenity, he did not possess. He *suffered* the struggles common to *all* imperfect men and women. He was tempted, as all are, to seek escape from the confinements of ordinary life. It is this emphasis on his limitedness, his experience of all ordinary human imperfection, which is one of the two distinctive assertions of the Gospels. The other, obviously, is that it was just *this* person whom God raised from the dead. Without denying the importance of the resurrection faith, it is often necessary to stress the fact that it was the man who suffered whom God raised up.

This assertion sets Christianity apart from all other religious traditions. Especially does it distinguish Christianity from those religions which arose out of the experience of the Indian subcontinent. There it is the suffering which accompanies contingent human life which is *the* evil to be overcome. It is desire itself which must be expunged. That this is often made to appear congenial to Christians is undeniable; that it cannot be reconciled to a faith grounded in the God who suffers must be clearly said. However much Christian piety has been nurtured by focusing on the wounds of the crucified body, these stigmata were from the beginning impressed on Jesus' mind, feelings, and psyche. The sufferings under Pilate—humiliation, physical pain, the inability to change his fate as a condemned prisoner—are undeniable. What needs to be seen clearly is that such limitations began with the birth of a helpless child (unlike Lao Tzu, he was not born mature), and they were the public and personal givens with which he struggled all of his life. That he managed to live an ordinary life without losing sight of its glory is inexplicable. This is *the* miracle to which some respond in faith; this is the inexplicable by which Jesus becomes the new (normative) humanity.

Our immediate work is to make these general assertions about Jesus' humanity more specific. To do so we will look at length at the temptations and, more briefly, at several of the tensions inherent in those relationships which are influential in human lives: family, outsiders (especially those readily condemned), the nation, and the religious tradition. In this discussion we are assuming that Jesus' life developed like that of every person: by genuine struggles with alternatives. It will not be an attempt to psychoanalyze him. The facts with which to attempt this are too few; and, did they exist, it is neither my desire, nor is it within my competence to do so. We will try to see, in what may be the unfamiliar language, customs, and situation of Judaism of the time, conflicts which are not unlike those experienced by people of all periods and places. Unless we do this, we will not be able to see what it might mean to be "saved" by him. For, like him, we define ourselves by the ways in which we respond to the various institutions and behaviors which would give us our identities. With reference to the basic issue of the trustworthiness of the divine initiative, the persistent temptation is to let oneself be defined in terms of some lesser loyalty. The issue for any Jew is always the radical question: in what or in whom do I find my identity? Does anything or anyone merit the trust which God alone should have?

Before turning to the New Testament, one or two things need to be said about my extensive use of language drawn from the social sciences, especially from the writings of Erik Erikson. In general I find his characterizations of the issues of the life stages useful. Whether or not his characterizations are complete or universal does not matter to me at the moment. Since what we call adolescence is a modern phenomenon, Jesus could not have experienced an adolescent identity crisis. What does matter is that some of the questions which create that crisis are universal and that, in the midst of such turmoil as characterized the centuries surrounding Jesus' life, those questions are not easily avoided. Such seems to have been Jesus' experience.

In the most general way I am assuming that between the cradle (or the manger) and the grave (or tomb) there are things to be learned about oneself and about one's relationship to the external world. As these lessons are acquired through the life stages, one is capable of ever more appropriate ways of relating to that world.

What also matters in Erikson's work are the assumptions by which it is informed: that, while the stages are generally chronological and particular configurations of forces are appropriate to each, the issues of all of the stages are present at all times; that each stage is characterized by the tension between what must become the dominant and subordinate poles; that chronological aging per se is no assurance of maturity or wisdom; that what he means by intimacy and generativity, while they usually involve sexual relations and reproduction, do not necessitate either of these. It will be more on such underlying assumptions than on Erikson's specific descriptions of the polar tensions that we will draw with reference to Jesus' development. However, I find Erikson's emphasis on generativity illuminative of and profoundly illumined by the Creed's insistence on the descent into hell. Is a more thorough identification with all suffering humanity possible?

Jesus' Temptations: Political

The environment into which Jesus was born and in which he lived and died was as turbulent and divisive as may be imagined. Primarily in response to the brute fact of Roman occupation of the country but complicated by the inroads Hellenism had made into the thinking—the Judaism of those decades was rife with conflicting and competing parties. Self-proclaimed messiahs were legion. It was anything but a leaderless situation.

Since the Maccabees there had been no single leader around which the majority of Jews could rally. The result had been decades of imposed authority which ranged from the intolerable desecrations of the Temple by Antiochus Epiphanes, which occasioned the successful, original revolt, to the smouldering conditions under the *realpolitik* of Herod the Great. For a people committed to belief in the divine initiative, it was an era in which poverty, oppression, and compromise led to many extreme reactions. I have mentioned the militancy of the Zealots—"The only good Roman is a dead one!"—and the withdrawal of the Essenes from contact with Roman and Jewish corruption. If the Zealots fantasized an eschaton to be accomplished by slaughter, there were those Jews whose fantasy envisioned the end of history with the arrival of an invincible army of heavenly warriors led by the Archangel Michael. That body of material which Christians know as the intertestamental literature is heavy with imagination-informed fantasies of Armageddon in which good and evil were to be permanently separated. With the gradual loss of hope in the possibility of improving their situation, the religious imagination was driven to the creation of a new literary mode—the eschatological fantasy—by which the need to hope became less absurd. What humans could not accomplish would be brought about by the God who had first called Israel into being and had sustained it in earlier adversity.

Such were some of the important ingredients of the environment into which Jesus was born, in which he grew up and lived his brief adult life. Recognizing that the Gospels are not an objective account of (even part of) his public life, we must be quite clear about what we are doing. From the limited material at our disposal in the New Testament, we are selecting some evidence of the ways in which Jesus' views developed. In particular, we suggest that he was quite aware of the issue of faith and fantasy and gradually resolved it. So equipped, he was able to withstand traditional obligations which compromise the faith stance which he had snatched from the teeth of fantasy.

While most of what we have said will help us to see more clearly the penchant for fantasy which underlies the temptations, we need to note first the way in which the pericope concludes. Tempting as it may be to naive faith to assume that when Jesus had settled an issue it was forever settled, that is *not* what the text reports. Quite the opposite. Having wrestled with the tormenting questions arising from his milieu, Jesus resolved them *for the time being*. Telling the story in a way that first-century persons would be able to understand, the Gospel writers report that, having done his best to lure Jesus into the realm of fantasy, the devil departed *for a while*. Momentarily put in his place, the devil clearly intended to try again to take advantage of Jesus' very human yearning to be utterly convincing to his audience.

It is not in the nature of real temptation to be destroyable. By temptation we are never primarily speaking about something "out there." Thus, stories which involve a devil, while they add dramatic excitement, are inherently misleading. Some provocations must be there, but they are only temptations when they are in some degree working elements within one's self. There may be many things by which others are tempted which, however strident the lures, do not tempt me. My temptations arise with reference to possibilities to which I have given a provisional "yes." Without the tentative assent there cannot be temptation: either the matter is of no concern to one (thus, outside the realm of possibility) or one's assent has to be complete (meaning the matter will be done with integrity). The devil could not tempt Jesus with something in which he was not interested; like any person, he could be tempted only by something which was at least part of his self-understanding. How big a part any particular temptation would play in his life's drama was a matter to be resolved only by allowing it to make its appeal. We can be tempted only by those things whose importance to us is undecided. The question always is this: is the tempting reality central or marginal to my being? If resolved as marginal it will, as the Gospels indicate, return at another time, a time at which it will again be possible for me to embrace it as primary rather than secondary to my self-understanding. Though the language may be radically dissimilar and the content of the issues quite unlike those which Jesus pondered out in the desert, passage through the life stages involves every person in similar experience. Tempted initially by the alternatives of trust and mistrust, every infant determines which option will have the larger part in its life drama. And at later stages the issues of childhood, adolescence, adulthood, and aging involve comparable temptations. As the tempter is put in its place at any time, the likelihood is that one will be better able to deal with temptation when it returns.

The second thing to be noted is that the temptations did not occur at a time of discouragement. It was an agitated "high": "Jesus, full of the Holy Spirit, returned from [his baptism at] the Jordan, and was led by the Spirit for forty days in the wilderness . . ." (Luke 4:1–2). It was not the case that he entertained fantasies out of any depression. He may have been uncertain but it was uncertainty which arose from, or in connection with, the solemn excitement of a spirit-filled baptism. It may be important to our argument on behalf of Jesus' humanity to distinguish between those fantasies of which people are capable at the nadir or the end of an unsuccessful venture and those which may occur at the apex or at the beginning of a momentous undertaking. Clearly, Jesus' temptations were of the latter type: strong options rather than desperate measures. They are akin to the cartoonist's recognizable "dreams of glory."

In the storied summary of Jesus' temptations, their sources are reasonably clear. He is famished. Further, the importance of bread, which remained central to Jesus' work, has deep roots in his Judaism. The eldest son in a perhaps by then fatherless family, he may have often blessed, broken, and distributed the Sabbath loaf. Certainly he had himself often eaten such bread and his Jewish-trained imagination was richly informed both with its symbolic profundity and with its daily necessity. In an environment of abject poverty it is not difficult to imagine the source of the desire to be able to convert a loaf-like stone into edible bread. It is understandable, even beautiful, and many have been similarly tempted; but it is sheer fantasy. Not even the most finely crushed stone provides nourishment. The temptation is the desire to escape the ordinary world by transcendent flight to the extraordinary. When the desire simply to be *for* God seems insufficient, one will be tempted to *be* God.

In an environment in which belief in the immediacy of extraordinary powers was widespread, it would not be surprising to find many who boasted such access. No more surprising would it be that people flocked to them. While some of those who claimed power were charlatans who exploited the credulous, I have no doubt but that people at least believed some of the things they "saw." I am not interested at this point in what *really* happened at such times. It is enough for the present discussion to recall that many followed Jesus initially because they were in awe of and/or interested in gaining access to powers he apparently possessed.

The distance in fantasy between these environmental facts and the temptation to put God to the test is not great. If a following could be had by those who apparently performed minor miracles, imagine the stir to be created by being uninjured in a fall from a great height. Whether the following would be for God or for the wonder-worker does not complicate the issue with which Jesus was tempted. If it was his own reputation he was tempted to enhance, he had to reconcile that with his desire for a covenant-vocation. If it were for God's glory that he was tempted to work wonders, he had to decide whether or not such persuasion would return people to proper relationship to God. Since Mark's Gospel begins Jesus' work with these words—"The time is fulfilled, and the kingdom of God is at hand; repent, and believe in the gospel" (Mark 1:15)—he had to determine whether such a dramatic announcement of the imminent kingdom as a leap without injury would also ensure that repentance would be people's initial response. As with the bread from stones fantasy, the same question resulted: were either miracle possible, would it have the desired effect? In this context the question is never whether or not a given technique will work; it is not the Madison Avenue product-testing to determine the market's readiness. The question is about the adequacy of the method to lead or to mislead. Not will they buy it but what will it do to them if they do.

In Matthew's report the dramatic progression climaxes in the offer of all power (to govern) in exchange for total capitulation to one's fantasies, i.e., total allegiance to the devil. It is the Faustian temptation though it need not have been as selfishly motivated. With the great tradition of the Davidic kings in his blood, Jesus might easily have included among the things which he pondered the possibility of solving all problems by thoroughly enlightened leadership.

Throughout these dramatic fantasies the issue is uniform: is it desirable to overcome the bewilderment and profound discouragements of ordinary life by means of fantasy? Always in dire circumstances the ordinary appears paltry. Under such conditions anybody who has any feeling left for self or for others is going to fantasize. Jesus was no exception. He is one with Faust in temptation: "Shall I make the spirits . . . resolve me of all ambiguities?" One more step was all he needed to take—then or at some later point in his work. That he declined that step is why there is a gospel. The reason for which he declined establishes the crucial difference between the way of faith, which affirms ordinary means even when they seem hopeless, and the way of fantasy, which breaks out of bewilderment by self-deception.

Each of the temptations is refused by citing a text from the Hebrew Bible. The point to be noted here is not that Jesus dismissed the devil by waving the Bible at him. This keeps both temptation and its resolution wholly external. Assuming that the inner reality of the temptations is to have great power, it is not resolved by texts but by being in touch with the reality to which the texts point. It was not just that "Scripture says . . . ," but that the man confronted by these temptations was able to recognize in his own tradition their lineage and source. They were fantasies to which prior Jews had been subject when they lost confidence in the adequacy of the divine initiative. Hunger has a long history, as does the yearning for a convincing sign and the experience of living under incompetent leaders. The need for bread, the hunger for persuasive evidence, and the desire for just and creative leadership are universal. It is always tempting to assume that the ability to provide one or more of these would assure life's tolerability. Jesus was not uninterested in any of these, but he recognized the potential in each of them to become an end in itself. He knew that God alone was the source of covenant faithfulness. Neither bread, nor assurances, nor leadership, however important all are, could substitute for life grounded in the adequacy of the divine initiative. His responses are not external refutations of an external threat; they reflect the ability to draw upon yet deeper resources.

In no way is the dynamic, internal nature of this experience clearer than in the conclusion of the report: "So, having come to the end of all his temptations, the devil departed, biding his time" (Luke 4:13, NEB). He would be back because, at best, one can only put undesired parts of oneself at the margin of one's life. They are never permanently dismissable.

Jesus' Temptations: The Claims of Family

In at least one important sense this discussion of the temptations may be a misleading introduction to the issues to which we now turn. It is true that Jesus' repeated resolution of such temptations was the necessary condition for dealing with other life-shaping claims. However, the cosmic nature of the temptations seems to support the assumption that all important struggles of the religious life are of monumental proportions. There are, I suspect, few such experiences. Rather, choices are made and character shaped in response to an endless series of small issues arising from one's ordinary activities. (The money—or time and energy—we are willing to assign to anything discloses the value we do or do not attach to it.) Seemingly inconsequential at the time, small decisions determine the direction in which a life is moving. As we shall suggest in concluding this chapter, the only important matter about any life is the direction in which it moves. As a much traveled people, overly impressed by great distances and quantities, this is not an observation which we readily find congenial.

Our effort to pay attention to Jesus' suffering will take us directly from the desert to the kitchen. That is not how the Gospel writers report the sequence of events, but it seems to me that we will be clearer about the realities of Jesus' development if we look first at his issues with his family before turning to the intra-Judaic conflicts which characterized so much of his public activity.

To understand the significance of his conflicts with his family we must recall two things: (1) the importance of family life and relationships in Judaism and (2) the radical nature of many of his statements about family. Especially if there are still those who misunderstand Jesus as endlessly meek and mild, it is imperative to be aware of such utterances as these.

> To the would-be follower who wanted only to say his good-byes at home, he said, "No one who sets his hand to the plough and then keeps looking back is fit for the kingdom of God." (Luke 9:62, NEB.)
>
> To the woman who praised his mother, this: "No, happy are those who hear the word of God and keep it." (Luke 11:28, NEB.)
>
> When his attention was called to the fact that his mother and brothers could not get through the crowd to speak to him, he replied, "My mother and my brothers—they are those who hear the word of God and act upon it." (Luke 8:21, NEB.)

Other illustrations might be adduced from the Gospels, but they would not add to the severity of these statements. That they are so severe possibly suggests a continuing temptation to allow the claims of family to have the importance for him that they had for other Jews. Were his identity fully grounded in his relationship to God, it would not have seemed necessary for him to speak so sharply. He was addressing men and women whose identity was in their families, and he was sensitive to the possibly brief time available to accomplish his work. The reasons for his sharp distinction between the claims of family and those of the kingdom are speculative. Whatever the proper weight to be given to the factors involved, the point is that, as the result of successful prior struggle with the temptation fantasies, he was able to distinguish the demands of his work from those of the most important institution in the Judaism of his day.

While there were contemporary ascetic movements within Judaism, it would be inaccurate to identify Jesus too closely with any of them. He may indeed have been influenced by the self-isolated Essenes (of Dead Sea Scrolls fame), but he was not one of them. Further, his attitude towards the marriage covenant indicates his disagreement with traditional arrangements by which a wife could be easily abandoned. More than most Jews of his time, he honored marital vows and would have made them less easily dissoluble. And could one improve upon his attitude to children? When the disciples would have dismissed them—perhaps on the assumption that his business was only for grown-ups—he insisted that they bring the children to him for ". . . to such belongs the kingdom of heaven" (Matt. 19:14). Yet he was no naive sentimentalist of the child. When he needed to speak to an audience about their disapproval of both John the Baptist's asceticism and his own worldliness, he compared them with children at games: unwilling either to mourn at the mock-funeral or to rejoice at the play-wedding. That women were attracted to him and that his was an exceptionally positive Jewish attitude towards them is one of the widely made observations by students of Luke's Gospel. At the end of his life, he was not indifferent to his mother's well-being. She was given over to the care of a beloved disciple (John 19:26–27).

He was deeply Jewish in his affirmation of family, but it was not for family that he was spokesperson. As he was of many Jewish institutions, he was critical of accepted marital practices which he saw as an accommodation to human, especially male, slackness. But it was not primarily the shortcomings of marital practice which he would set aright. It was the temptation inherent in family life to become an end in itself. As the closest analogy to a person's relationship to God, it was endlessly tempting to absolutize its claims, to act as though one's identity were to be found there rather than in the covenant faith. Having wrestled through basic issues in the desert, he knew what needed to be said when an appeal to family threatened the clarity he had gained.

That he was able to do this must not obscure the reality of the conflict about the importance of the claims of family which he had to resolve both prior to and during the course of his public work. In this he was like every person: in part the product of a basically good institution, the relative importance of which each must gradually decide. The options range from unbroken dependence on family to pathological rejection of it. Neither extreme is informed by a sense of identity which enables one to affirm family relationships without absolutizing them either positively or negatively. The struggle to develop such an identity was experienced as vividly by Jesus as it is by any human being.

Before turning to the second area by which to illustrate the reality of Jesus' human development, it might be well to remind ourselves of the reasons for this undertaking. We are saying that the stages of life are among God's ordinary means for our humanization. He calls us to serve by calling on us to be ourselves. So also was it with Jesus. It is that person's complete identification with humankind which heartens us to begin to act our age. Further, one of the most important characteristics of each stage is the tension which must be resolved in favor of the positive pole without destroying the negative. In combination with the risk involved in moving from one stage to the next, the need to embrace such polar ambivalences at each stage is too much for us. We refuse the "curriculum" by which God intends to keep us in touch with our real lives and with others and to equip us to perceive the divine initiative amidst ordinary experience. This is the human plight: we are unable to engage the instruction which inheres in progress through life. The evil which results from this sin is to be seen in the quality of lives, the quality of relationships, and the inability to see in Jesus Christ the normative humanity by which our lives may be put aright. Part of the solution lies in correcting widely mistaken notions about Jesus' humanity. In place of a "savior" who was inherently above it all, who only appeared to struggle with the issues which torment and destroy ordinary human lives, I call attention to his recognizable struggles. It was by resolving these in covenant faith that Jesus achieved normative human wholeness. It is in relationship to this humanity that pretense becomes unnecessary. To the extent that he possessed that wholeness from birth, or prebirth as the logos Christology of the Fourth Gospel suggests, he does not share our humanity. As such he may save us *from* life, which is not the good news, but he cannot save us *for* life. Since it is more abundant life now that is promised, we must find in the New Testament evidence of his full identification with humankind. It is not enough to say that he understands our struggles. That would be but empathy without salvation. Nor is it adequate to say that he rescues us from our struggles, which would be but salvation without empathy. He must identify fully with the human condition without being destroyed by it.

Believing with Paul that Jesus was tempted as we are, yet without sin, we must see the specificity of that faith. The incarnation may not be reduced to an idea. It is with flesh and blood reality that we deal. It is because of Jesus' successful struggles— and my emphasis is on their ordinariness—that we have reason to believe in the meaningfulness of engaging our own comparable tasks. All efforts to explain his successful struggles remain just that: varyingly suggestive efforts to account for the inexplicable. That God was in Christ I do believe. *How* this was I do not know. What I do know is that this assertion is meaningful to the extent that I can see a similarity between the developmental challenges which I face and the issues which he successfully resolved. In relationship with him I find evidence of the divine initiative in issues which I would otherwise refuse to engage. Whether or not I will thereby be able to resolve those issues properly is less important than is the fact that my energies have been freed to undertake what seem to be the right tasks. I am suggesting an agenda for human effort which will be fatiguing, as it was for Jesus, *because* it is our proper work. It is the alternative to the exhaustion felt by those who waste their effort avoiding the work which God gives in the stages of life. It is one thing to have to deal with the fatigue which results from failure at tasks which we do affirm; it is quite another to be unsure that any effort is meaningful and to have to conceal our uncertainty. One recovers from the former fatigue; from the lassitude of the latter, there may be no escape. It is central to

Jesus' work to rescue us from the hopelessness of the latter for the excitement and fatigue of the former. It is the opportunity to begin to live our own lives.

This takes us back to what we said earlier about the two natures of Christ. There is a subtle Christian understanding of the relationship between God's grace and human initiative. Too much of the former and there is no human responsibility; too much of the latter and we are in humanism. To tread the delicate path between such coordinates is the work of Christian theology. Theology always requires a dialectical balancing of realities such as the understandings of God's transcendence and immanence, of eternity and time, of the two natures of Christ. He is not just a man. However, whatever he is must be seen through the fullness of his humanity. It is this vision of what one's life may yet be which exposes the inadequacy of every alternative for those created in the image of God. There may be more to such an understanding of one's life than the work of the life stages. It is Jesus' successful struggles with his developmental tasks which make it possible to seek the work of one's stage of life. The sufferings which arose from his humanity are our struggles.

Such a vision is easily lost, but there is an ongoing, inclusive community within which people struggle to keep the vision of humanity in sharp focus. It does not all depend on the individual, yet in that fellowship of saints and sinners there is no diminution of the importance of each person.

Beyond Scorn for "Ordinary" Experience

The kind of people with whom Jesus eventually associated was a source of conflict with other Jews. His work initially was exclusively with his own people. It was to fellow heirs of the covenant that he proclaimed the announcement with which Mark begins his public work: "The time is fulfilled, and the kingdom of God is at hand; repent, and believe in the gospel" (Mark 1:15). That John's ministry was to the compromised elements of the house of Israel, those who thought it sufficient to be lineal descendants of Abraham, and that there were similarities between his message and that of Jesus, supports the assumption that it was a Jewish audience whom both men addressed.

The surprise was not that Jews in some number responded eagerly nor that there was eventual Jewish opposition. Rather, it would seem that Jesus was not prepared for the sources of some followers. Some of the statements attributed to him—that his work was with the house of Israel, that Samaritans were unfit to feed at a Jewish table—suggest an insular attitude which experience caused him to modify. While the precise chronology of his work and of the sequence of reported utterances are not establishable, we must note the sharp contrast between some of his (early) statements (about Samaritans) and the inclusiveness of such a parable as that of the Good Samaritan. I am not suggesting that I can document his development with reference to such non-Jews as Samaritans, but it seems reasonable to assume that (possibly unanticipated) experiences required him to revise his understanding of where his audience was to be found. We should not make light of this requirement. These experiences involved another fantasy with which he had to come to terms. We have no reason to believe that Jesus had other than provincial training and experience prior to his appearance in Galilee. Beyond this parochialism he may have been associated with ascetic Jewish sectarianism; he was certainly not an urban or cosmopolitan person. With John the Baptist as both predecessor and possible tutor, we have no evidence that Jesus envisaged a ministry to other than Jews. Events pushed him beyond the boundaries of his original assumptions. While we know little about the content of his regular prayers, it must have been about such matters that he sought guidance. Not to be accepted by those by whom he had been shaped but to be welcomed by those to whom he did not think he belonged represents a major demand for growth. That Jesus accomplished this and that disciples had to learn the same lesson largely accounts for the universal character of the Christian community. Neither the Holy Land nor the people of the covenant were able to confine the faith to which Jesus broke through. His relationship to God was driven to deeper levels as events forced him to recognize the inadequacy of his fantasy of reforming Israel.

We might have emphasized in this section Jesus' conflicts with some of the parties within the Judaism of his day. It is to these conflicts and to the resultant clarifications emphasized in his teaching that the Gospels give primary attention. There were few aspects of his life and work—from the people with whom he associated to his attitude to Sabbath observance—which were not sources of such conflict. In the present context it serves little purpose to explore these conflicts in detail. What is important to see is the issue at stake in all the disputes. Underlying all the differences is disagreement about the nature of covenant faith and about the behavior appropriate to those who professed it. It was with Jesus' understanding of what this meant that the opposition disagreed.

It is important to realize that, depending on the time and place into which one is born, part of maturation involves coming to terms with public factors which compete for our allegiance. In part, we develop an identity by the causes which we support or resist. Such God-given decisions were as much a part of Jesus' experience as they are of our own. In his time it was through the various political forces within Judaism that he had to thread his distinctive way. Those parties ranged from those who prepared for an apocalyptic resolution of all issues to those readying for a bloody "apocalyptic" expulsion of the occupying army. Somewhere between were Jews willing to make accommodation with Roman administrators and perhaps Jesus' primary antagonists, those who insisted on scrupulous observance of the many commandments of *Torah*. The multiplication of these commandments over the centuries and the anomalous behavior inherent in contradictory requirements were prime sources of disputes between Jesus and the Pharisees.

With the possible exception of the Sadducees, whose willingness to negotiate with the Romans involved them in maintenance of the status quo, there is no basis for passing negative judgments on any of these groups. Under the trying circumstances of military occupation, and as bearers of a great and rich tradition, they probably had evolved all of the possible major options. This was the situation in which, as a young Jew of provincial origins, Jesus found himself. Men of his generation were attracted to all of the options; by a generation after his death they flocked in great numbers to and died in the Zealot cause. If we assumed that, confronted by such an array of alternatives, Jesus always knew his course, we assign him a prescience inconsistent with his humanity. I believe rather that he was as bewildered as was any young person who took seriously the claims of the tradition into which he had been circumcised. The conclusions at which he arrived and the skill with which he advanced them were distinctive.

As the reader may now expect, the point I wish to stress is that Jesus had to suffer to reach those conclusions. Clearly, he suffered their consequences, and that, too, is central to the Christian story. If Jesus merely endured the consequences of convictions which he did not struggle to reach, we would have a different story, and not one that would have endured for ages. While we can neither explain why he persisted in his search nor describe the process by which he reached distinctive conclusions, we must not conceal the reality of the search. In the assent to such uncertainty, if not in the persistence of his efforts or in the significance of the conclusions reached, lies his kinship with humankind. And that kinship is, in my judgment, the key to the role which, as risen Lord, he has played in the lives of many. It is by the reality of his struggles to fathom the divine initiative as the source of his being that our own struggles are both judged and put aright.

The error against which I would guard is the assumption that Jesus' life was untroubled. The agony at Gethsemane was not an exception, brought about by the betrayal of one of his intimates, to an otherwise general rule of equanimity. Such sweat was the price often paid before, and paid in full on the following day, for the vocation to which he felt himself called.

By this language of calling I do not intend to imply resources which lie beyond ordinary human reach. Whereas thousands of others were able to satisfy their desire to live responsibly as Jews, within one of the existing options of Judaism, Jesus was unable to do so. His search forced him back behind the Jewish traditions varyingly embodied in the major parties to the deeper and long obscured sources of Judaism itself. Each party may have embodied some part of the tradition. Had it been possible to assemble them, neither any single group nor all of the parties together would have grasped the source of that tradition. Consequently, as he came to believe, all were distorted by overcommitment to their part of the truth.

Since this is a story with which many are familiar and since the Easter outcome is such a vindication of the effort, it is comparatively easy to minimize the suffering involved in both the search and in the conclusions reached. Progressively alienated from and eventually threatened by his own people, initially responded to but eventually abandoned by his own followers, we are speaking of a man left with nothing but God. His subsequent arrest, trial, and condemnation must have made that presence less than fully convincing. The hard-won confidence of the previous night, "yet not what I will, but what thou wilt" (Mark 14:36), must have quickly eroded under the rapid developments of the following hours. There is a sense in which every person must face the fact that, born into a relationship, we shall die alone. Ordinarily, however, this does not occur as the result of successful search for the costliest of pearls. The dying ordinarily get what they have deserved: loving concern and gratitude or one of the options between that and neglect. In Jesus' death, however, the consequence is in every way discordant with the prior struggles: he who had become aware of God's universal concern dies by himself. The suffering to which his sufferings had brought him was total.

At the heart of Christian faith is the conviction that God is present in the life, death, and resurrection of this man. Since such an assertion is not fully comprehensible, the temptation is to assume that it means that Jesus *appeared* to be human but in fact was subject to no such limitations. It is my contrary suggestion that he knew no more than others—and less than some, that he was subject to misleading fantasies, that unanticipated events caused him to rethink and revise his mission, that he may have been discouraged. This is the distinctive, life-giving assertion at the heart of the gospel: that it is in an ordinary, limited man's faithful effort to live the covenant faith that we see and have access to the divine initiative. Jesus is not superman. Every temptation to obscure this reality reflects a hardly concealed triumphalism which wants God to do what we refuse to do for ourselves. He does not bear all of our burdens nor solve all of our problems. Every effort to obscure Jesus' humanity conceals an inability to affirm the inherent worth of all God-given life. The burden he bears is the otherwise hopeless weight of human ordinariness. Able by faith in him to affirm its God-givenness, we must make of our particular situation what we can. The source of this intentionality is the cross: it is out of weakness that we are to be made strong.

The point which we will not grasp until we see Jesus' ordinariness is that there is an alternative to the pretenses of present life. The new is to be fashioned out of the familiar materials of the present. It was this—nothing more or less—which Jesus did: to make of an ordinary, first-century, Jewish life the normative humanity which death could not contain. It was precisely because he had to struggle with conflicts akin to our own and did so by driving his identity to ever deeper levels that God raised him from the tomb. This does not explain *how* he was able to reach these depths. The consequences of this may not be as anticipated. Everything is *not* now to be done for us. Every necessary thing has been done in Jesus as the Christ. The humanity of which we had lost sight has been re-presented: *this* is what it is to be a person. We are not cut off from the divine initiative: God's grace is to be seen in the successful ordinariness of Jesus. There is no longer need to pretend or to overinvest trust in unreliable institutions; we can trust our own resources, however uncertain or modifiable their lead may be, *to the extent that we recognize them as God-given*. The sufferings of

Jesus—the acceptance of limitations, the final indignity of public execution—do not take us away from ourselves. From falsely grounded lives we are led away in order that we may see in our limitations, as we have seen in his, the glory of human ordinariness.

The radicality of Christianity is impossible to overstate. In his farewell discourse, Jesus assured the disciples that they would do even greater things than he had done: ". . . he who believes in me will also do the works that I do; and greater works than these will he do . . ." (John 14:12). In faith the believer will learn to draw upon his or her own God-given resources. Jesus must depart in order that this may happen.

The believer has not been given a new personality. More importantly, she or he has been given reason for taking a new attitude to the old. In Christ the believer is free for the first time to take seriously the actual givens and the potentialities of his or her life. The debilitations of pretense and deceit have been exposed and their power challenged. While the temptation to revert to these attitudes persists, persons of faith are free to get about God's business with whatever resources they possess and may yet develop. It is with no other resources than these that every person may do some (great) good.

The good news is inseparable from the human limitations with which Jesus suffered successfully. The consequence of trust in a reliable other is increasing trust in oneself. The evidence from the last days of his life suggests that Jesus finally could trust only his own understanding of God's trustworthiness. The point of the crucifixion is its utter isolation from all human support: the large following diminished to nothing. However tormented he may have been by this unforeseen fact, it was the final reality with which he had to come to terms. As in his numerous conflicts with fellow Jews, he was able to center his life in that trust in God which had deepened over the course of his work. Either this was madness or it is the disclosure of God's grace in a way which has the most dramatic consequences for our lives. It appears absurd to claim the latter and the possibility that one will find it so should never be dismissed. But neither should the radical consequence of affirming that faith: in relationship to the God who is ultimately trustworthy we are *free to trust in ourselves*. In such relationship we are able to affirm both the worth of our ordinary lives and our responsibility to live them to God's glory. There *are* limits to what we can do, there will be endless temptation to wish things were otherwise than they are, and we will succumb to many of them, but the root source of despair has been removed. In Christ the believer knows the divine initiative and senses the relationship of ordinary lives to it.

There is no cheap grace here. Throughout the chapter we have stressed the reality of Jesus' suffering. No less suffering will be experienced by those who respond positively to him. The effects of habitual ways of thinking and behaving will have to be seen for what they are. No area or arena of our lives will be unchanged and even the changes must be covert. We will no longer even be at liberty to boast of our accomplishments for they will not simply be ours. It was Paul, the original theologian of mid-life, who struggled to understand the relationship between his own initiative and God's grace. It was his sin-informed self which caused him to do those things which, in conscience, he abhorred. It was Christ's indwelling which brought him to life that he had been unable to achieve himself (cf. Rom. 5–8). The price to be paid for one's new life in Christ will be paid to the end. Every negative option in the course of the life stages will tempt us. The devil bides his time. One can only believe that the rewards of working at one's proper business are more nourishing, even in adversity, than those to be found by working successfully at somebody else's.

The work of self-reform will be trying and endless and may not be minimized. It should not be stressed as a demand to which only men and women of heroic stature can respond. It is *not* a moral code for superior people. Quite the opposite: its appeal is to all, especially those who know themselves to be weak.

The business of the Christian life, traditionally identified as the work of sanctification, is not undertaken apart from a continuingly renewed relationship with Jesus as the Christ. Sanctification is not a process accomplished only by one's own efforts. The continuing self-reform is undertaken in consequence of one's engagement with Christ. The old symbols around which life was organized have been abandoned in favor of the empowerment of the cross. It is in this event, and Jesus' prior thorough identification with humankind, that believers find the divine initiative which enables them to embrace irresolvable conflicts. As Erikson put it in his psycho-historical study of Luther, ". . . Christ's life is God's face . . ." (Erik H. Erikson, *Young Man Luther*, New York: W. W. Norton, 1958, p. 312). So understood, it is Christ who frees the believer from the burden of having nothing but beautiful thoughts. It is by faith in Christ that we are able to be present to ourselves *just as we are*. No longer is it necessary to conceal the excitement and the threat of our conflicted feelings and desires. Nor is it license to do one's thing. Rather, it is to be freed to acknowledge our actual condition in all its chaos or its deadness and to determine in Christ what is to be made of it. Gone is the urgent need for either deception, by suppressing aspects of our conflicts, or of rejection of our present condition in favor of an idealized past or future. In faith it is always the challenges and opportunities of the real present which are to be embraced. When so embraced, the believer is free to be present to others' realities. Deep satisfactions in such authenticity need not obscure the continued suffering as the believer relinquishes ever more of his or her old life. But this suffering derives from working at rather than avoiding God's curriculum. The difference is dramatic.

Jesus' suffering under Pontius Pilate may not be confined to the days at the end of his life. That suffering was real enough but it was possible, and only barely such if we hear in his cry of dereliction the devil's final temptation, as a consequence of prior suffering successfully borne. It is the reality of human limitations, of the unavoidability of conflicts not easily resolved, which was his distinctive affirmation. It was this affirmation which drove him into ever deeper relationship with

God. It was from these depths that he affirmed from God the final limitation of a brutal death. It is by grasping the kinship of this person to ourselves that we are enabled to affirm the particulars of our lives also as from God. In this grasp of God's grace, we become willing pupils of the life curriculum in which we now recognize the divine initiative.

Throughout this section I have tried to suggest that Jesus' humanity was like our own: subject to numerous limitations which, in fantasy, we are tempted to try to transcend. His identification with humankind, which is crucial to the good news, is convincing. Equally important is the fact that, unlike others, he was not destroyed by affirming his limitations and grappling with his fantasies. Rather, it was just this faithfully human being whom God raised from the dead. In his identification with humankind and in God's triumph through him, we are able to embrace as from God our peculiar lives.

Regarding the Creed's affirmations about Jesus' crucifixion, death, and resurrection, I am able to add little to what has been said. So executed, he really died and was appropriately buried. That God raised *this* man from the dead *is* the nub of the good news. It is both more exciting and more troubling than any concept of immortality. The Gospels and the Creed stress the point that this resurrection may not be separated from Jesus' public life and work. As the church has repeatedly done, we are proposing another possible understanding of the relationship between the events of his ministry and his risen presence.

It is my belief that, in response to the recognition of grace in the conditions of one's life, God desires the believers to live out these conditions responsibly. That means initially the acceptance of limitations. Such acceptance of one's creatureliness is the precondition for exercising one's vocation in the world. Such acceptance signifies that, whereas one intends the full development of one's powers for good, one does not intend to play God. Since limitations are never easily identified, I have suggested that we include such realities as the ambivalences inherent at all stages of human development and the inability to know in advance the consequences of any risk taken. By the former we identify those tensions which one must resolve while retaining permanently a grasp of both elements; in the latter we see the source of all uncertainty about risk and changes, all conflict between the forces (both within lives and in social structures) for continuity and for change. Something like this is my understanding of God's curriculum which truant "pupils" avoid at all costs. A less trying assignment is a clear-cut and permanent resolution of conflicts and the elimination of risk. Utter clarity of intention and comparable assurance as to the outcome of one's actions are sin's desiderata.

Generations of truancy progressively confirm people in their aversion to the prescribed syllabus. Evil compounds itself and the resultant blindness is nearly total. God has not abandoned the original intent for humankind. What was needed was a person who would faithfully enroll in the divine curriculum. In Jesus a man was found to manifest the divine initiative by living out the limiting conditions of the life into which he was born. Since the power of death is fear and the source of fear is pretense about one's condition, death could claim but not confine an authentic human life. Without fully understanding what it means, I acknowledge that God raised this man from the dead.

Not to be thwarted in the desire for good life for all creatures, God raised Jesus from the tomb. Death is the last word only to those who pretend an invulnerability which they never had; death is final only where fear controls. When faith informs a life death is only the penultimate word. He who was raised on the third day is he who struggled successfully in circumstances akin to our own for just such faith. This is what we need to understand about the resurrection if it is to be the basis for affirming as God-given the particulars of one's life. Through God's raising up of Jesus we see clearly the divine initiative both in his life and in the possibilities of our own. It is in his human sufferings willingly undertaken that we see the divine initiative. Thus has the church rightly insisted on the full humanity and full divinity of Jesus as the Christ.

As a unique event, the resurrection remains a mystery. Without abandoning any of them, we may note the contradictions inherent in the Gospels' reports of the resurrection appearances. Every attempt to speak of the unspeakable encounters the same difficulty. All that we can do is to be clear about the claim made from the outset and continuingly reaffirmed against every attempt to destroy the tension: that he who appeared after his death was he whom they had known in his public work. On this understanding rests the ongoing witness of those who have affirmed the glory of all human life.

The Descent into Hell

In its emphases on Jesus' descent into hell and his judgment on the living and the dead, the Creed reminds us of human solidarity. The apparent incompatability of the descent and the judgment is resolved in the recognition that while God's grace is intended for all people there is no way to escape either the consequences of past or the condemnation of present sin. The intent is to make lives whole but the consequences of past brokenness are not obliterated. They could not be without extricating individuals from the social matrix by which they have been shaped and which, despite their new life, they continue to misshape. The indissolubility of humanity is, for good and ill, one of the God-given facts of human life.

To assert that the crucified Jesus descended into hell is a vivid way of insisting on his complete identification with humankind. A more thoroughly generative attitude toward the world is not imaginable. It is a literary extension of one of the central themes of his public life: that it was not the "well," those satisfied with their lives, but the "sick" whom he came to heal. Jesus' descent into hell bespeaks his identification with men and women of all times and places who have lost sight of the divine initiative. Further, the descent into hell acknowledges a fact of Jesus' public experience: response to his work came from Jews and Gentiles. There are no limits of race or sex or circumstance from which the good news is excluded. The gospel is universal.

The descent into hell brings into sharp focus an understanding of the nature of sin often obscured in individualistic emphasis. Sin is cumulative. Every generation bequeaths to its successors a deeper bondage of blindness to the divine initiative. Unless faith is renewed in each generation, it is being eroded. This understanding was the source of Jesus' hyperbole in exchanges with those Jews who considered themselves righteous because they were Abraham's lineal descendants. Unable to find faith within such hardened hearts, God would animate the stones to shout like proper children of Abraham. The deterioration of faith might occur over two or three generations: from a grandparent's animating beliefs to a child's imitation of parental practice to a grandchild's indifference. Nothing of a living faith is necessarily transmitted from one generation to the next; each must undertake its own search for evidences of the divine initiative. Unless new bases for faith are found in each generation, the darkness of its absence is compounded. Things not only do not get better, they worsen. Jesus' descent into hell, thus, acknowledges the lineal as well as the universal character of sin. The possibility of new life requires the identification of where it was that things began to go awry, which is the theme explored in William Golding's novel, *Free Fall*, (New York: Harcourt, Brace & World, 1962). There is the source of evil to be located and its consequences for successive generations to be eliminated. The descent into hell is a pithy way of recognizing these realities and that Jesus' ministry was to them. The Gospels are not an objective, historical report of a part of Jesus' life. They are post-resurrection documents written out of the conviction that in Jesus as the Christ the writers encountered both normative humanity and the grace of God. In him they saw total humanity and total divinity fully combined. The church goes as far as imagination allows to suggest the range of the effectiveness of his work: he descended into hell.

That he will (return to) judge the living and the dead is implied in what we have been saying about the nature of sin. It is not easily eradicated. It will not, for example, be painless for the present generation to modify its misguided attitudes toward aging. The effect of such violation of the God-given life stages, which involve growing older, is never confined to those who hold such attitudes. Such attitudes damage individuals by making them averse to aspects of their own lives. It is not healthy to hate the fact of one's own aging. Energy, time, and money are diverted in concealing reality which is capable of nourishing those who embrace it. The consequences of pretense and concealment are not merely personal. As is true of sexist and racist attitudes, our negative feelings about aging get expressed in deeds committed and omitted. It is not enough just to learn that. In Christ, one's sins are forgiven. That is the vital first step which frees us from the continuing need to pretend. But a lifelong attitude built onto generations of similar pretense is not painlessly changed. Layer after layer will have to be stripped off of individual lives and a beginning made to reverse generations of destructive attitude and practice. It is in this sense at least that Jesus' normative humanity is experienced both as mercy and judgment. Forgiveness not only doesn't preclude judgment; it is the precondition which makes judgment tolerable. Sinfully self-satisfied lives have to be gradually conformed more closely to the divine initiative perceived in Jesus. That we are forgiven the sin is crucial to the process; without that we have no alternative to concealment of and/or rationalizing the evil. A new life has begun in Christ, and it is his presence which both requires and enables the believer to persist in the process of personal and institutional reform.

I put in parenthesis the Creed's insistence that Christ will "return to" judge. Whether or not there will be a final judgment, I do not know. However, such language implies a remoteness of which all are tempted to take advantage. Judgment in some indefinite future tends to defuse the urgency of present reform. By also obscuring the inseparability of God's mercy and judgment, it may contribute to the postponement of the reformation of lives in the direction of that humanity perceived in Jesus. Judgment need not be minimized in order for it to be more appealing than the self-deceptions which destroy us.

Finally, the point to be stressed about self-reformation is

that it too is a process which goes on for as long as one lives. It is not something to be accomplished in one great act of heroic transformation. We did not get into our misshapen condition by any such single decision but by small, often unnoticed, increments. The process will be similarly reversed. The important thing is not the thoroughness of the reform but that that is the direction in which one's life is very gradually moving. This may not excite high-spirited people. There is, however, no exception to the fact of slow growth. There are heightened times in all lives—the adolescence and mid-life which we discussed in the opening chapter—and there are crises in personal and public life which may alert people to question the direction in which their lives are headed. At such times of questioning and self-judgment one may be more than ordinarily receptive to evidences of the divine initiative. Should such prove to be the occasion for a fundamental change of direction, I do not minimize its importance by stressing incremental growth. To change direction is all important, but it is not everything. It is not arrival at one's new destination; it is only to be headed there. Of the numerous hazards en route, none is more dangerous than that the experience of judgment become immobilizing self-condemnation. It is by regular reacquaintance with God's mercy, seen in the glory of Jesus' ordinary humanity, that the intention of a reformed life is renewed.

A Role for Fantasy?

One matter requires clarification. Having insisted throughout this chapter on the sharpest distinction between faith and fantasy, we must discover the function of fantasy in the life of faith.

We have identified Christian faith as that perception of the divine initiative which enables one to embrace the particulars of one's own life. That is, faith's acknowledged relationship to God is the means by which one affirms the curriculum for wherever one is in the life stages. The alternative to such affirmation is the rejection of that curriculum with the consequent pretenses to conceal one's refusal. We were led to this understanding of faith's function from the evidence of Jesus' relationship to the particular realities of his life. His search for an ever deeper relationship to God was occasioned by issues within his own experience with which he had to come to terms. It is in relationship to God that one is able to come to grips with realities which it is tempting to ignore. Faith is the means by which the believer is able to move beyond repugnance for ordinary life to an appreciation of its glory. Given my emphasis on the absolute importance of life affirmation, and with Doctor Faustus as the model antihero, we identified fantasy as the ultimate refuge of all life rejection.

I believe that fantasy often functions in lives as a substitute for life engagement. Unable to derive adequate satisfaction from one's particular life involvements, it is understandable that people are driven to fantasize better worlds. However, the further we withdraw, for example, from the contingencies of the natural world or the injustices of the social order, the more inflated become our expectations and the more predictable our disappointments. Circumstances which require acknowledgment of one's own limits are instructive; those which we master easily are less so. The former may yield an appreciation for both life's inevitabilities and one's own capacity for initiative; the latter result in hopelessness. With the latter comes the desire for fantasy's escape.

Religious faith has its own tendency to rigidify. The very biblical tradition to which we have attached such importance may be viewed as a running record of periods of vital faith followed by periods of deterioration in which "faith" progressively insulates against ever more of the world. Vital faith's ability to take risks gives way to a defensive "faith" calculated to guard against the possibility of loss. Courage is overcome by timidity.

Within religious communities at such times fantasy will flourish. Unable to find adequate nourishment in perpetuating traditional observances, feeling the adverse effects of professing belief in a living, caring God but acting as though that God were dead or withdrawn, some persons will, in imagination, begin to search for the route to the vital springs of faith which once nourished the community. Without utterly demolishing all existing practice, which always sustain some flicker of the original faith, fantasy-informed reformers appear to melt the stasis in a renewal of vital faith. Within, but not confined by, this prophetic tradition Jesus stood: "I have not come to abolish [the law and the prophets] but to fulfil them" (Matt. 5:17). In my understanding fantasy is a source of renewal to the extent that it operates within the limits of a given community and for its reformation. While I am here assuming the Christian community as the constraint within which fantasy may bring about renewal, the point is that all fantasy needs the constraint of human community if it is to be guarded against solipsism. The product of individual imagination, fantasy functions creatively only if the imagining person understands him or herself to belong to and to care for some larger community. Unrestrained, it leads rapidly further into the limitlessness which breeds despair. As the resource of a tradition, it may be a priceless human agent for faith's continuing reform. The need always is not for spirits but to ". . . test the spirits (the fantasies) to see whether they are of God" (1 John 4:1).

It is to this task that we now turn.

V. | Holy Spirit and Demonic Spirits

When we turn to the third article of The Apostles' Creed we move from elaboration to terseness: after ten christological clarifications we find three words of belief in "the Holy Ghost." By this brevity may we assume the affirmation to be self-explanatory? Hardly. However imprecise any inference may be from our own experience to that of Jesus as the Christ, there are no obvious parallels from what we ordinarily know to belief in a Holy Ghost. That the Spirit is inseparable from Jesus as the Christ is the only anchorage for our discussion. It is never to some general spirituality, some special (religious) feelings, that one refers. Always the referent is to that Spirit who enables men and women to achieve the wholeness which is seen in Jesus Christ. It is the gift of the Holy Spirit so to enable people to discern the divine initiative that they may become more intentional about God's curriculum for their particular lives. With this clearly in mind our task will be to suggest some of the functions of belief in the Holy Spirit with reference to that curriculum about which humankind is so truant. Since this truancy arises in connection with the lures of other spirits, we shall see that the central work of the Holy Spirit is to expose and to combat the demonic spirits. This takes one back to the words with which we concluded the last chapter, ". . . test the spirits to see whether they are of God."

How Determined Are Lives?

To honor Paul's exhortation requires us first to identify what might be meant by those spirits which are not of Christ. Anyone with a clear and limited sense of approvable behavior could make quick work of it. They might simply extend the prohibitions of the Ten Commandments. I have two problems with that way of identifying spirits which are anti-Christ. First, it confuses conformity to a behavioral code with moral behavior. Second, and more important for our present purposes, it apparently ignores the social sources of evil. Deviant individual behavior, behavior which violates the God-given agenda for one's lifestage, is always partly the consequence of misguidance from one's society and always serves to strengthen the grip of those false leads. Thus, while it is for the reformation of lives that the Holy Spirit works, it is always to the social sources of truancy that the Spirit calls attention. We have seen that it was with temptations that arise from such sources that Jesus grappled successfully.

In order to come at these determining influences more accurately, it is necessary to make a confession about much of the preceding material of this book. We have largely proceeded on the widely held assumption that individual lives are self-determining. We must now expose the fallacy of this assumption. Personal freedom is constrained by many fairly obvious factors, ranging from one's finitude and general situation in time and place to such specifics as health, wealth, and capability, and to the obligations which one has to others. While some of these are less fixed than others, we will miss entirely the point of the work of the Holy Spirit if we confine our understanding of the constraints on human freedom to such individual particulars. Behind such realities, and always informing them, are the attitudes and the institutionalized practices of the society to which one belongs. Not frequently acknowledged, these are what Paul refers to as the principalities and powers (Rom. 8:38). We manifest our allegiance to them in almost everything we believe and do. No institution, including those of religion and education, is exempt from their influence; every person who has grown up in any human society has been shaped greatly by them. So ubiquitous is the influence of these forces that the temptation is either to take them for granted as the unchangeable "givens" or, if one is disposed to combat, to identify one or more as the particular sources of evil and to wage war on them. The latter is an appropriate Christian strategy providing one realizes that the very agency one attacks is but part of a network of complicity. In part it is to this network that the doctrine of original sin points.

The sins which western religion punishes are possible only because of a prior condition of sin. By this acknowledgment I do not intend to excuse particular sins, though I would hope to soften the all too common tendency to pass judgment on the failings of others. The issue is not as simple as either to acquiesce in social determinism or to hold individuals absolutely responsible for their deeds. The latter is the tendency of those who equate moral behavior with conformity to a behavioral code. But, ultimately, this is not a more dangerous attitude than that which refuses to hold persons accountable for their deeds. This is a Scylla and Charybdis between which to navigate: on the one hand, to acknowledge the power of societies to shape lives without abandoning the reality of individual acquiescence; on the other, to insist on personal accountability for behavior tempered by the realization that, given the circumstances, little else may have been possible. It is on such fragile foundations that societies are built; it is with such subtle relationships that Christian ethics must deal. Years ago Niebuhr put it thus: "Sin is necessary but not inevitable" (Reinhold Niebuhr, *The Nature and Destiny of Man: A Christian Interpretation*, I, "Human Nature," New York: Scribner, 1941, pp. 251 ff.). He did not thereby solve the dilemma but he did state it clearly and succinctly.

By insisting that sin is necessary, Niebuhr acknowledged that human lives are socially conditioned. Many theologians hold that such conditioning is absolute and that the Bible holds no other view. Rudolph Bultmann, possibly the most influential New Testament scholar of this century, is unequivocal about it.

... it is the conviction of the New Testament that man needs first to be restored to his true nature through the event of redemption accomplished in Christ. Until this event has taken place ... he is alienated from his own true nature ... and in bondage to death ...

... He is totally unconscious of his enslavement. He has not the least notion what he is doing when he strives to attain life ... by his own efforts. (Rudolph Bultmann, *Primitive Christianity in Its Contemporary Setting*, New York: New American Library, Meridian, 1956, p. 189.)

Perhaps because I have been more influenced by American than by continental scholarship or perhaps because I am a product of American "principalities and powers," I find Bultmann's consistency unconvincing. By his position he apparently honors the absoluteness of the divine initiative, but he does so by negating that grace, however minimal, which resides in God's creatures. Unlike Niebuhr, he insists on sin's inevitability. If men and women are absolutely conditioned by social circumstances into which they are born, then there is neither grounds for holding them responsible for their deeds nor is there reason for renewed hope in the new humanity seen in Jesus Christ. If he is not one like ourselves but completely able to transcend the conditioning effects of his particular circumstances, he cannot be the means by which persons are freed to make what they can of the "givens" of their lives.

Behind these differing judgments about the extent of social conditioning there probably lie dissimilar estimations of the worth of social structures. Acknowledging the inevitability of such structures, people disagree about the values inherent in any social arrangements. It is one thing to recognize that most social arrangements tend to claim more validity than is warranted. They are tempted to pretend an absoluteness which the believer reserves to God alone, and are based on some, often covert, exploitation. It is quite another thing to refuse to recognize that every historical arrangement both maintains some degree of social order and has been subject to change. In such absolute societies as ancient Egypt, change may be slow to come. This does not invalidate my assumption that vestiges of God-given humanity are never fully expunged by any social arrangement. Basically, the Creator did too good a job with the creatures to permit any arrangement to destroy every shred of their humanity. They may be trapped in attitudes and institutional arrangements which distance people from themselves and from caring relationships with each other, but the evidence is that no social arrangement, including such believable fictions as George Orwell's 1984 (New York: Harcourt, Brace & World, 1949), has managed to dehumanize all of its citizens.

I argue in this apparently conservative way not because I believe that any society merits more than one's provisional allegiance. Every society is in need of endless reform in the direction of ever more inclusive justice. I do so, rather, because I believe that evidence of the divine initiative is never completely lacking in any viable social arrangement nor from any individual human life. Some societies more desperately need reform than others; all are inadequate to the full humanity of their members. It is such an understanding of every society as inherently imperfect which allows me now to illustrate what is meant by the social conditioning of the "principalities and powers." On that basis we will be able to suggest more clearly what is the necessary work of the Holy Spirit. Since any exhaustive catalog of ways in which we are conditioned would be more exhausting than illuminative, I shall only suggest ways in which society impinges on human development through the life stages. In this way we will see why it is crucial that we be able to test the spirits to be sure that they are of Christ.

In order to explain how lives are shaped and misshaped in our society, I must restate my understanding of the purposes of the life stages. In one sense the passage through time is simply a biological process of physical maturation followed by a usually longer process of aging and death. This we share with all living things: "Dust thou art, and to dust thou shalt return." (Gen. 3:19).

However, as self-conscious beings, life is not as automatic a process for humans as it seems to be for other creatures. Onto the biological facts humankind grafts social needs. Thus, in considering the development of human lives, account must be taken of both hereditary and environmental data. Kin to the world of nature, human beings are also able to transcend that world in thought and imagination. The ability to rise above some biological limitations finds expression in both social attitudes and arrangements. Some of these complement the biological promptings; others do not. Many of the things we do and believe contribute to the survival of the human species; others do not. At the extreme, every thought of self-sacrifice may serve societal purposes at the same time that it jeopardizes species survival. Such fundamental tensions are at the heart of human experience. They must constantly be resolved; they will not permanently remain so. It is never enough either to be selfish or self-sacrificing. Neither extreme takes full account of what we actually are in our biological and social dimensions. We are not free, without doing violence to our dual nature, to become either merely animals or utterly to transcend limitations.

To be stressed here is the fact that human life is inherently conflicted. Less obvious is the assertion which I believe to be the Christian response to the basic fact: the endlessly rewarding and demanding human task is to embrace the reality of conflict. To assume that anything else is enduringly possible is to attempt to substitute a fantasy for a fact. As we shall see, tensions are not confined to those arising from our common biological and social involvements. The latter is the source of a spectrum of conflicts with which all people deal constantly. These range from the obvious conflicts at the level of power politics to the concealed struggles within every person between the desire to relate to others and the fear of doing so. It is with these socially-derived tensions that we shall be primarily concerned. That such tensions continue to be biologically influenced and that there may be important evidences from biological data about the effects of these tensions, I have no doubt. However, these matters lie beyond our present concern. Human beings are the products of both nature and history. Neither source of renewal and deterioration—cyclical/seasonal and linear/chronological—may be ignored. Neither one may be allowed to dictate constantly to the other. To understand oneself created in the image of God requires acknowledgment both of natural kinship with all things and historic involvement with all humankind.

Demonic Spirits: Selective Aversions

I suspect that every society derives its peculiar dynamic from assumptions which minimize these tensions or resolve them in favor of one of the ingredients. Here we see the basic source which undermines commitment to the tasks of the human stages. Every inclination to obscure the inherently conflicted nature of human life tempts men and women to believe that they should aspire to nonconflictual lives. While I am not, I trust, a romanticizer of conflict, I believe that temporary relief from conflict only comes after conflict has been fully engaged and resolved, and that each such rest is both an end in itself and leads to successive struggle. More passive societies may accomplish this by stressing the natural rhythms with which life must accord; the more dynamic by appealing to the vitalities latent in a sense of historical distinctiveness. Probably no society is purely committed to but one of these emphases. Whatever the emphasis chosen, there are irrepressible realities which arise from the part neglected. The vitality of Germany under the Nazis arose from the myth which "explained" historic difference by the natural selection of a superior race. Herein is the demonic: where historic contingency is ostensibly grounded in natural fact or where it is assumed that natural fact may take only one historical form. The comparative health of less rigorously consistent societies results from the recognition that biological fact takes no necessary political shape. Whatever may be true in nature, it is not only the case that societies differ from each other. Beyond that, every conceivable human adaptation of biological "givens" is to be found in every society. Thus, in terms of our concern with human development, the task is to identify those ways in which historically derived predilections militate against growth which is latent at one or more of the life stages.

Since it is at the level of such predilections that we encounter Paul's principalities and powers, we may now illustrate ways in which American society wars against the God-given agenda of the life stages. Consider first the matter of aging. Clearly, not all people age at the same rate or from the same specific causes. Heredity and/or accident may debilitate some, while others of their age continue to thrive. Regardless of the timetables, however, all do grow older and die. I assume that there are important lessons to be learned over the course of this process. While such learning is not inevitable at any of the life stages, some things become more likely as one grows older. At the very least one might expect a person to become increasingly aware of his or her finitude. That this, and the more dramatic imminence of death, may engender fear is one of the possible reactions to such awareness. With or without the fear, one might hope for the gradual emergence of wisdom about many matters which less experience might not have yielded: an increased appreciation for the great diversity of viable human lives; an increased awareness of the particularity of one's own life, recognizing both the gains and losses which resulted from the way one has lived; gradual acceptance of the fact that gains are always complemented by losses; a growing realization that, whether or not one might have lived somewhat differently from what one did, in no case could one have lived both as one did and as one might have. Without pretending that these suggestions exhaust the wisdom to which aging might lead, such awareness would undoubtedly result in some changes, especially in one's attitude towards society and its future. I can imagine such a wise, older person learning to speak out on behalf of the richness of diversity and to resist every ideological tendency to approve only one kind of life. I can imagine such a person moving beyond the deceptions inherent in the roles of his or her prior life into the greater honesty which accompanies more accurate self-acquaintance. As we have seen in several, notable older persons over the past decade, I can imagine an aroused concern for the welfare of children and youth and a deepening impatience with those who are either careless about the world's future or indifferent to flagrant social injustice. (We need to remind ourselves of Erikson's insistence that chronological aging per se does not assure the presence of such understandings. Immature older people are common evidence to the contrary. Further, we must remember that it is at least theoretically possible for a much younger person to possess such self-acquaintance and social concern.)

Whether or not this is an adequate characterization of the wisdoms of which older people are capable is immaterial. I have meant only to suggest some resources which elders have made available to societies more receptive than is our own. The point I cannot overstress is that, at the level of our deepest societal assumptions, we have no resources for embracing the universal reality of aging, no way of affirming aging's inevitability. That this does grievous harm to all persons as they grow older must be obvious: forced to pretend to be what one no longer is, denied access to the limited ways in which one is able to offer the possibility of meaningful life to people, kept from such growth as might lie within one's capability. Less obvious is the deprivation to society as a whole which results from our inability to encourage men and women to live out their lives with self-respect because they continue to be needed for what they know and who they are. By our ideological denial of aging and death, which is another of the sources of our society's peculiar vitality, we deny the desirable wholeness of the social fabric which we ostensibly would enhance. To the extent that any group within a society is denied bases for self-respect then all must find ways to settle for less than the wholeness of their humanity. No societal wholeness is possible where some segment is required to suppress significant aspects of its experience. It is the work of the Pauline principalities and powers to render us content with such a truncated existence.

Before identifying what we believe to be the whole-replacing part, we must not lose sight of the fact that our central concern is with the work of the Holy Spirit. It is not my observations about society which matter except as they enable us to see how the demonic spirits frustrate God's curriculum. Only as this is clearly recognized does the believer become able to recognize those forces which the Holy Spirit would have us resist.

It is one of the Spirit's works to keep us in touch with the stages of life through which we may pass. At each stage we have something important to learn about ourselves, and because what we may learn applies not just to our individual life, we have something important to teach others. For example, Jesus, who is the model because he persisted successfully with the demands for growth which came to him, rightly said that it is perilous to lose touch with the child within. Whatever else he may have meant by "unless you turn and become like children . . ." (Matt. 18:3), he indicated clearly that we must not assume that we completely outgrow the child we once were. Thus, to act one's age always provides for the presence of the inner child. It is my present contention that it is no less dangerous to be oblivious to the aging one within every person. To act one's age is to be able to draw upon resources from one's present stage of life and from one's past and imaginable future. In this view the work of the Holy Spirit is twofold: (1) shepherd-like, to help the believer hold together those varied parts of oneself which the society urges us to undervalue and to isolate from each other and (2) prophet-like, to identify and resist the sources of such misvaluing and fragmentation. The Holy Spirit is both the advocate of personal wholeness and the adversary of all that undermines the pursuit of such wholeness. Consider the matter of our attitudes towards aging.

The process of aging is undervalued. Therefore, we must search out the spirits which inform our society to determine whether or not they are of Christ.

The literature on aging is voluminous. Few thoughtful people both in and out of Scripture have failed to address themselves to the fact of growing older. The difficulty is that poets of all generations have conflicting judgments about it. Two voices are always to be heard.

The issue is put clearly in Psalm 90. There we read the petition/exhortation, "So teach us to number our days that we may get a heart of wisdom" (Ps. 90:12). Note that the psalmist offers no assurance that chronological aging necessarily produces wise hearts. Such wisdom is possible but not inevitable. The opinion of poets over the millennia is contradictory.

An examination of parts of two other Psalms produces diametrically opposite judgments. The report in Psalm 31:9–12, NEB, is utterly bleak:

> My life is worn away with sorrow
> and my years with sighing . . .
> my neighbours find me a burden,
> my friends shudder at me;
> when they see me in the street they turn quickly away.
> I am forgotten, like a dead man out of mind;
> I have come to be like something lost.

In sharpest contrast are words from Psalm 92:2–14. Of the righteous, who flourish like a palm tree, the psalmist says they:

> . . . still bring forth fruit in old age,
> they are ever full of sap and green . . .

Confirmation of both voices is found throughout later poetry. Robert Browning clearly reflects one perspective on aging:

> Grow old along with me!
> The best is yet to be,
> The last of life, for which the first was made:
> Our times are in His hand
> Who saith, "A whole I planned,
> Youth shows but half; trust God: see all nor be afraid!" ("Rabbi Ben Ezra")

To Browning, however, we must add contrary judgments of two, earlier English poets. If he shares the hope of one psalmist, they embrace the despair of the other. In his description of the seven ages of man, Shakespeare describes the stages beyond mid-life as follows:

> . . . The sixth age shifts
> Into the lean and slipper'd pantaloon,
> With spectacles on nose and pouch on side,
> His youthful hose, well saved, a world too wide
> For his shrunk shank; and his big manly voice,

Turning again toward childish treble, pipes
And whistles in his sound. Last scene of all,
That ends this strange eventful history,
Is second childishness and mere oblivion,
Sans teeth, sans eyes, sans taste, sans everything. (*As You Like It*,
II. 7. 157–66.)

Alexander Pope is hardly more hopeful:

Behold the child, by Nature's kindly law,
Pleased with a rattle, tickled with a straw;
Some livelier plaything gives his youth delight,
A little louder, but as empty quite;
Scarfs, garters, gold, amuse his riper stage;
And beads and prayer books are the toys of age;
Pleased with this bauble still, as that before;
'Till tired he sleeps, and Life's poor play is o'er! (*An Essay on Man*,
Epistle II, 11. 275–82.)

Perhaps one more pair of illustrations will confirm the ambiguity of texts regarding the outlook on elders. A cartoon in *The New Yorker* (10 February 1975) depicts two elderly gentlemen at some Union League Club. One says: "As the days dwindle down to a precious few, I say to hell with everybody!" The contrasting text might be that in Luke 2:25–32 regarding the comparably elderly Simeon, who, having seen the child at the Temple in Jerusalem, spoke these words:

"Lord, now lettest thou thy servant
    depart in peace,
according to thy word;
for mine eyes have seen thy salvation
which thou hast prepared in the
    presence of all people,
a light for revelation to the Gentiles,
and for glory to thy people Israel."

How shall we explain the despair of one man, the life-giving hope of the other?

For every affirmative text there is always contrary opinion. Thus, literature per se does not simply urge the embrace of aging. Let us see if we can discover some of the sources of the negative feelings we all know. Perhaps this will begin to clear the way to Browning's assurance that the best lies ahead.

Of the reasons why elders may say, ". . . to hell with everybody," I would like to identify two which may be important. Among the sources of our aversion to aging may be our so-called youth cult and our understanding of "adulthood." While the former seems to be aging's adversary, I suspect that it is less important than our "adulthood." It is this concept which society advocates as the part which shall be the whole!

Many observers insist that America is a youth-oriented society. No doubt there is some truth to this. Most people prefer to look younger than their chronological age. To the extent that we adulate youth we should acquaint ourselves, for example, with the beautiful old Jewish men in some of the paintings of Marc Chagall. Is the inability to appreciate both forms of beauty a serious social liability?

Whatever the judgment, I suggest that we have little sympathy for either youth or age. Both are rejected because of our overriding commitment to the real enemy of both youth and age: our absolutized norm of "adulthood," from which there is no escape and which is characterized by two central traits: largely externalized lives and the capacity to produce/consume. We have taken a stage of life generally applicable between youth and aging and insisted that all ages conform to it. One of the bases upon which people of whatever age are approved in our society is their ability to produce and consume. There is no better recent illustration of the centrality of productivity as a norm of an acceptable "adulthood" than in the article, "Now, the Revolt of the Old" (Time, 10 October 1977). The case made by the magazine is that older people should not be retired as long as they are able to produce. That many "elders" share this view suggests the power of our absolutized vision of "adulthood." The emphasis results in externalized lives preoccupied with the markers (holidays, anniversaries, birthdays, trips, etc.) and the roles we play rather than with the internal meaning of lives.

We have so absolutized "adulthood" that we are intolerant of the "deviancy" represented by both youth and age. By all possible means youth are encouraged to move beyond uncertainty into vocational and familial commitments which assure both productivity/consumerism and externalized lives. Whatever "deviant" agenda may be appropriate to their advanced years, elders are essentially forbidden to depart from the criteria of our normative "adulthood." I appreciate that many older people can remain active, and more should be so encouraged. But must we assume that such continuing activity alone justifies lives? Older people have other important lessons to learn and to share. They must not be confined to the agendas of earlier life stages.

Part of our tragedy is our inability to share Chagall's appreciation for the beauty of age. As the Negro had to learn that "Black is beautiful," so we must learn to embrace the beauty of the aging one within each of us.

I indicated earlier that we have something both to learn and to teach at each stage of life. Infant, child, youth, adolescent, young adult, adult, mid-life, aging, death: at each of these we learn something both for ourselves and to share with others at our own and other stages. Each life stage has its appropriate and distinctive contribution to make to all the others. To the extent that we isolate any age group, we deny all others access to their understandings. The ". . . fruit in old age . . . ever green" is needed by those presently younger. As much as is true for any other lifestage, elders must be encouraged to share lessons that cannot be learned elsewhere.

Two such lessons seem to be central: the emphasis on one's internal life and the development of a new relationship to the external world. In these beautiful developments of which aging is capable, we have the evergreen fruit about which those uncritically committed to "adulthood" need to know. They may not yet be ready or able to eat that fruit but should know in advance of its existence. Let us look at these briefly.

Perhaps the most beautiful fruit latent in aging is the rediscovery of one's own story. Having lived largely externalized lives, lives often short on meaning because of indifference to it, men and women desire reacquaintance with their own lives. Roles, which provided certain stimulus for decades, no longer satisfy. One desires the rewarding truth rather than the unrewarding appearance. The long-neglected internal must be reembraced.

The elderly become beautiful as they come to realize that to be alone is not necessarily to be lonely. Alone, one may get in touch with one's inner life and become progressively at home with others. Eliot put the matter nicely:

> We shall not cease from exploration
> And the end of all our exploring
> Will be to arrive where we started
> And know the place for the first time. (T.S. Eliot, "Little Gidding," *Four Quartets*, New York: Harcourt, Brace & World, 1943, p. 39, 11. 240 ff.)

And not only the place but the self of that and many other places. It is with one's own, complex story that each of us needs to be in touch. It is the privilege of aging to help us to see the beauty of lives so connected with their stories.

The route inward also yields a new relationship to the external world. If the effect of the externalized lives of "adulthood" is a rapacious attitude toward the external world, the rediscovery of one's own story enables one to begin to enjoy that world in and for itself. If "adulthood" prompts us to try to possess the world outside of ourselves, it is part of the beauty of aging to begin to appreciate without needing to devour. This capacity should have been nurtured in us earlier. Since that is rarely the case, it takes experience to teach us that we cannot possess anything or anybody outside of ourselves. It takes experience to teach us that not only can we not take it with us but that we do not need to. One of the things reported in the *Time* article to which I alluded was a statement by S. I. Hayakawa. Retired from university administration and recently elected to the United States Senate, Hayakawa said of aging people, "We are no longer on the make." While such detachment is in part the result of many disappointments, I am suggesting that it is one of the beautiful fruits which the aging may have to share with the rest of us. To discover that one has a genuine story of one's own makes it unnecessary to compensate for "adult" indifference to one's story by attempting to justify ourselves by our possessions.

Perhaps the simplest illustration of this new relationship to the external world is to be seen in the difference between grandparents and parents. Gone is the parental anxiety about properly shaping young lives. In place of this burden to both parents and children is the capacity for enjoyment, for appreciating the desires of one's grandchildren to mature appropriately to their own time and place. Both are less plagued by the burden of roles—elders having outgrown them, youth having yet to grow into them—than are "adult" parents. It may not be desirable for "adults" to be other than they are, but must they be so absolute about it? Were we more in tune with the child and the elder within us, we might be less rigid in defense of "adulthood."

I have suggested that we all have much to learn and to teach at each of the life stages. I have tried also to show why our societal emphasis on "adulthood" makes it difficult for elders to learn their appropriate lessons and for the rest of us to learn from them. It is perilous to be shut off from those developments which are the peculiar privilege of aging. Whatever the consequences for "adulthood," we must no longer allow that norm for a given stage of life to impose itself on all stages. To do so is to imperil the beauty and wisdom which aging has to share. Should anybody be denied access to the beauty which the psalmist saw in those who ". . . still bring forth fruit in old age, . . . ever full of sap and green . . ."? Who does not need the wisdom which will enable one to say with Simeon, "Lord, now lettest thou thy servant depart in peace according to thy word"?

Unfortunately, it is not aging alone for which no adequate provision is made by our society. Having suggested that it is in the productivity of "adulthood" that we pretend to have found the part of the whole which defines all of the life stages, let me indicate now one of the ways in which youth is denied the moratorium necessary to its proper development. The justification for this lies in the understanding we are advancing of the nature of the Holy Spirit's work. Rather than being partial to any single stage of human life, as demonic spirits are, the Spirit's concern is for those stages which a society would neglect or isolate from the total life process. In part, the Holy Spirit is a twofold shepherd: (1) caring for each stage which, like sheep, tends in self-preoccupation to get separated from the whole and (2) guarding the entire flock from marauders. How are we to translate this pastoral imagery into late twentieth-century terms? For the moment it may be enough to recognize that the Spirit's work is always to make us more rather than less ourselves.

Both exceptional and ordinary experiences have the potential power to bring us to ourselves. War and disorder in the public realm and individual calamity in the personal may open our eyes to realities to which we are usually "blind." In the "ordinary" experiences of going to school for the first time, graduating, reaching one's majority, getting married, becoming parents, getting older, or being terminally ill, we may be especially reachable by God. Because ordinary experience is universal, or nearly so, we tend not to think of it as part of God's "classroom" for self-clarification. However, the fact that so much of our life is quite commonplace means that, if God acts as the believer holds, that initiative must be within familiar events. To think otherwise is to be ignorant about the cumulative shape of one's inner life. Ignorant, that is, until negative developments reach a point where dramatic measures are required. In everyday life one thinks of couples who ignore too long the destructive patterns in their relationship. In Oscar Wilde's novel, *The Picture of Dorian Gray* (New York: Penguin, 1949), we have the tragic story of a bargain with Satan by which the world was kept ignorant of the deterioration of the protagonist's inner life. Would that there were for all people a hidden portrait of our inner state and that, with such information about our "health," we might act to reform rather than finally to take our own life.

The problem is that modern women and men largely do not appreciate the mundane. Basically, we simply underrate the importance of ordinary days and times. Virtually everything in our society by which our attitudes are constantly being shaped—television and the press—stresses the exceptional. Our appetites are regularly overstimulated to desire the unusual: the trip to some exotic, remote place; the new appliance or this year's "completely new" version of the same; some holiday memorabilia. By these lures are we misled; by our knee-jerk response to them our lives are trivialized. The consumer society demonstrates that Pavlov's findings have wider application than he imagined: run a juicy ad and watch the acquisitive salivate and flock! When only the extraordinary holds promise, when we are deaf to all but the loudest noises, it is impossible to attach importance to the ordinary. We are acutely disadvantaged when it comes to hearing Elijah's "still, small voice." But what if God's call, or the neighbor's cry for help, or the word from within is voiced *sotto voce*?

The spiritual consequences of this are lethal. Progressively schooled to believe that meaning inheres only in the unusual, we are progressively out of touch with our own lives. To have lost this connection with ourselves means simply that we are not where God can reach us. And where we "are" satisfies us so briefly that we are on an endless treadmill, trying to satisfy appetites with nonexistent nourishment. A clever movie, *If It's Tuesday, This Must Be Belgium*, exposes some of the fallacies of the whirlwind tour of anywhere, as did Charlie Chaplin our pathetic acquisitiveness.

Spiritual Consequences of Self-alienation

Here is the question we should ask: what does life in our society do to people? What does it teach us that is important? What good? Especially should we ask, what does such a society do to youth who are making some basic decisions at a time when they have inadequate experience and, understandably, too little knowledge of themselves?

I would like to come at possible answers to such questions

indirectly, looking first at public evidence of what is happening
to many people in their middle years. I do so on the assumption
that there is an important relationship between what is now
popularly known as the mid-life crisis and some of the "decisions" of adolescence and early adulthood. I suspect that we
are seeing in the restlessness of many middle-aged people an
important effort to get free from the consequences of lifestyles
overly determined by culture. That affluent hearts are restless
only confirms Augustine's experience that, short of God, nothing satisfies long. By the time a person is forty, she or he has
become aware of some important, ordinary realities largely ignored. As parents and even contemporaries die, one is almost
unavoidably reminded of one's own mortality. The prospect of
death must be acknowledged. It is also difficult in this context
to avoid asking some questions about the meaning of one's own
life and the worth of one's pursuits. Activities which were
pleasant, or at least endurable, at twenty-five or thirty may be
intolerable at fifty. Something within the person has changed.
When time seemed limitless, certain attitudes were possible;
when the years are more clearly finite a changed outlook may
occur. The facts which we read may be disturbing news; they
may also be evidence of some people's heartening search for
their soul. It was C. J. Jung who said that, at bottom, the problems of all middle-aged people are religious (Jung, *Modern Man
in Search of a Soul*, p. 110 ff.; the entire chapter, "The Stages
of Life," is rewarding.). There are decades in responsible lives
when the normative clamor and pace utterly deafens us to other
aspects of God's call. We may learn to be thankful, if pained, to
discover through the ordinary process of growing older that
God may be getting us back in touch with ourselves. Thus does
our *ordinary* experience become preparation for, if not the actual means of, God's grace.

Finally, we must ask how it was that we got so out of touch
with ourselves. Increasingly I am persuaded that part of the
answer lies in the pressures put on sons and daughters to make
premature decisions. Especially where parents are ambitious
for their children or nervous about "appearances," the young
are unable to resist the obligation to make some basic choices.

Since it is also educationally efficient to "know" what eventual work one wants to do, the circle of coercion is complete. Parental pressure combines with educational "efficiency" to force youth into vocational commitments for which they may not be ready. This is the material out of which mid-life crises are made. Do not assume from these remarks that I am hostile to youths' desire to find a work to which to give themselves. Quite the contrary. It is wholly appropriate for young people to want to know that they will be needed. In the process, however, two conflicting realities need to be made explicit: (1) well-educated youth need time to sort out the numerous ingredients of responsible vocational choice and (2) parents often want inappropriately to hasten the process. Evidence accumulates to suggest that adolescent haste leads to mid-life waste.

Believing in the lures which society holds up to the well educated and wanting to believe in the soundness of parental exhortation despite ample evidence to the contrary within family and neighborhood, youth takes the bait. Largely swept along by the current of uncritical societal enthusiasm for schooling and prestigious careers and largely out of touch with their own feelings, many students make heroic efforts to show academic interest, and many young adults pretend the same zeal for their jobs. If they marry and have children, houses, boats, snowmobiles, they are trapped until public or private misfortune, or mid-life itself, rings the bell on this merry-go-round. (Nikos Kazantzakis, *Zorba the Greek*, New York: Ballantine Books, 1952, p. 93. "The Full Catastrophe" is one of the songs in the film produced and directed by Michael Cacoyannis, New York: 20th-Century Fox Record Corporation, 1965.) Years ago, T. S. Eliot wrote an obituary for the modern world.

> . . . Here were decent godless people:
> Their only monument the asphalt road
> And a thousand lost golf balls! (T.S. Eliot, "Choruses from 'The Rock,'" III, *Selected Poems*, London: Faber & Faber, Ltd., 1965, p. 116.)

This is *not* to suggest that there are no rewards, *no* possibility for significant growth even in commitments which don't endure. Virtually no lifestyle lacks some blessing. It is to say, however, that much about our life and goals, especially as we try to perpetuate ourselves by imposing these goals on our children, is demonic. The fortunate fact is that increasing numbers of people are becoming aware of the inauthentic "adulthood" of the consumer society. Are they not prophets recalling an alienated people to themselves? Disenchantment may be part of God's tutelage.

There are people who object strongly to my social determinism. They insist that "the young *can* resist, though they may *feel* unable." The opposite seems to be more accurate: they may feel able but actually are not. As I reflect on my own experience, I recognize that only certain possibilities were encouraged by those who were important to my life. Given the circumstances into which I was born, it was almost inevitable that education would be important. However, we have to remember that despite societal influences, each of us is accountable for the "choices" we make. Thank God, there were inconsistencies in the influences, and we each *did* choose from among such as were actually available to us.

It is important at this point to stress the relevance of life's inconsistencies to human freedom. The charge that I was inconsistent used to bother me. In part, it was as a father that I became more comfortable with my condition. I realized that it was through my inconsistencies that our children learned how to accomplish for themselves what would have been much more difficult had I been monolithic. A great virtue of having two parents is that the inconsistencies increase at least arithmetically. This gives children greater maneuverability for their own growth. Part of the hard lesson that these auspicious conditions eventually bring home to children is that they embody in themselves many of the inconsistencies which their parents never resolved. Thus, to honor one's parents, as the commandment requires, involves our acceptance of the tensions of our own lives which result from the inconsistent parents to whom we were born.

For reasons "explained" only by reference to sin, it is never easy for God to recall us. In an affluent and arrogant age the means to conceal the presence of the Holy Spirit are both numerous and clever. Only the possibility of disenchantment with many of the unrewarding lures of our society may save us, though that may take us through the valley of despair. If mid-life is the time when the ill-resolved and long-repressed issues of adolescence reassert themselves, this could be another of the Spirit's means of getting us back in touch with God by getting us back in touch with "strayed" parts of ourselves.

The Spirit's Holistic Work

In order to suggest the nature of the work of the Holy Spirit, we have illustrated a few ways in which the predilections of American society inhibit the progress of men and women through the life stages. So unequivocal is the commitment to "adulthood" as the norm for all development that we cannot get youth into the circle fast enough nor will we allow the aging graceful escape from it. In our distortion of the shape of the lifeline, we are not different from all other societies; all achieve distinctive vitality by comparable inflation/deflation of one or another of the life stages. As products of a particular society who also profess interest in the Spirit's work, however, our task is to recognize and to learn to resist the particular distortions of which we are the bearers and the victims. To do this it will be helpful to look somewhat more closely at a few of the characteristics of that "adulthood" which has absolutized the importance of the ability to produce and to consume. Having considered some illustrations of the ways in which "adulthood" undervalues specific life stages, I want then to note the adverse effect of several of its central emphases on one's understanding of the life process. As these are more clearly recognized, we will be better able to see what it means to affirm belief in the Holy Spirit.

We begin with two demurrers. First, that what we are calling "emphases" are so much a part of the way we live as to be hardly recognizable. We suffer their effects without ever having looked at them carefully. Second, the emphases which we shall identify as characteristic of our society have been selected from among many possibilities because of their particularly adverse impact upon people's efforts to progress through the life cycle. What follows is neither an exhaustive characterization of the most important qualities of the demonic spirits in our society nor a negative attitude towards particular stages of life. Rather, the intent is to identify qualities encouraged in modern society which jeopardize that wholeness in which the Holy Spirit would fashion us.

While it is central to my argument that there is deep resistance at all times to God's curriculum for our humanization, I want now to identify some of the attitudes peculiar to these present times which make sin necessary if not inevitable. I do this on the assumption that the likelihood of success in one's effort to live meaningfully is improved to the extent that one recognizes what and where the enemy is. In *The Courage to Be* (New Haven, CT: Yale Univ. Press, 1952), Paul Tillich indicated the successive challenges with which faith had to come to terms over the centuries. The devil bides its time and changes attire from the Greek anxiety about mortality to the medieval preoccupation with guilt and to the modern threat of meaninglessness. Concern about one's mortality and/or one's guilt persist but as relatively minor problems in an age threatened by life's apparent absurdity. Similarly, the societally-derived, Jewish issues with which Jesus successfully came to terms have not been, per se, the issues which successive generations have had to resolve. They were the issues of humanization *for his time* thus making them only somewhat relevant to our tasks. The form taken by the devil in the desert will not be that which late twentieth-century people encounter. The ultimate issue remains unchanged; however, the ways in which the question arises and the temptations to respond negatively vary with time and place. It is some of these subtle temptations which we wish to expose. To have recognized them will not result in their defeat.

Of the many ways in which such exposure of the demonic

spirits of this time could be organized, the simplest will be to draw upon our earlier discussion of continuity and change. This discussion underlies three characteristics of demonic spirits which inhabit our life-cycle progress: they mislead by causing us to believe that issues must be viewed as either/or, that limitless change is possible, and that constant change is both possible and desirable. Let us take a look at each of these demonic attitudes in some detail.

At least since Kierkegaard the emphasis on either/or has been an important source of much modern theology. It remains misleading. (It has long interested me that we find in the Gospels two versions of an utterance by Jesus: "He who is not for us is against us" (Luke 11:23) and "He who is not against us is for us" (Luke 9:50). Scholarly arguments for the greater authenticity of one of these undoubtedly say as much about the predisposition of the scholars as about their exegetical skills.) Regarding such enduring fundamental realities as continuity and change, it is demonically misleading to insist that one must prefer one or the other. In the development of a life there must be both for any viable identity: who one is must connect with who one has been; who one becomes must reflect changes which will have occurred. Amnesia is the condition of the person who cannot connect present and past; stagnation is the plight of the person who remains indifferent to and uninfluenced by recent and present events.

This is not to say that persons are not inclined to favor either continuity or change. They are. Some people live out their lives without apparently modifying their basic stance. We probably all know lifelong political conservatives or liberals. Others fluctuate from basically conservative to equally liberal stances. Adolescence may be a more change-oriented time of life than is advanced aging but it would be misleading to obscure either the adolescent's profound need for assurances of continuity or for the older person's yearning to escape a well-established rut.

It is inadequate to insist that maturing people see continuity and change as mutually exclusive. Yet this is precisely the mentality bred into us by the prevailing principalities and powers.

It is such a mindset which undermines our capacity for embracing the ambivalences which inhere in every person's progress through each of the life stages. This defeat-the-enemy mentality is *the* enemy of all human growth. It is the mentality which assumes, contrary to the evidence, that when Jesus bested the devil that that was *the* end of temptation for him. Such an us/them mentality is peculiarly lethal when one is trying to deal responsibly with internal conflict. It leaves no way for young persons to incorporate within their identity any ingredients from their subordinate sexuality. The accolade, "He's all boy!" misleadingly implies that such a child will become a *real* man. Actually, he will avoid becoming a machismo monster only to the extent that encouragement is given to those resources which eventually make intimacy possible—the ability to care for others, and to allow oneself to be cared for. Why is it that there is no occasion, other than illness, when male adults feel free to acknowledge dependency on others?

Only the deepest fears about aspects of oneself begin to account for this either/or mentality. If it is fear about latent capacity for rage and for the violence to which it could lead, which underlies some people's docility, it is equally true that others' insistence on toughness conceals fear of their inclinations to tenderness. In both cases the fear indicates that such people are out of touch with integral aspects of their own lives. The unconnected parts of one's self really are demons, and they must not be acknowledged. The groundless fear is that they would take over if recognized; therefore, they must be suppressed, minimized, and even concealed. If only it were that easy! Such feared, unacknowledged parts of ourselves do not just disappear. Like the devil they bide their time and grow because they are ignored. They thus require more of our energy. Had Jesus refused to engage his demons, there would have been no energy for any public work. If we persist in the either/or determination to destroy the indestructible, to ignore the non-ignorable, we shall never experience the Holy Spirit's efforts to lead us to wholeness. That perfect love casts out fear I am certain. That perfect love includes a proper love of self I am equally confident. Fear of parts of the self is cast out as the Spirit frees one to embrace and to assign proper roles to all the parts.

My emphasis on acknowledging the "unattractive" parts of ourselves does not imply that all aspects of our lives are equally important and deserve comparable roles. Not at all! Jesus engaged his demons, but this did not result in his assigning them lead parts in his life's drama. Demons need to be regulated; they are not expungable. They become unregulable only as we insist that they be expunged or as we refuse to recognize them. I suspect that the most heinous qualities which we try to conceal have their origins in our social rather than our biological part. No animal is capable of any behavior even remotely approaching the evil done by antisemitism. The way to deal with inimical qualities from our universally natural and distinctive historical pasts is not denial. That way leads to the dissipation of energy and to directing the unacknowledged qualities at inappropriate objects and people—Jews, Blacks, strangers.

The task is to acknowledge always that for everybody life is a mixture of strengths and weaknesses. Each individual is responsible for the deployment of these "givens." Whatever importance we assign to any of the parts reflects both their inherited strength and our willingness to be accountable for ourselves. Our inherited features and qualities vary so greatly, as does the conditioning to which all are varyingly subject, that there are experiential reasons for agreeing with Jesus that, but for God, no one is good. That we are also exhorted to be perfect, as God is, means to me only that we are required to be the acknowledged stewards of our particular inheritance. To desire to be such a custodian might lead one in search of the Holy Spirit; to find that Spirit might enable one finally to believe that one had a vocation.

The point of this exposure of the fallacy of either/or is to enable us to see that both parts of every polarity are functional and must be affirmed. At specific times it is crucial to know one's mind about the roles to be assigned to continuity and change. Always to be opposed or committed to either, however, is the mark of a person who refuses to make those discriminations which distinguish one occasion from another. To be ideological about either continuity or change is to refuse to honor the God-given distinctiveness of every human occasion. For all their apparent similarities, there is no greater mistake one can make than to assume that a given situation is indistinguishable from others in the past. Déjà vu is an understandable response to experience only by recognizing that the feeling arises from the refusal/inability to take the trouble to pay careful attention to the distinctive situation at hand.

Before proceeding with the identification of ways in which societal attitudes mislead us, we must fully understand the religious importance of being able to encompass *both* continuity and change. Let me repeat my understanding of the religious significance of progress through life's stages. It is not that there is anything inherently religious about any one of these stages or about them in their entirety. Aging, for example, is not a more inherently religious time than is mid-life; childhood is not more potentially spiritual than is adolescence. Nor will the passage of time from birth to death assure either personal maturity (despite physical maturation and senescence) or the nurture of any religious inclinations. Physical developments are inevitable and societies will continue to shape "desirable" citizens without the process of either continuity or change assuring any readiness for a religious understanding of the meaning of human experience.

I have a different hunch and it arises from my suspicion that preparation for faith is *potential* in progress throughout life's stages. It is because of this hunch that I have identified the stages as God's curriculum. Everybody is capable of some such progress; for most the *potential* for continuing growth is endless. That comparatively few persist does not invalidate the reality of the divine initiative to be discovered during the life process. It does suggest, however, the many obstacles and how persistently we resist the cost of genuine growth. The preparation for faith has less to do with the content of any of these stages than it does with the kinds of realities which one encounters in the course of struggling to master the content of every stage. It involves recognizing many things: the determining influences from the past, the legitimate yearnings and needs searching for roles that they will play in one's life, and the fact that the casting director must find parts for all applicants. None may be dismissed. Further, progress through the life stages is a potential *preparatio fidei* to the extent that a person acknowledges that concerns from other life stages may complicate the ever-changing configuration, that every celebration of a gain unavoidably involves grief for what has thereby been lost, that most relationships can be deeply and mutually rewarding. Finally, faith becomes a possibility inasmuch as one can admit that no negotiation of the life stages approximates either the ideal adjustment which social scientists describe or the hopes that one may have had for coping with any particular stage. The preparation for belief lies in experiencing the fact of human limitations and in acknowledging the ambivalences which inhere throughout life. In these experiences one may perceive the graciousness of the divine initiative. Alternatively, the vision of what might be and the lack of hope for its realization may evoke despair. It is about the subtle and fragile complexity of life that progress through the stages may instruct.

To the extent that one's society allows one to learn about such matters, the life cycle holds potential for the development of faith. Having learned from progress through the stages, some will despair. Life really is as hopeless as one had long feared. Sensing evidence of the divine initiative, others will search for the Holy Spirit. From that Spirit they will learn first about the grace of God: about how it never was possible or necessary to prove anything by one's efforts alone. They will also learn that, with nothing cosmic to prove, even the most unpromising human resources may do some good. Not all good, or even a great deal, but *some* human good. Having been given a vocation, they are free to go about the ordinary business of their lives and that of their society with an appreciation for the glory in life's ordinariness.

It is for such reasons as these that progress through the life stages is not optional for Christians. No other experiences hold comparable potential for enhancing appreciation of one's humanity and for driving ever deeper the roots of one's identity. No other experiences have the ability to instruct about the inseparability of gains and losses, about the satisfactions inherent in modest achievement, nor about the potential in all behavior for both good and evil results. That human relationships are sustaining under such circumstances without obscuring the ultimate solitude of lives prepares some people to seek that understanding of the ultimate source of life which the believer calls faith. It is for such reasons also that it is essential to be able to recognize what one's society is doing to assist or to hinder access to such experiences. It is dangerously inaccurate to assume that society is ever indifferent to the kinds of experience one may readily have. Having recognized the inadequacy of misleading attitudes about continuity and change, let us look at further misguidance about change itself. Since we are ostensibly a change-oriented society, one might expect sound guidance to assist our progress through life.

In few ways are we more disserved in our desire to undertake the work of the stages of life than in prevailing attitudes towards change. We are misled to believe two inaccuracies: (1) limitless change is possible and (2) constant change is both possible and desirable. Both of these misleadings seriously undermine any effort to undertake the tasks of the life stages. I shall say relatively less about the harm done by these attitudes toward needed social change. It might be misleading to try to work at both public and personal change simultaneously. The reader who has followed the argument to this point will have little difficulty extrapolating for society from what shall be said about the inadequacy of these attitudes for understanding personal change.

Myths About Change

To believe that there are no inherent limits to the amount of change possible in any life obscures the varying limitations to which every life is subject. By acknowledging the reality of limits, I have no intention either to define these for anybody else nor to discourage anybody from trying to move beyond any present confines. There is an important truth captured in society's misguidance: for any person, the limits are not determinable a priori. This uncertainty is the source of the dynamic of life in the west. However, while nobody should allow anybody else to set limits and while there are glorious stories of persons who have achieved beyond all expectations, these should not obscure the fact that everybody needs to be able to embrace both temporary and permanent limitations. To be able to thrive, or even to survive, in the modern world we need something more than the misleading assurance that the sky is the limit. To that exhilarating permissiveness we need the complementary resources which permit graceful acknowledgment of particular limitations. Actually, there are unrecognized burdens in the fallacy of limitlessness.

There are relatively fewer restraints today as to what a person may do with his or her life. Personal freedoms and upward mobility are, in an expanding economy, available to greater numbers of people than was true at the turn of the century. That this hardly includes the most disadvantaged of minority groups is not its only oversight. It conceals the fact that a general broadening of opportunity does not mean that inherent limitations have been overcome. For hosts of reasons we are not free to become anything we may be able to think. While we may be motivated to buy or to steal the products which merchandisers dangle before us with the assurance that life will be good if we only have their article, there are limitations not to be overcome by either purchase or theft. In the language of the New Testament, we can add neither to our height nor to the number of hairs on our head. Raised heels may enable us to appear to be taller, and there are various devices for the balding, but they are both pretenses. Nothing has changed but one's appearance. We need an understanding of our lives which will enable us both to keep pressing for ways to move beyond today's confines *and* to be able to acknowledge limitations without feeling defeat. We need to be able to combine hope and realism, an awareness of life's inherent dynamic and of the inevitability of stages. Society's single-minded exhortation to endless self-improvement is demonic. This is its power: it feeds fantasies.

It is the contrary function of the life stages to concentrate upon the modest but not easily accomplished tasks of any particular stage of one's development. In this area there are no giant strides, no dramatic transcending of limitations, but by small and precious increments, there may be an accumulated ability to aspire and simultaneously to be resigned without despair. Clearly, this is no easy achievement, especially for people as misled as we are about the absence of limitations. In the balance of this discussion of societal misinstruction about our capacity for limitless change, I want to stress three things: (1) the pain inherent in the discovery of one's limitations, (2) the wisdom about these matters to be found in so-called simpler societies, and (3) the relevance of Christian faith.

Two things which should be clear often are not: (1) not all things are possible and (2) the discovery of one's limitations is always painful. Since neither is readily recognized, let me illustrate both from the pages of an eighteenth-century diary. Out of many possibilities, I chose this for two reasons: I find touching the language in which a mature man describes a poignant disappointment; that he lived in another era suggests the ubiquity of the experience of personal limitations in romantic relationships.

Jeffrey Whitaker was an educated, English, bachelor landholder of about age forty when he fell in love with a widow. This experience had the transforming effect which a genuine romance has on most people. He came alive with pleasure and hope. Even his dreaming was renewed: on December 10, 1740, he recorded that he had "Dreamed a pleasant Dream that I was married to Mrs. (Adlam), with all the pleasant circumstances thereof." With ever increasing initiative by Jeffrey, the courtship flourished over the following months. It was not until May 19, 1741, that the first negative note appeared: ". . . apprehensive of being Sleighted by Mrs. Adlam and jealous of F. Fricker, but however danc'd with her in the Evening." As his journal entries for the following days indicate, his uncertainty about her affection mounted rapidly. Finding himself increasingly "vext and disappointed" and that he and Mrs. Adlam were "... Awkward Company and (unable to) be free with the company of each other," he had to act. He records May 23, 1741, as follows:

> ... Being resolv'd to know Mrs.' mind more perfectly, she discharg'd me quite and will hear no more on that head. Her mother vext about it ... her Brother saith he should have been glad if she had accepted me. No objection was made against my person, Character or Circumstance but as I think Mrs. ' being naturally brisk and airy *and I being used to Reading and Study am thoughtful and grave in Countenance which she cannot like* and perhaps willing to try another. Oh! most unfortunate Journey this Week to lose my chiefest delight in this World! (Marjorie Reeves, *Sheep Bell and Ploughshare*, Bradford-on-Avon, Wilts, England: Moonraker Press, 1978, p. 27 [italics added].)

As most adolescents discover without disaster though usually not without distress, who they are—"thoughtful and grave in Countenance" or "naturally brisk and airy"—does not necessarily make them attractive to everybody. There are limits. That some cannot like us as we are may be a matter of indifference; that others, and a special other, cannot, is the source of grief akin to that of Jeffrey Whitaker. Most adolescents not only survive such unavoidable experiences but are wiser if temporarily sadder. At mid-life a first such disappointment may be one's last. Jeffrey Whitaker remained a bachelor and probably became yet more "thoughtful and grave in Countenance." The experience of limitations did not free him to try another.

> "24 May. at Home all day being greatly vext at my late disappointment can hardly bear up under it. God of his infinite mercy either turn her heart or Support me under all trouble this being the greatest I ever met with." (Ibid., p. 28.)

Several weeks later he made his final, written reference to the episode. "15 June ... am very thoughtful about things since May 23 last. I hope my health nor senses will be impaired" (Ibid., p. 30). His worries about his physical health proved unnecessary. A larger understanding of health as a lifelong movement towards wholeness, of being rewardingly in touch with the range of his sensibilities and those of others, he never gained or further sought.

Perhaps the residual Calvinism of his rural nonconformity helped Jeffrey Whitaker to heal his wounds. If so, he did it by a resignation which simpler people manage to avoid. This, at least, is the view of two English scholars of peasantry. In sharpest contrast with our society's misleading guidance about the limitlessness of change, the primary tendency of the peasant is fatalistic. Immersed in nature and endlessly subject to its vicissitudes, it would be understandable if peasants were simply resigned. Utterly clear-eyed about death, they possess the ability to combine an appreciation of inevitability with a capacity for initiative.

> One can learn from peasants. As they know, nobody's exempt [from contingency], and the world is not only what we want. To a very great extent there are processes which are stronger than us— social, biological, physical. It's not a question of accepting them, nor of surrendering to them, but it is a question of understanding inevitability as a part of them. (Teodor Shanin in an interview with John Berger, "Can Peasant Society Survive?" *The Listener*, 21 June 1979.)

Wise first about processes which are stronger than people, they are able to find niches where initiative is proper and possible. Misled about our capacity for initiative, we are largely unable without despair to acknowledge the reality of limits.

For most modern men and women the road back to the tutelage which gives peasants a distinctive wisdom is closed. Yet we continue to experience the reality of limitations which was forced onto Jeffrey Whitaker. Not everything is possible. But *some things are possible.* For the sake of life progress, two related facts must be learned: (1) only some things are within our capability, and (2) acknowledgment of limits is the beginning and not the end of our freedom. As we shall see more fully in the final section of this chapter, the assertion that there are no limits is not merely misleading; it is bondage. Rather than freeing, it imprisons. When everything is theoretically possible,

no particular achievement is of much value. The more relent-
lessly one affirms the theory, the more inevitable is it that every
achievement is but instrumental to the next. In itself it is nothing. Thus are we driven—like beasts by a maniac who lacked
all understanding of beasts' limitations. We drive ourselves as
somebody whose primary instruction came from machines
rather than the animals with which we have kinship. But we
are not machines whose parts can be replaced when they wear
out. It is this fact which prompted a wag to observe that, "Death
is the body's way of telling us to slow down."

That there is an alternative to the misleading myth of unlim-
ited change is suggested by one of the central characters in
James Michener's *Centennial* (New York: Random-House,
1974). Levi Zendt, a rebel from a strict family in Pennsylvania,
was among those forced to stop short of the Oregon destination
on which he and his young bride set out. After her death he
married a half-breed and was an early settler of Colorado. He
was able to assist many of those of differing interests—who
came in the following years. It was these conflicting interests
which provided much of the drama for the novel and for unfolding Levi's character. Shortly before his premature death and
in response to the problems which plagued his daughter, he
said two things which summarize what I have been trying to
say about the myth of limitless change. "We cannot choose the
time in which we live. We can only try to change things a
little—if we will" (Ibid., p. 136). This statement accords more
with my own experience than does the exhortation to pursue
limitless change. The need is not for an impossible dream but
for self-understanding and the consequent ability to persist at
those changes which are possible.

The related myth about change accounts for the maniacal
pace of much of modern life. Lest any should escape bondage
to the assumption that change has no limits, we insist also that
change must be constant. It is for this reason that we find it
difficult to tolerate those who even seem to be unoccupied.
Long having apparently abandoned belief in the devil, we are
still convinced that idleness is the devil's opportunity. What do

we make of the mountaineer who spent much time on his porch rocker? When asked how he occupied himself, he replied, "I rock a good deal." As to what he did when not rocking, "Oh! I just sits." I suspect that there is wisdom here which remains hidden to those of us who are endlessly busy.

I am incapable of arguing for a completely passive life. Not only do I lack experience with which to make such a case, I believe that passivity is as misguided as is our compulsive activity. What we need, and the life cycle holds the potential for instructing us, is an understanding of our lives which includes time and energy for both action and nonaction. Like all of the polarities about which we have spoken throughout this book, this balance is not easy to achieve or maintain. The claims of life endlessly tend to unsettle every equilibrium. What we lack is the ability to appreciate the inherent appropriateness of the need for being both active and quiet. In its cycles of growth and being dormant, nature is wiser than we are.

In an important book, *Contemplating Now* (Cambridge, MA: Cowley Pubns., 1983), Monica Furlong attempts to ground such an appreciation in the ongoing pattern of our hearts. They do their crucial job of maintaining the supply of oxygen and ridding the system of wastes by alternating action and rest. Unlike the constant running of a brook, the heart produces its energy by a thrust and by a relaxation. As a proper understanding of one's blood pressure readings indicate, the level of one's diastolic "rest" is at least as important to health maintenance as is that of the systolic action. We cannot survive without both the pumping and the recovery. Contrary to the understanding of blood pressure as only the systolic reading, what is equally and relatedly important is the reading of the pressure at rest. Can the heart's pattern be irrelevant to the lives we are able to lead because it continues to work *and* rest? Because what goes on within our bodies is autonomic, we are largely unaware of its potential for instruction until it malfunctions. In view of the fact that cardiovascular diseases are so widespread in the so-called advanced nations, we have some evidence of the depths of commitment to the myth of constant change. Many are driven to premature deaths by their inability to incorporate into their lives appropriate times for both action and nonaction. The resultant dependence on drugs to stimulate and relax is widespread. Lacking all natural wisdom we rely increasingly on pharmacological skills. This may not be profitable to the users, but if the extent of television advertising is any clue, it clearly is to the producers of the products.

It is the consequence of compulsive busyness for one's progress through the life cycle which we must note. To do this we shall first quote from a book about the Norwegian sculptor, Gustav Vigeland. It was a brief exposure to his work in Oslo that first prompted me to begin to pay attention to the ambivalences in my own life. To my knowledge no artist had acknowledged as powerfully the tensions—love and hate, relationships and solitude, physical vigor and infirmity—which persist over the course of the life stages. At that time I was unaware of Vigeland's grasp of the diastolic/systolic rhythm of progress through the life cycle. For that I am indebted to an essay, "Youth and Adolescence," which introduces photographs of Vigeland's sculpture.

> The cycle of development of the human form does not progress in a straight line, but rather in a rising series of sequences. *After periods of growth and expansion the living functions on a plateau before it begins a new phase of development.* Vigeland understood this rhythmic nature of human form very well, and he was particularly sensitive to the underlying emotional meaning of the periods and their direction of change.... (Nathan Cabot Hale, *Embrace of Life*, New York: Henry N. Abrams, Inc., [n.d.], p. 210 [italics added].)

Life on the Plateau

We could not find clearer or briefer refutation of society's misguidance about the constancy of change. Change is possible over the entire course of life but it is not constant. Humankind is not under obligation to be constantly seeking change any more than is the heart only to pump. There is a systolic/diastolic rhythm as one moves through life's stages: each achievement of growth requiring expenditure of time and energy is to be followed by a period of rest and rejoicing, consolidation and integration. Let's look briefly at those aspects of the diastolic plateau.

The "activity" on the plateau is quite different from that which was required to reach it. On the way, one struggles to move beyond the resources of a previous plateau. For example, the adolescent who has achieved a viable identity next encounters the opportunity of intimacy. In an intimate relationship one is asked both to reveal oneself and to be able to receive the self-disclosures of the other. To have achieved adequate self-understanding is the precondition of such mutuality. The capacity for commitment is determined by the adequacy of one's identity. Most initial commitments are provisional and short-lived. This is why it is important for budding sexuality to seek its way to intimacy during the adolescent years. Among the lessons one may learn then at the least cost are these: (1) that who I am is not equally attractive to all people and (2) that it is not fatal to find out that one or the other of the parties in an intimate relationship must withdraw from it. Despite its poignancy few adolescents die of heartbreak. Without such experiences one would know neither one's own capacity for injuring and being injured nor of the ability to recover from such injury. Lacking these understandings, one would be incapable of moving from tentative to enduring relationships.

The point of this clarification of the activity distinctive to arrival at a plateau was to be able to recognize the "activity" distinctive to the plateau thus reached. While no intimacy is long problem-free, the agenda on each plateau has a different character from that worked through en route. It is a deserved opportunity for rest and celebration. It is an appropriate time for enjoyment. Simply to be able to be with and for the other is sufficient and right. It needs no other justification. None other is possible. A person celebrating a birthday is not necessarily required to demonstrate or accomplish something. Neither should persons arriving at one of life's several plateaus be expected to do anything more than to sit, or perhaps to rock a little. This basic need to celebrate and enjoy is undermined by society's emphasis on constant change. It may well be this emphasis which has radically impoverished our ability to enjoy anything. When busyness and rush are the imperatives of our lives, we become progressively unable to recall today anything of yesterday. We are no longer able to enjoy the familiar and that may be the most pathetic consequence of our belief that change must be constant.

A second characteristic of life on the plateau is that it is a time for integration and consolidation. In the process of its maturation a healthy plant naturally abandons parts which were functional to its early growth. No so with human beings' inner life. Unless the plateaus are times of integration, of recognizing the changing importance of resources from prior stages, one will draw upon them appropriately and inappropriately. Unless time is taken to sort through the experiences en route to the plateau, they will be like a quiver filled with arrows and golf clubs and asparagus stalks. The process of accumulation is not necessarily accompanied by the process of selecting and discarding. Part of what should occur on the plateau is to recognize the somewhat new self which has developed while getting there. Unlike self-admiration, this involves recognition of both one's strengths and weaknesses, of the fumbling and ineptness as well as the grace by which the growth was gained. The process further reminds one of the limiting "givens" of one's life and teaches one to search for those means by which their limitations may themselves be limited. Failure to do this assures that one's "givens" will be seeking ways to extend their limiting influences. This is singularly important for the person coming onto the mid-life plateau. For this is both an extended stretch of "space" and the time when many have a crucial opportunity to take stock of the effects of their acceptance of societal misleadings. That there have been gains in one's life is usually recognizable; the realization that one's commitments have resulted in unanticipated but undeniable losses is what often makes the middle years particularly traumatic. Whether or not to persist in well-established life patterns is the troubling question not easily put down.

That there are unavoidably gains *and* losses in every movement through life's stages is the third acknowledgment to be made on the plateau. That we are ready enough to welcome the gains is why I stressed this as also a time for grieving. Those who find this language unacceptable to describe their experience need to recognize that each plateau is a time for letting go of aspects of the past which have become less functional. For example, few people in this society reach that stage of life when they are capable of responsible commitments without having developed quite a competitive sense. While the desire to compete may continue to be functional in other areas of one's life, its persistence as a dominant factor in a mutual commitment is a source of endless mischief. While I am not so naive as to assume that competitiveness can be quickly or easily eliminated from such a relationship, I am quite clear that a mutual relationship of intimacy presumes the desire to deepen and extend one's capacity for cooperation.

Perhaps it would be useful to distinguish between the life circumstances in which cooperation is expected of us. As children, in an involuntary and clearly unequal relationship "cooperation" was one thing; in a voluntary and essentially equal situation of intimacy it may not be as easily confused with obedience. We must learn both to want to get along with the other and how this is to be done consistently with one's integrity. That the desire to compete will not easily be subdued for the sake of the relationship is on two counts a source of grief: (1) it is painful to relinquish it and (2) it *is* an aspect of the old self which is being reassigned.

Even while acknowledging the gains which derive from the relationship there is no need to obscure the reality of the loss. There is a lifelong process of dying to misguided or passé aspects of the self. Without these "deaths" there is no possibility of resurrection to new life. To deny that grief accompanies such a process is both unnecessary and undesirable. To mute the losses curtails one's capacity for celebrating the gains.

In one sense, then, it must be admitted that change is constant. It may just be the contemporary urgency of it to which I take exception. Certainly such a frenzied approach to life's stages excludes even recognition of those plateau periods in which at least the *rate* of change is different. In addition, however, I have tried to show that the nature of change varies at these times. There are losses as well as gains with which to come to terms; there is a gradual process of integration and consolidation of hard-won gains; there is opportunity for enjoyment. All of these are imperiled, as is the future growth which depends upon them, if one is rushed on by an imperative to yet more immediate growth. Growth will come when one is ready and when evocative circumstances exist. It can be forced and there are exceptional occasions in every life when time is not available for the slow processes we have described. There is a high price tag attached to all forced growth. When all of a being's energies are artificially evoked, that being requires more than ordinary time to recover. Surely the implied guidance in this fact for human growth is more relevant than any analogy we may see in machines which run round the clock.

On the assumption that every society derives its distinctive character from its basic values, I have discussed a few of the governing attitudes of modern, industrialized society. I have done so in order to suggest the ramifications of these attitudes for people's efforts to progress through the life stages. I am convinced that our society both encourages and discourages particular aspects of the growth process. For example, every encouragement is given to maintain the assumption that only productivity matters: little encouragement is available for those who are ready to move into life's final stage. In particular, we looked at three attitudes towards change—its relationship to continuity, its supposed limitlessness, the expectation that it must be constant—in order to discover their consequences for human growth through the stages.

To the generally negative conclusions reached we must add the deeper recognition that there is an irresolvable tension between society's expectations and the actual experiences of individuals. Improvements to which we are exhorted—sustaining weight loss—usually prove much more difficult than we were led to believe. The assumptions which underlie all social organization are at odds with actual experience of life, and the more consistent those assumptions are the more persons are required either to suppress their experiences or to be deviants. I am unable to call this tension an actual contradiction. Since people are, in large part, the products of society it is impossible to be completely at odds with one's society. At the least, however, we must recognize that contradictions are experienced within people between some societal calls and some inner promptings. It is this precious experience, often the key to potential growth, of which we must not lose sight. It is on these promptings, if they are of Christ, that the Holy Spirit encourages growth. Some degree of societal inconsistency is necessary if people are to be able to honor their own experience as the basis for their maturation. It is with reference to such reality that I understand not only work of the Holy Spirit but of the church also. While it is with the reformation of lives in the direction of Christ's humanity that the Spirit is concerned, the prior task is to recognize and to learn to resist the deformations caused by the demonic spirits peculiar to one's society. The most serious mistake one can make is either to ignore the incredible power of these spirits or to assume their easy dismissability.

The convulsions which racked the United States for a decade, and continue to undermine confidence, resulted from the inability of society's leaders to believe that there was any alternative to "total victory" in Vietnam. Mounting public defiance, coupled with reluctant recognition within military circles that the war was not winable, eventually subdued this absolutism. We will be poor students of the Gospels if we assume that this devil has departed other than for a season and bides its time. The militaristic language of President Carter's energy address of July 1979 suggests that he still believed that Americans were arousable only when sacrifices are justified in terms of the eventual "victory" of self-sufficiency. The need for such extreme language with reference to issues as obvious as the energy crisis should alert us to the difficulty of arousing concern about the negative effects of social attitudes to the needs of something as subtle as life's stages. Different issues have varying powers to appeal for action and those of quantity will always outshout those of quality of life.

The fundamental assumptions which sustain a society are the principalities and powers with which Paul saw Christ having done successful battle. As Paul makes quite clear, the victory was in principle only. This victory is the Christian basis for hope in the amelioration of society; to accomplish actual changes in social values and behavior requires both recognition of ways in which these are inimical to human well-being and a basis for organized resistance to them. The church should be one of the latter. No individual can prevail against such powers; those who defy them are either exiled or destroyed.

Testing the Spirits

This is pretty dramatic language. Some may feel that I have inflated realities in order to enhance the importance of those matters about which I am concerned. I do not know whether or not to hope that such an accusation is true. If the obstacles to human development are less formidable than I have suggested, I shall be glad. What I suspect, and this is only minimally influenced by the recognition that we are overstimulated and underinformed, is that it is not possible to overstate the ways in which the demonic spirits are arrayed against the possibility of human development. The work of the Holy Spirit is to help us test the spirits to determine whether or not they are of Christ. Even this task of analysis is more difficult than is usually recognized. Not only do the spirits always serve some good purpose, but they are exceptionally able to present themselves in the best possible light.

My view of the irresolvable tension between society and the person results from the conviction that, whereas society abhors contradiction, personal experience is inherently contradictory. Societies and individuals tend to move in opposite directions: society towards more consistency, persons towards greater diversity; society favoring either/or clarity, persons favoring both/

and comprehensiveness; society preferring that single life stage which best serves its purpose, persons searching for ways to include all of the stages which they recognize to be within them; society honoring single-mindedness, persons trying to honor the ambivalences of their experience. Please note these as my understanding of *tendencies*. I am not convinced that society is evil and individuals good. One does need to be on guard against society's inclination to claim more loyalty than it warrants, but it is equally the case that within each person there is resistance to God's curriculum which, paradoxically, is rooted in human freedom. The spirits/values which empower any society are rarely inherently evil; some shred of the divine initiative persists in them. It is human well-being which they exist to serve. The problem seems to be both that that which exists to serve humanity wishes in time to be itself served and that persons, finding the burden of human freedom intolerable, allow themselves to be enslaved by that which should serve them. Many words of Jesus have a radical edge but few cut more deeply into the root of error than these words: "The sabbath was made for man, not man for the sabbath" (Mark 2:27). That is, there is no institution, however good, which people should serve. There is only One who should be so served because it is only in relationship to that God that the burden of human freedom is bearable. Every other relationship seeks to absolutize itself—to become like God—and thereby are people enslaved.

There is no inherent evil anywhere. Rather, there is the capacity for evil everywhere. This is the complex and fluid situation with which we are trying to deal, but it is impossible to understand a situation in which all of the pieces are moving. We must stabilize momentarily by stopping the action; there must be a temporary suspension of the social and personal streams of consciousness. What we see in this "still" is that our society creates obstacles for the God-given life stages which men and women are unsure that they want to occupy. Since it seems pointless to urge people to desire more deeply that about which they are at least uncertain, the only course open to us is to dismantle some of society's obstacles in order that the beauty of the life stages may exercise more appeal to the imagination. To do this we must recognize that this is the beauty which the believer sees in Jesus as the Christ. An initial problem for many Christians is that this beauty has been obscured by mistaken things they have been led to believe about him. His beauty, in which we see the presence of God, is that of a man refusing every option which would distance him from his own experience. Rejected by all institutions and persons, he stands witness to the validity of the relationship with God; executed by the spirits he defied and by the timidity of his followers, he refused to abandon though abandoned. Ultimately, the believer finds that the beauty of that life was vindicated by the God in whom Jesus believed his experience was grounded. Society's misleadings and the power of human apathy are unable to obscure the divine initiative.

Men and women need to be encouraged to recognize and to trust their own experiences, and this is where society is most remiss. It offers goals to which to aspire with the assurance that their pursuit will bring rewards. It recommends methods by which to reach those goals. Rarely are we encouraged to pay attention to our actual experience; never are we reminded of how much of ourselves must be sacrificed to single-mindedness; never are we invited to consider what is happening to our freedom to choose. When we check any of these matters with our actual experience, which is what often happens in mid-life, we may find that the goals were misleading; the single-mindedness was either unachieveable or at excessive cost to other parts of our lives; the last occasion when a choice was made is so remote that freedom is felt to be a threat. It is of our own experience that society frightens us.

For that experience is in tension with society's goals and assurances. We are not people who are satisfiable by something as inherently unfulfilling as the pursuit of success; we yearn for those relationships of affection and trust which the "bitch-goddess" abhors. (Cf. *The Bitch-Goddess SUCCESS*, New York: The Eakers Press, 1968. Opposite the title page is the statement by William James, ". . . the moral flabbiness born of the exclusive worship of the bitch-goddess SUCCESS . . . is our national disease.") It is only their pretense which she can use. We are either incapable of the recommended single-mindedness or astute enough to recognize the inordinate price it exacts. We cannot embrace either continuity or change because our experience shows that we must have both. Our capacity for change is not limitless; we are restrained by innumerable limitations both genetic and historic in origin. The insistence on constant change is intolerable; we tire, we sense that precious things are being lost in the haste to be on. We are not paragons whose every desire is realizable in the demands and rewards of a career; we know that that euphemism for vocation derives from a French word for horseracing which is all too much like the rat race of our lives. We are unable to fit enough of ourselves into the roles by which the world would recognize us. There is, thank God, always more to us than is accounted for in society's programs.

The guidance available from one's experience may not always be sound. We do need constantly the reality check from others' experiences. But it is, ultimately, our distinctive experience with which the Holy Spirit would teach us to work. The "givens" of our lives are our particular limitations; it is they with which we must learn again to start. The opportunities of our lives are our particular opportunities and it is with them that we must learn to do some good. The gains and losses of our lives are the particulars with which we must begin to come to terms. The growth of which we are capable is the growth for which we must strive. I emphasize the fact of our unrepeatable distinctiveness. It is this which the society obscures by suggesting that we can become anything we want to be. We cannot. We can, however, become something by first recognizing that we are already someone. It is this limiting and liberating fact which we must learn to embrace with confidence.

There is an affirmation central to Judaism and Christianity which illumines these matters: men and women are created in the image of God. If one's experience enables one to perceive the presence of the divine initiative in life one may realize that this historic belief means something quite modest and vital: I am free under God to make what I can of what I am. Not with what I should or might be but with what at this moment I am. This and nothing more or less is my vocation: called into relationship with God, created *imago dei*, I am free to trust my experience and do such good as my limitations permit. That these are never precisely definable is both the glory and the curse of my life; that they are undeniable is also my curse and my glory. Much that has been written about vocation suggests that awareness of one's calling should be actively sought. I once believed this. That I no longer do has been liberating. Whether or not one has a vocation may well be determinable only after the fact. In retrospect, others may recognize that one lived with some consistency as though called of God.

The effect of society's misleading is to equip us for either despair or for flights of fantasy. The intent of the Holy Spirit is to help us to recognize the potential for good which inheres in the limitations of every particular life, and, in lieu of either despair or fantasy, to help us to discover the possibilities for real choices which accompany the embrace of limitations. It is the Spirit's work to enable us to begin each day with gratitude. This is the source of real freedom and freedom is always the distinctive mark of the human. The task is to be clearer in our minds than society's tutelage makes us as to where the opportunities for exercising freedom are to be found. Since the work of the stages of life is the primary, ordinary opportunity for making choices and for learning to live with them, it is imperative to begin to identify both those external forces which distort the cycle of lives and those within which refuse the risks which freedom always involves.

For the believer, Jesus is the model. It is for this reason that the work of the Holy Spirit is always to help us to become more accurate about testing our values to determine if they be of Christ. It is by such critical reliance on our own experience that we become equipped to care for others. It is this conviction, coupled with a concern about the impoverishment of so much contemporary life, which justifies such a book as this in an era dominated by major social problems. That there is so little concern among the privileged about the fate of the Boat People or about other than selfish solutions to the energy crisis suggests that we are cut off from significant aspects of their own experience. The root of compassion is sufficient self-acquaintance to be able to identify with another's plight. Such a sense of self and kinship, which is the Spirit's gift, is one of the marks of membership in the church, the community of support and defiance. It is to this article of the Creed that we must turn.

VI. Community of Support and Defiance

Accurate analysis is one thing; to be able to act on such understanding is quite something else. While there is no substitute for rigorous inquiry and reflection, they do not in themselves assure change. As we have seen in the previous chapter, social pressures are sufficiently powerful to discourage individual innovation. One may be aware of the causes of suffering without being able to change anything. The person who desires to effect change, especially changes in the society, needs a community from within which to address his or her challenges to the larger world. It is with such considerations in mind that we turn to the next articles of the Creed.

The brevity of its affirmation of the Holy Spirit is matched by the succinctly stated belief in ". . . the holy Catholic Church; the communion of saints." In these affirmations lie resources without which the present argument would be impotent. Those sensitive to the forms of human bondage which we have sketched will recognize the need for some base from which to defy societal pressures, some communion within which to renew one's vision of the curriculum in which God would keep us enrolled. Thus, we look to the church as a community of support and defiance.

Those who are unsympathetic with institutions generally and with religious structures in particular may find such a characterization laughable. Acknowledgment of need for support will be dismissed as weakness. To the assertion that religious institutions are defiant, others will insist that churches largely mirror and often attempt to sacralize social values. Neither charge need be denied. Those who embrace religion do so, in part, because of an acknowledged inability to make sense of experience on purely human terms. Those who prefer self-reliance will always object to the inadequacy which faith presupposes. The point at which and the reasons for which faith is affirmed vary with individuals. Further, we must admit the truth of the observation that the church *largely* reflects society's values. While this is the fate of all institutions, it is especially objectionable when the institution claims a source of authority which transcends the particulars of societies. The relationship of the church to the institutions of the world remains endlessly problematic. That it may not, however, acquiesce to the world's judgments on all matters is decisive for its responsibility to encourage the development of human lives. As the bearer of values only partly affirmed by society, the church's self-understanding must include capacity for both support of persons and defiance of structures.

Since there are many forms of loving criticism, it is necessary to clarify how we intend in the present context to use such language about the church. Two assumptions are central: (1) progress through the life stages is God's ordinary curriculum for men and women and (2) individual efforts to defy social pressures to conform are doomed. There is no Archimedean lever for single-handed movement of society. What is needed is membership in a community which both affirms the life stages and intends the well-being of society even in its defiance of social pressures. Despite a recurring tendency to make a common cause with the powers-that-be, I believe the church to be such a community. Thus, it will be from commitment that I shall ask how the church may be both supportive of persons struggling to maturity and defiant of social pressures which aggravate those struggles.

The problem for all institutions which insist on both affirmative and critical relationships to society is to know when to support and when to resist societal directions. As H. Richard Niebuhr demonstrated in *Christ and Culture* (New York: Harper

& Row, 1951), there are many ways in which the church has understood its relationship to the larger milieu of which it is a part. Between the extremes of Erastian subordination to society and the chronic defiance of sects unalterably opposed to the pretensions of all cultures, there are traditions which understand the relationship of church and society more dialectically. My commitment is to this tradition which would transform society: endlessly seeking wider justice and means for humanization, aware of its complicity in social and personal evil but not thereby immobilized, nurtured by a source of hope which neither the defeat nor the success of particular projects may extinguish. To stand in such a theocentric tradition is to be as skeptical of religion as of an ever enlarging state. The institutions of religion must endlessly devise ways to discourage society from moving destructively and to encourage constructive social change. Those who prefer a religious ghetto will always be able to criticize the greater vulnerability of this dialectical understanding. We are less concerned with the style of affirmation or criticism than with the reasons in any instance for which support is to be given or withheld. Since those reasons lie at the heart of the church's self-understanding, it is to the terse article of The Apostles' Creed that we must now turn.

Life in Christ: Holy and Catholic

Our community of support and defiance is identified as the holy, catholic church. Each word has occasioned both volumes of scholarship and centuries of piety. Few triads combine as do these words both natural denotations and transcendent referents. This is undoubtedly the source of their enduring power to inform the lives of believers: they both can and cannot be understood. As symbols they manage to suggest enough of their meaning to satisfy the inquirer at the same time that they point beyond themselves to realities which transcend time and place. Demurrers are appropriate in attempting to speak of matters which are ultimately unspeakable. The urgency of the task requires that the risk of trivialization be taken.

Of the three words the first is the most intimidating. The history of its usage is so largely confined to devotional and liturgical ascriptions to the Divine Person that it is ordinarily difficult to imagine what human holiness might mean. Further complication comes from the fact that such use about humans is largely restricted either to men and women who lived their holy lives far removed from ordinary human intercourse or to exceptional deeds designatable as miraculous. As ascribed to saintly persons, we may be impressed from a great distance, but we are little informed in ways that matter to our ongoing lives. Most people are neither monastics nor miracle workers. Such persons may indeed deserve to be called holy, but their experience has usually been too remote to be able to revive abandoned interest in personal growth. We need understanding of holiness with which the contemporary imagination might connect.

More promising was a usage of pre-Elizabethan English, which reflects an era in which the relationship between the transcendent and the immediate was still affirmed. It was not then uncommon for a person observing a child engrossed at play to exclaim, "There is a holy child!" About such a child there was a wholeness which was as obvious as it was precious, a wholeness both natural and inexplicable, both ordinary and evanescent. Health was a clue to holiness. Fully in touch with itself but not aware of itself; able to draw upon all of its resources as the activity required, so completely engaged in the immediate game as to be beyond the need to draw upon the resources of conscious will: these were among the recognized ingredients of Anglo-Saxon holiness. So understood we may be able to affirm the appropriateness of first identifying the church as holy. Such a community derives its self-understanding from one God characterized by such wholeness. One who lacks nothing. In consequence of its source, the church has as its vocation to be the agent of wholeness in the lives of all people and adversary of all that fractures lives.

What may be said about the church which exists to serve God is always informed by what is known of Jesus as the Messiah. About him during his brief public life there was sufficient suggestion of wholeness to enlist a following. It is clear that many who "tuned in" initially, "tuned out" when they failed to hear what they sought. Even among those followers who persisted, who could not ignore the appeal of Jesus' wholeness, they preferred their association with him while it demanded relatively little of them. That the followers heard what they would has been brilliantly suggested by George Benson, an American psychoanalyst, in a book entitled *Then Joy Breaks Through* (New York: Seabury, 1972). Benson suggests that Jesus was no more inclined than is the therapist to do for others what they must and can do for themselves. Therein do we see the nature of Jesus' wholeness: he took with unfamiliar seriousness the God-given potential for wholeness of each human life. The compliment was irresistible—until the disciples realized the cost at which the Other gained his wholeness and the price yet to be paid for it in their own lives. This was the time of those second thoughts which we see overtaking disciples during Holy Week. Especially while it was assumed that the Other had already paid for their wholeness, the invitation to follow was attractive. It became less attractive as it was clearer that there was to be no cheap grace. It was only the resurrection appearances which arrested their flight and enabled them to accept the fact that they were not to be abandoned while they learned to do for themselves what nobody could do for them.

The relationship of the believer to Jesus is more subtle than ordinary piety recognizes. The difficulty is that popular salvation language—the signboard's assurance that "Jesus saves"— both illumines and obscures important realities. It is the illumination which is eye-catching: that which we cannot do for ourselves has been done for us in Jesus Christ. For the Christian nothing may be allowed to obscure that decisive "fact." The problem is that this central reality may also be used to obscure reality which is no less important. The point of believing gratitude is that, in Christ, the person of faith is able to see reality afresh. For the believer "morning *has* broken, like the first morning." Thus, it is not Jesus per se but what one is able to see as the result of his indwelling which is the occasion of gratitude and of new life. What is adorable is not Jesus but the goodness of God's creation, including one's own life. It is in Christ that the new vision is possible—one's blindness has been overcome—but it is now with one's God-given eyes that one sees for the first time. The consequences of this clarification are momentous.

Life in Christ is to be freed from all dependent human relationships. It is the Holy Spirit's work to free us from all those relationships which fundamentally undermine hope, in order that we may take on the excitement and terror of our own vocations. As the disciples discovered at Pentecost, this means even being freed from dependence upon Jesus. In the course of what we call the farewell discourses, Jesus said several striking things. That they have been less emphasized than passages which encourage passivity and dependency probably speaks for itself. For example: ". . . it is for your good that I am leaving you. If I do not go, your Advocate will not come . . ." (John 16:7, NEB); ". . . he who has faith in me will do what I am doing; and he will do greater things still because I am going to the Father" (John 14:12, NEB). In order that we might experience the exhilaration and the accountability of being fully children of God, it was necessary that the Way get out of the way. Only as Jesus' ministry to us concludes with his departure may we get on with our portions of God's work in the world. Before God alone are we children. Whereas we have often been told only to lean, God assures us we can stand; whereas we were encouraged only to listen, God urges us to speak.

How unfamiliar this is! In virtually all of our lives we are either willingly dependent or impotent protestors of our dependency. Rarely do we experience relationships in which we take both ourselves and our neighbor seriously. Either we are preoccupied with ourselves and oblivious to the other, or we are utterly out of touch with our own feelings because of our intimidated dependence on the other. Such patterns are commonplace and unhealthy. They evince nothing of the life in Christ, which combines humility and audacity, sacrificing neither. Before God alone are we both dependent children and people capable of radical independence.

Life in Christ is noncoercive. Love is the ability to care without holding on tightly. The inability to let go, which often masquerades as love, is either dependency or the determination to keep others dependent. Most relationships of our life are of this type. Think about three of these: parents, teachers, friends. What is love's role other than, in the interest of wholeness, to release powers otherwise inaccessible? All too often the helper tries to do something for us, thereby keeping us dependent. Parents, friends, and teachers should not have such helping relationships. It is their tasks not to do things for us, not to keep us dependent upon them, but to free us to assume responsibilities commensurate with our humanity. The parent, the friend, the teacher who cannot let us go does not know the presence of the Holy Spirit and all suffer the consequences.

The sad fact is that we are often all too willing to be and remain dependent. We often even receive approval for such behavior: "very cooperative of you," "thanks for going along with that proposal." I am convinced that we betray Christ's Advocate whenever we encourage dependency in ourselves or in others. In the Spirit we are free both to think our own thoughts and to listen and respond to others. To betray this Advocate is to profess to love Christ rather than loving like him, to insist only on seeing him rather than trying to see the world as he sees it. Faith and deeds are inseparable. The former is never a substitute for the latter, and the latter is sustained always by the former.

Against every attempt to ascribe to Jesus an unearned wholeness—whether at birth or baptism or at any other time in his human life—we insist that access to his divinity is only by embrace of his full humanity. The decisive miracle to which the New Testament witnesses is not that divinity could convincingly appear to be human. All too common among believers and nonbelievers, though serving opposite purposes for each, that attitude not only violates the earliest Christian testimony, it undercuts the gospel which encourages pursuit of that wholeness which God intends for all lives. That God raised Jesus from the dead *is* the good news because, being mortal, it was a man who gained that wholeness for which all yearn. He was not divinity in human guise. However unable we are to explain the miracle of it, and we need not abandon any New Testament effort to acknowledge its inexplicability, *the* christological assertion is the inseparability of his divinity from Jesus' *humanity.* It was through his pursuit of that wholeness and his inexplicable willingness to pay the price such wholeness required, that hope is renewed in the possibility of greater wholeness in one's own life. That which lures and eludes *is* our destiny.

Perhaps that is the best way to speak of the holiness which characterizes the church: without pretending to *possess* his wholeness, it is a community captive to the person in whom such holiness is found. The paradox is that, being a person, the effect of his presence both judges the believers' failures and frees them to attempt whatever may be their modest next step in the direction of greater wholeness. The judgment is not immobilizing because it is not experienced as the disapproval of a punitive institution but the chastisement of a person who desires our good. *Always the emphasis in lives must be on the direction taken rather than upon the distance covered.* This may be the most difficult assertion for a quantitatively oriented society, but it is the crucial quality of a supportive community because it is freeing of false burdens. No set of accomplishments is obligatory upon all. Without obscuring the important similarities of all lives, we stress the distinctiveness of each human life. Neither the same expectations nor the same burdens may be laid on all. In such basic matters as temperament, the ease with which some are comparatively anger free is an achievement by which others will be defeated all of their days. What is assumed within the holy community is that all desire to move, however modestly, in the direction of that Wholeness to whom they are captive.

The support to be found in a holy church will vary with the needs of its members. At one extreme it will be a place of refuge for those who have been wounded in struggles with a world offended by wholeness. At another the support will take the form of cadre-planning to marshall votes on behalf of a particularly humane legislation or to resist discriminatory politics. Basic support for those committed to the advancement of life-cycle wholeness will be found in the very composition of the community and in its regular liturgical practices. While exceptions exist such as suburban ghettos of young marrieds and their children, or institutional chapels, it is generally true that Christian community is composed of all ages and stages of life. It includes all sorts of men and women. Racially and socially inclusive by definition, I stress here the life-stage comprehensiveness which characterizes the supportive community. An intentional milieu encompasses people from birth to death; none may be excluded. Nor is any particular age or condition regularly honored above the others. Attention is paid to the common ventures through which all pass in the movement from birth and childhood to age and death. The very presence of all of the life stages is a constant source of support for those whose experiences often isolate the generations from each other. Here children and adolescents, vigorous adults, the ailing and the elderly are encountered and may teach each other.

If, in the present context, the church is to be criticized, it must be for its failure to take seriously the needs and resources of those men and women from all of the life stages which constitute its wholeness. It deserves criticism also if, having the rich variety of human life within its membership, it fails to fashion means by which the generations may learn to support each other. Not only do all of the generations have instruction to share, but by that sharing many are encouraged to persist in their particular struggles. The temptation to abandon the desire for greater life-cycle intentionality is chronic. To be more fully in touch with the many unrealized potentialities of one's life, both for oneself and for others' benefit, may be alluring. To begin to work at the process is to discover resistance both within oneself and in the reactions of others. Encouragement to persist is not only desirable, it is necessary. Some support comes from the explicit approval of friends. More often people take heart by observing what others with comparable or less potential have accomplished. About these matters the supportive community encourages a candor uncommon in the society at large. What I eventually understood was that the experience of many people at mid-life was peculiarly aggravated for as long as they thought the feelings to be idiosyncratic. There is no more unnecessary curse than to be isolated because of the failure of others to assure one of the normalcy of troubling experiences. By my own candor about mid-life matters, which were not widely discussed a decade ago, some have been helped to avoid the unproductive isolation which accompanies the suspicion that one's afflictions are unique. Such sharing does not solve anybody else's problems. That remains their task. What it may do is to free another to acknowledge the reality of his or her situation. This is the necessary first step which is made unnecessarily difficult without the accepting acknowledgment of it by others. Often it is just such acceptance which frees one to begin to deal with the situation. The resources at hand may be quite modest but they *are* one's own. They may not take one very far in a more creative direction, but that is immaterial. The distance that any individual may be able to move never was important. What does matter is the direction of greater wholeness in which one seeks to move and the fact that it is with one's God-given resources that the attempt is made. Despite all efforts to pretend otherwise, there really is no alternative to this recognition. Membership in a supportive community enables one to embrace these facts as one's vocation rather than to be resigned to them as one's fate.

It is important to recognize emerging questions about human development which are often prompted by work-related experience. For example, the conflicts within families resulting from the amount of time and energy which the primary wage earner spends at work are common enough for some corporations to provide opportunities for groups of couples to work through the issues under professional guidance. In discussing work-derived awareness of deeper issues, we should locate other people who find themselves similarly conflicted. Within the holy community are both peers and elders who have been there before us or who share our plight. Such people may be able by their candor to help us to embrace questions we might otherwise deny.

This is not a form of support distinctive to the Christian community. Such assistance, wherever found, is much more important than initially may be apparent. The process of chronological aging may be inevitable, but it does not follow that anyone gladly embraces his or her appropriate life tasks. *There is often as much reluctance to undertake the work of the next stage of one's life as there is desire to forge ahead.* Popular misunderstanding of this matter, arising as it does from the mistaken assumption that maturation accompanies the obvious fact that everybody *is* getting older, is probably the most serious handicap to understanding the central contention of this book. At least two hazards are always involved in growth: risk and loss. Both of these—the uncertainty that one will be "up" to the demands of the next set of life tasks and the certainty that one will no longer be quite the same person if one succeeds— call for encouragement. There are inward urges to get on to life's emerging agenda, but one is always cautious about making the move to fuller adulthood; and there is often social pressure to delay movement to some of life's stages.

Life in Christ: Comprehending All Stages

One of the chief sources of encouragement to get on with one's life is other people. In others we may see both positive and negative guidance about the imperative to maturation. Negatively, we encounter men and women whose development was arrested at one or another of the life stages: grown people trapped in infantile selfishness or adolescent self-preoccupation; aged people never capable of a generative concern for the future. These are pathetic illustrations of opportunities lost by the inability to have taken risks. We see occasionally in the eyes, physical movements, social concerns, and/or capacities for empathy and compassion of men and women of all ages the evidence of past and present willingness to take the risks which justify the losses. To know such people is to be encouraged in the desire to embrace as from God the tasks and opportunities of one's particular stage of life. It is inherent in the composition of the supportive community and in its understanding of the common ventures of life so to encourage all. With that support we may learn that the losses which accompany successful risk-taking are not to be compared with the pathos of lost opportunities. The paradox of these dissimilar experiences is akin to Jesus' insistence that those who would protect their gains will surely not succeed, that one must lose one's present certainty in order to find that certainty which endures.

The support which is inherent in the age inclusiveness of the holy church is to be found also in its liturgy. Indeed, some of its enduring formal practices reflect the presence of all sorts and conditions of men and women. It is, for example, a rare instance of public worship in which attention is not drawn to the sufferings of the ill and the aged, to the needs of those who mourn. Nor is it inappropriate or rare at such a time for a child to be baptized or for marriage bans to be posted. In the context of the worship of God the whole range of human experience is regularly rehearsed and the corresponding range of human emotions—from glee to grief—appropriately evoked.

The support which this provides for those who seek greater intentionality about their present life is both modest and massive. On most occasions one will be only ordinarily responsive to the evocations to add one's joy to those who rejoice and to weep with those who grieve. The human imagination is simply not regularly responsive at a deep level to others' good or ill fortune. However, the cumulative effect of being regularly reminded of the larger context of one's life—both where one has been and has yet to go—is often significant. The vision of the possibilities and limitations of human life is constantly rehearsed in the ongoing liturgy of the church. On rarer occasions the effect of such prayers, announcements, and exhortations can be massive. When the inner conditions are right, it is not even necessary to have known the person alluded to for the supportive effect to be experienced. At a church in England brief posthumous remarks were made about an elderly Miss Bennett, long known and beloved in that congregation. While I had never met her, I was struck by the range of humanizing feelings evoked on this occasion of public worship. That my own life would one day end was made more believable in that context than by many other reminders of my mortality. The fact of my eventual death was, at least momentarily, transformed from an undesired fate to an embraceable aspect of my total vocation under God. That very morning, congregational song was accompanied by a quintet of adolescent musicians. Without regret for the loss of my youth, the young violinists put me back in touch with enduring aspects of who I am; without yearning my own death, I gained from an unknown Miss Bennett a posthumous gift which enabled me to anticipate aspects of my own future. Is this not the ongoing support of the communion of saints?

Why I was peculiarly receptive that morning to gifts from the living and the dead, I do not know. The inadvertent juxtaposition of the contributions of youth and age was surely part of it. The cumulative experience of public worship, often apparently negligible in its regular benefits, occasionally heaps its rewards on those desiring life-stage intentionality. That the cumulative and the exceptional experiences are interrelated seems obvious. The likelihood that one will be able to make creative use of exceptional experiences, rather than being either baffled or merely entertained by them, depends upon the extent to which the extraordinary is relatable to the ordinary. The point always of exceptional experience is whether or not one possesses resources for incorporating into ordinary life the gains which are latent in the unfamiliar. When this is the case, significant growth may occur; when one is unable to connect the exceptional to one's previous experience, one has merely been titillated or mystified.

Our emphasis on the support to be received for life-cycle

intentionality within the holy community may obscure one important ingredient of such membership. Each person has as much to give as to receive. It may not be with any arrogant assumption of superiority that one associates with the community; more often the affiliate is quite aware of his or her deficiencies. While a proper humility is initially appropriate and will be nurtured by association with *grace-full* persons within the community, this emphasis on humility should not be allowed to hide the fact that *all* persons have resources to share. Members are both aware of their need for encouragement and prepared to draw upon their experiences as they are germane to others' need for support. Central to the Christian life is acceptance of one's combination of strengths and weaknesses. Each person has negotiated the several life stages in ways which were both healthy and unhealthy. There is neither perfect nor utterly imperfect passage through the stages. It is the work of the supportive community to acknowledge this imperfection while enabling all to recognize that even their imperfect lives may be of some help to others.

Often this has been brought home to me during years of association with the holy community. Let me share three instances. I recall officiating at the interment of a person I had not known, a long-retired member of the faculty. Around the grave stood a dozen elderly persons, former colleagues and friends of the deceased. Since all that I knew of the man was external information, I suggested that they share some recollections. After a very long silence they began to talk. The result was a glorious, late-winter celebration of a particular life and, by extrapolation, of life generally under God. They, who may have come expecting me to support them in their grief, had resources with which to support one another and to serve as I was unable to do. Each has something to give.

In another instance on a Maundy Thursday at the church to which I belong, I found myself taking a simple meal with a retarded woman who had lived much of her life largely in the isolation of a local residential school. When it came time to read the appropriate, precommunion lesson, somebody suggested that "Mary" might like to do it. I doubt that I shall ever be addressed as deeply by the Gospel's report of the Last Supper as I was by that hesitating reading. Out of Mary's "inadequacy" my "adequacy" was served. Each has something to give. Often what we have to share may be quite unknown to us. Perhaps this is the best of gifts.

I recall the members of a tiny congregation I once served on the West Side of Manhattan. It was a racially, ethnically, and nationally mixed group of largely elderly men and women. It was during the saying of the Lord's Prayer that I regularly found myself supported by these people. While the entire service was conducted in English, for this prayer several reverted to their native tongues. Below the murmur of English and Spanish, I often heard the Italian of the woman of Waldensian origins and the French of another who was native to a tiny Huguenot village. There was no way in which I was able to convey to them as they unwittingly did for me the catholicity of the holy community to which we belonged. Each has something to give.

At the outset of this chapter, we distinguished briefly between healthy and unhealthy forms of support and defiance. While all people occasionally need to be able to be thoroughly dependent on others, (when one is ill) and while there is a profound sense in which religion encourages acknowledgment of ultimate dependence on the Other, I identify as unhealthy those forms of support which perpetuate and deepen dependence. On this understanding I believe the support found in the holy community to be healthy. It is probably the paradox of Christian life that the effect of acknowledged dependence on God is greater confidence in one's own resources. A possibly helpful analogy to this assertion is to be found in the wise things which Erik Erikson has written about the development in infants of a sense of trust in the world. The result of such a sense is a growing trust in oneself. The infant comes to trust its own "judgments." Something akin to this occurs also in the believer's relationship to God: regularly renewed acknowledgment of one's dependence on God has the effect of acquainting one accurately with one's capabilities and of enabling one to trust them. Acknowledgment of one's dependence on God also yields greater accuracy about one's limitations. Freed of the Promethean need to possess all power or at least freed to conceal whatever one lacks, the believer is more able to be just a person of certain capabilities and limitations. Free of the burden of pretense, one is able to enjoy and to use what one has.

At least three ongoing aspects of the Christian community contribute to the healthiness of the support provided for those desiring greater intentionality about their present lives: (1) the age inclusiveness of the membership, (2) the concerns for and the celebrations of the various stages of human experience which regularly inform the liturgy, and (3) the Scripture by which worship is shaped. For it is by its literature that the inclusiveness and the sensibilities of its membership are determined. The holy church of which we are speaking is not just another institution amenable to social science analysis. It is such an institution of society, but primarily it is the bearer of a tradition by which the society itself has been shaped and is judged. It is a humanistic tradition in the sense that the well-being of the human is its concern because that is the central concern of the God whom the tradition exists to honor and to serve. The concern for social justice which informs so much of the Hebrew Bible makes sense only as one assents to the primacy to God of human well-being. And the centrality of the human, in whom God is seen, is the key to the New Testament. Informing the supportive function of the holy community, these Scriptures are also the source of its mandate to defy the larger society when the human is imperiled.

Against Societal Parochialism

The history of the holy community's defiance of the larger society is quite uneven. Examination of contemporary churches will reveal that the relationship of religious institutions to the world ranges from those willing to be subservient to their state, which results in some form of civil religion, to those who either withdraw into religious ghettos or belligerently resist all public authority. There are good reasons why the relationship of church and society must and will be subject to endless reclarification. The safest guidance is to affirm the relative autonomy of *all* institutions on the assumption that there will be mutual influencing and the ability to resist excessive outside pressure. Anyone familiar with the history of higher education in Europe and North America will recognize that it was such a self-understanding which the universities had to reach in order to be able to make their distinctive contributions to church and society without undue influence from either. As this history makes clear, this is not easily achieved by any institution traditionally subservient to another.

The relationship of church to society is further complicated by the fact that there is usually much in a society to support. An analogy may be seen in the pulling and pushing of the adolescent within the family. Unable to survive without the family and appreciative of its strengths, the adolescent is also vividly aware of the family's shortcomings. The task, which is never easy for the person in transition nor for a vital institution, is to be able appropriately both to affirm and to resist. The requirements of intellectual clarity about the issues at stake and the courage to take what may be an unpopular stand often exceed the capability of both the young person and the church.

In order to move this discussion beyond such generalizations, we must ignore many crucial areas of the church's relationship to the larger society: issues of domestic and international politics. For most people these areas may be both more familiar and more important than those on which we shall focus. It will be self-evident to many that the portion of national resources spent for defense or the passage of legislation inimical to the environment are both more obvious and urgent matters than the less easily discernible effects of societal attitudes to participation in the life stages. I wish to acknowledge the force of those concerns for public issues. In part, it is by our decisions about such matters that the quality of life possible in a society is determined. To many it will be ludicrous, if not evil, to be concerned with questions of quality of life when it is life itself which is imperiled. While such matters are undeniably important, they will not be our immediate concern here.

I am convinced that progress through the life stages is God's ordinary expectation for men and women. To be in touch with the operative realities of one's stage of life means several things: one is capable of the enjoyments appropriate to that stage, one can recall and draw upon the resources of earlier stages and be willing to move on to the next, one is able to relate appropriately to people of ages and circumstances other than one's own, one's concern for the well-being of future generations is ever being deepened, and one's awareness of inimical forces is more accurate. These I take to be reasonably self-evident and desirable. Comparatively unfamiliar is my central thesis: in the struggles with the ambivalences of any particular stage of life and in the gains and losses of movement from one stage to another a person may gain a relationship with the God whose initiative is seen in the life, death, and resurrection of Jesus Christ. Life-cycle experience may be religiously instructive; to be denied access to one or more of the life stages both arrests desirable human development and imperils concommitant maturation in faith. Such developments of self and faith are the source of effective concern about public issues. That relationship, however, awaits explication elsewhere.

From this central conviction about the God-givenness of the life stages two important consequences for the supportive and defiant community may be drawn. First, it is of the church's vocation to support and extend every social attitude and arrangement which encourages all men and women to seek such maturity as lies within their capability. Second, the obverse is that the holy community must resist every attitude and arrangement which discourages such developmental pursuits. This may seem something which society obviously does. Especially for the privileged that is often the case. However, even for the privileged, there are many unnecessary barriers in the path of those who seek maturity by life-cycle intentionality. The restrictive, prevalent understanding of "adulthood" as limited to those capable of both producing and consuming goods demonstrates that many people at both ends of the life spectrum, and those within that spectrum who for such reasons as ill-health are nonproductive, are denied full human status. Consequently, and importantly for our purposes, they are forced either to pretense or to resignation to their "inferiority." In both instances they are, by those who define "adulthood," denied access to those experiences and aspects of themselves by which their relationship to God might be enhanced. Inability of the young to remain youthful and of the aging to become elderly are but the most striking illustrations of this socially-engendered deprivation. Thus, for the well-being of all persons, it is part of the church's task to support attitudes and programs which encourage people to embrace their particular stages of life.

While they are now concerned with a broad range of public issues and their membership ranges from adolescents to the retired, The Gray Panthers was organized by a group of older people in order to raise the public consciousness about the needs of the elderly. Such groups as the Gray Panthers, whose founders were largely persons of Christian conscience, illustrate the initiative which should emerge from the concerns of a supportive and defiant community. They challenge destructive social attitudes and advance programs to serve a disadvantaged age group within the society. Social attitudes discouraged the elderly from embracing the reality of aging; social policy, which denied adequate income to many of the elderly, added the humiliation of poverty to the stigma of being old. Such punitive arrangements must be defied for the sake of the elderly; such attitudes must be resisted for the sake of the whole society. While it may be desirable that the Panthers have broadened the range of their concerns, one would hope that the deprivations which first aroused their passions will not be lost as they address themselves to larger issues.

Even when groups focus on single issues, they are preferable to the impotence of single voices. The concerned individual may be able to arouse others and to organize. If this fails to happen that person's cause will founder. An organizationless individual has rarely, if ever, effected significant social change in the modern world. The individual not only needs the group for personal support but as a basis for effective defiance of undesirable social patterns. This has not been more clearly demonstrated recently than in the Civil Rights movement. Unlike the Vietnam protests, which had the commendable but limited goal of stopping that war, the Civil Rights movement both defied long-established racial discrimination and advanced a vision of a more just society. There were individual leaders of the movement, many of whom also were motivated by Christian conscience; they needed the group as much for support, including physical protection, as the group needed their leadership. Isolated from the group, individuals were not only largely voiceless but, to the extent that what they said was threatening to conservative elements, their very lives were imperiled. The discipline within the Civil Rights movement, especially as the result of guidance provided by the Southern Christian Leadership Council, was the key to its effective support and defiance.

The two groups—the S.C.L.C. and the Gray Panthers—well illustrate the capacity for support and defiance which characterizes the holy community. Unsympathetic with societal attitudes and institutions which destroyed human dignity, sensitive church people created structures for social change. Rarely will a local congregation have such a single mind about any controversial issue that it will be the agent of social action. The holy community's intentionally diverse composition and the different ways in which decisions are reached within various religious structures largely militates against frequent agreement on divisive public issues. At the extremes of polity we have hierarchical churches and those organized in a radically congregational way. Whereas the former are able to address some issues through authoritative officials, of which the Pope is the clearest illustration, such groups as the Quakers are able to await the guidance of the Spirit with reference to every controversy. Most Protestant congregations lack either the authoritative person empowered to speak for all or the active patience of the Society of Friends. Sometimes it is possible to work through a controversial issue to the general satisfaction of the members. For example, while a few people left the congregation over the issue of draft-counseling a decade ago, the church to which I belong did assent to the presence of such counselors as part of its ministry to young men struggling with a profound issue of conscience. In this instance we were able to move beyond the all too common attitude of "my country, right or wrong." What moved us was the plight of a particular age group: conscriptable young men who, as the result of public legislation, were prematurely required to resolve the conflict between the claims of conscience and the obligations of citizenship. Because the moratorium within which adolescents are normally allowed to clarify such issues was drastically foreshortened, the church had to defy the patriotic zeal of both some of its members and of the larger society in order to minister to the aggravated needs of one of its life-stage constituencies.

Constructive steps are possible when a congregation is unable to act. In some churches there is regular opportunity for persons to address fellow worshipers about matters of conscience. From the congregation to which I belong, here are several illustrations of the sorts of issues which have recently resulted in ad hoc action: after a visit to the Soviet Union a member aroused a number of people to write to the United States Vice President on behalf of a Russian family which had taken refuge in the American Embassy in Moscow, a concerned young man collected money for telegrams to be sent to those being held in the Embassy at Teheran, letters to Minnesota senators were solicited in support of the SALT accords, frequent appeals are made by the Community Action Center on behalf of a wide variety of local human needs. Probably there are members of this congregation who turn deaf ears to all such concerns. The point, however, is not to insist on 100% participation in any particular matter; the formation of individual conscience is too subtle for this to be possible very often. It is necessary that there be regular opportunity for persons to be able to locate within the membership those who, on a particular issue, are kindred spirits prepared to act. If the issue is divisive enough to preclude agreement and sufficiently important, the ad hoc group will seek others of similar concern in the larger community. Coalitions are organized and the issue pursued on the broadest possible base of support.

We should acknowledge that there may be those who are uncomfortable with ad hoc responses to issues. Apart from standing committees responsible for monitoring developments about matters agreed to by the entire group, I see no alternative for democratically ordered communities. Actually, there is a distinguished history for such an approach in the practice of at least one group of churches. The precedent is known as the congregational meeting and may occur as frequently as each week or on a monthly basis. Often held immediately after an occasion of public worship, one question is asked: in consequence of having been intentionally together in the presence of God, what matters of conscience are uppermost? Acknowledging both a commonality of intent and the persistence of individual distinctiveness, the group creates the opportunity regularly to ponder the possible leadings of the Holy Spirit into public life. The response might range from the recognition of a local concern for a distressed person or family to a grievous public issue about which it is no longer possible to remain silent. By whatever name such a meeting might be called, the point is that it is a necessary ingredient in the life of a supportive and defiant community. From one perspective what occurs during a liturgy and sermon might be thought to be a purely personal matter. That this is never the case is the inevitable consequence of the God worshiped. In neither Judaism nor Christianity is there any basis for public worship which supports indifference to issues of social justice. For reasons which John Donne suggested in his observation that "No man is an Iland, intire of it selfe . . ." (John Donne, *Devotions Upon Emergent Occasions*, XVII, London, n.d.), these religious traditions lead one to a grasp of one's identity as part of all humankind.

We conclude this discussion by calling attention to the findings of two social scientists who are concerned with the future of the city. This question prompted their research: Who are the people most active in the pursuit of *public good* in American cities? Their conclusions conform to what we have been suggesting about the characteristics of the holy community. Those who make a positive difference in urban life combine three ingredients: (1) a comprehensive life purpose, often a religious outlook, (2) membership in a supportive group, often a church, and (3) active participation in the give-and-take of public life, usually through membership in a political party (cf. Karl A. Ostrom and Donald W. Shriver, Jr., *Is There Hope for the City?* Philadelphia: Westminster, 1977). Since it was such a combination of faith, church, and public responsibility which informed my theological education, it is no surprise that it also underlies my understanding of a community of support and defiance.

Depending on the comprehensiveness of one's definition of catholicity it may overlap the communion of saints. We proceed on that assumption. *The emphasis on catholicity counteracts every inclination to parochialism.* By catholicity we identify the universal witness, in all of its variety, to the Lordship of Jesus Christ. While it may be true, as the church into whose ministry I was ordained insists, that the *whole church* is present in spirit within the life and worship of any properly ordered local congregation, *it was in order to recover* what they deemed to be a lost, or at least dangerously suppressed, understanding of catholicity that they took their radical position. To their sixteenth-century minds, anything that impinged on Christ's lordship was to be defied. For the left-wing of the Reformation, bishoprics and presbyteries, represented at least misleading approaches to the understanding of catholicity. For the radicals the lordship of Christ allowed nobody, by whatever "religious" means, to escape the issue of faith. In their recovery of the radical nature of that faith, mediated by but not identifiable with church structures, they made a most important contribution to the modern person's self-understanding. By their emphasis on the centrality of trust in Christ's lordship, we may see the source of Christian responsibility. Freed from all structures which might obscure that lordship, the believer takes responsibility for his or her own life and choices. In this double movement of faith and accountability, we have the Puritan understanding of vocation. Each person is responsible for his or her own decisions; each is also responsible to all because of the universality of the lordship by which individuals have been freed. Christ's lordship alone is the source of catholicity. That these congregationalists belonged to all others who affirmed that lordship is quite clear from their ecumenical activity. Distinctive to them was the insistence that participation in the universal church depended on the volition of each local congregation. They took membership in a national church, which appeared to be so much more "catholic," to be the perpetuation of patterns by which Christ's lordship was often more obscured than revealed. That their convictions were the source of much mischievous parochialism is evident from almost any familiarity with their history. That Christ's lordship is the key to Christian understanding of catholicity and that there are innumerable ways to avoid affirming that radical lordship is no less clear. It is these convictions which inform our present discussion.

To affirm belief in the church catholic is to insist that there are no restrictions of race, culture, age, sex, social status, education, etc., to those who may find the divine initiative and their consequent identity in the person and work of Jesus Christ. The churches are the ordinary means by which this initiative and identity are to be found. While the living God neither was nor is confined to the Hebraic tradition and its Christian and Islamic offspring, the catholic affirmation insists that no person is inherently unable to apprehend the grace of God in Christ's lordship. Thus, the emphasis on catholicity involves the joyful embrace of the most comprehensive community of believers: the great variety of contemporary men and women, those of earlier times and other places, and those who are yet to apprehend that grace. To acknowledge membership of the church catholic means to include as constitutive of one's self-understanding men and women of circumstances quite unlike one's own from past, present, and future. Every attempt to limit the universality of the gospel's ability to illumine and empower lives is prohibited by the insistence on the church's catholicity.

The implications of such belief become apparent upon realizing the narrowness of one's Christian experience. Many years ago Daniel J. Fleming published a small but useful book, *Each with His Own Brush: Contemporary Christian Art in Asia and Africa*, (New York: Friendship, 1938). Even those unable to read could not miss the point of the reproductions of Christian artwork from around the world. Every painting and piece of sculpture readily suggested the culture within which it was fashioned. It is not possible to confuse the technique of a Chinese painter with that of a neighboring Indian, nor that of an African sculptor with that of a Latin American. Yet all were attempting to give aesthetic expression to their varied experiences of the divine initiative perceived in the lordship of Jesus Christ. Because of the variety of artistic technique the person familiar only with Western art might, at least initially, deem them alien. Such a reaction demonstrates that the opportunities for parochialism are limitless. However, the Creed's insistence on the church catholic denies the validity of every such parochial judgment. Each person unavoidably encounters the gospel in modes—aesthetic, verbal, organizational—particular to the circumstance into which she or he is born. Against every temptation to absolutize those modes and their consequences for self-understanding stands the affirmation of catholicity. Without abandoning the unavoidable particularity of having one's origins in a specific time and place, the understanding of one's identity in Christ must take account of the rich diversity of experience denoted by belief in the church catholic. Ultimately nothing which has been experienced or expressed "in Christ" may be excluded from the believer's self-identity. It is this fact which permits us to see how affirmation of catholicity illumines our understanding of the importance of the life stages. However, it may be as difficult to affirm aspects of the life cycle as part of our present self-understanding as it is to be informed by statements influenced by unfamiliar artistic traditions.

Actually, I suspect that many people are better prepared to embrace the culturally unfamiliar than they are to get in touch with past stages of their own lives and to anticipate their own futures. For all of our parochialism, it is difficult not to be exposed daily to cultures other than our own. This may involve little more than an intellectual awareness of Japanese or West German products and the once unfamiliar names of their manufacturers. More likely, through popular magazines and public television, Americans' awareness of the aesthetic products of non-Western civilizations has at least been broadened in recent decades. We not only know but in varying degrees appreciate what was once alien. In not being as insular as once was the case, we are also better able to be nourished and challenged by some of the products and concerns of previously voiceless segments of the church catholic. The ready reception by some Western theologians of the concerns of Third World liberation theology is a case in point. We are beginning to appreciate that the understanding of the gospel which was informed by our socioeconomic myth that "bigger is always better" just may not be the last Christian word. Of the sources of that parochialism which obscure the claims of catholicity, few are more powerful than such myths which have exhalted quantity over all other considerations. The simple fact, as the Creed's emphasis on the catholic church has always implied, is that every part of any complex—an individual, a religious tradition, a particular society—urgently needs the correctives which are to be found in the other parts of the whole.

Every particularity distorts in its own way. If we are to avoid some of the worst consequences of unrestrained distortion, we need the perspectives of other particularities. Since there is no single, endlessly contemporary, universal model by which to be self-correcting of one's particularity, we have access only to the corrective inherent in catholicity. We may move beyond our particular distortions to the extent that we are able to recognize kinship with those who are apparently different from us. The key to this possibility lies in our ability to trust that there is enough similarity beneath cultural differences to be able to benefit from perspectives other than our own. Only so will we be able to move beyond the bondage of parochialism. However esoteric this may sound, it is in fact a daily experience. Every instance in which one senses in a member of the opposite sex the human kinship beneath obvious sexual differences illustrates the ability to transcend an inherent, universal limitation. The world simply has a different appearance from the other side of the line which separates the sexes, races, life stages, social-economic statuses, and/or the cultures. To be able to cross that line is a mark of catholicity.

Even less familiar than the need to be able to benefit from unfamiliar cultures is the argument which is central to this book. We contend that it is vital for our human development and for our growth in Christian faith that we embrace the various developmental stages which are normally parts of maturation. Few might quarrel with a theory of developmental stages. However, there are strong societal forces which discourage active pursuit of all of the stages. The fact of human aging illustrates an unavoidability which many struggle to avoid. Avoidance or neglect of one or more of the stages of normal human development is analogous to the refusal to acknowledge the kinship which connects us with "alien" cultures. Both are serious violations of the claims and rewards of catholicity.

Let us come at this discussion by first reconsidering the relationship of a part of anything to the whole. Without reducing any particular part to but an aspect of the whole, we insist that each part exists to enhance the whole. This will be clearer when we confine the discussion to the development of any human life. However, given the tendency to think from mechanical models in which the whole is absolutely dependent on the proper functioning of each part, it is important to emphasize that, in human affairs, there is ongoing tension between the claims of the whole and those of the part. We affirm this tension believing it to be one of the important sources of human creativity and well-being. That this belief is often contradicted by evidence of the destructiveness of such tension only forces us to recognize that there is no foolproof resolution of the tension between the part and the whole.

Within each human life there are many parts. Paul grapples in his letters (cf. 1 Cor. 12) with the fact of human differences and of the one Spirit which maximizes the contributions of which the varieties of gifts are capable. The important thing in any life is that the greatest number of one's parts be able to make their contribution to personal well-being. Of the many ways in which to think of the parts of a human life, I want to stress the developmental stages. I do so partly because there is increasing information from the social sciences about the actual issues which may be dealt with in the progress of lives from birth to death. While some of this has long been recognized and appreciated as a source of wisdom, recent study has produced both quantities of data and some suggestive theories about the life stages. Beyond this, I believe that intentional grappling with the ambivalences inherent at every stage is the ordinary means by which the question of Christ's lordship is encountered. Whether or not to relinquish the security and the satisfactions of a particular stage of life in order to engage the uncertainties of the next raises as vividly as may be ordinarily possible the question of the depth of one's trust in the goodness of the divine initiative. One's present satisfactions may be undeniably diminishing. In itself this will cause few to abandon them in favor of the unknowable, and possibly unachievable, satisfactions of the next stage of life. In addition to what are often unpersuasive lures from an uncertain future, we must acknowledge that it has never been a simple matter to trust in the living God. Taking comfort in the God of one's forebears or wildly hoping for some beneficent future are counterfeit forms of faith. Neither antiquarianism nor apocalypticism should be confused with the risky willingness to discern and to conform one's life to the divine initiative in what is always the perplexing and urgent present.

From this appreciation for the nature of the stages of human life, I sense within every life realities relevant to our discussion of catholicity. Not only is it imperative to move with the passage of time from one stage to the next, dying to former securities in order to be born to new risks and rewards, one needs also to realize that in that progress the past is never lost. It is only as one attempts to sustain the pretense of the past stage that it vanishes. In order to keep it, one must be willing to let it go. Although the accomplishments of all prior stages are instrumental to one's achievements in the present, they are not just that. Each stage of our lives had, and in an important sense continues to have, a life of its own. Nothing that we have been from the day that we were helpless infants to the present is gone. There remains within every adult both the terror and the glory of each of the stages through which we have passed: all of the helplessness and dependency, all of the achievements and consequent capacity for independence. Nothing that is human is alien to us *to the extent* that we are in touch with our own lives. There is a catholicity, a universality, about every life. A decade ago a book, *I'm OK, You're OK* (Thomas Anthony Harris, New York: Harper & Row, 1969), which left much to be desired as a guide to human relationships, made an aspect of this "catholicity" popular in its emphasis upon the continuing presence within all people of what were called the "tapes" of our inward child and adult. I am urging recognition of much more of the past as livingly present than just the voices of our parents and our childhood reactions to them. There is a great cast of characters—noble and base, major and minor—which move in and out of the "script" of our daily lives. To the extent that we acknowledge the size and variety of the cast and with the gentle hand of a stage director allow them their appropriate entrances and exits, we will be threatened by nothing that we encounter in the world. Nothing is inherently alien to us to the extent that we are familiar with our own continuing drama. Herein lies the importance of an understanding of human development for a discussion of catholicity. To the extent that we are conversant with the many selves which are part of our present self, however convenient it may seem to be at times to ignore one or more of them, we will be more aware of our kinship with the varieties of men and women whom we would often rather ignore. To the extent that we are so aware we will at least be less threatened by those who otherwise might appear to be alien.

There is a parochialism of the present self against which we need to be protected just as much as we need to be able to transcend the insularity of our particular community. The difference between these forms of parochialism which we have been using as though they were identical needs now to be noted. For as long as we pretend to be only what we appear to be at the present, that is for as long as we are out of touch with the many "characters" which constitute our own lives, we will be unable to affirm catholicity in anything but an intellectual way *at best*. If our present self is strong, we will be unable to relate constructively to forms of weakness as we encounter it in others. If our present self is weak, we will relate self-destructively to strengths we find in others. The simple point is that it is only as we are free to recognize the many components of our actual identity that we are able to affirm the church catholic. To believe in the catholic church is not to compound our all too natural inclination to think of "we" and "they." On the contrary, the affirmation of catholicity is the consequence of having discovered in Christ's lordship the great internal diversity which underlies one's identity. With this saving knowledge one is able to begin to recognize one's kinship with all sorts and conditions of men and women. So much of Scripture will spring to life because awareness of the complex self enables one to hear the words addressed to oneself rather than to others only.

I have suggested that the inward change comes before the ability to relate anew to what had been seen as "alien." While that is the order of experience which I wish to stress, it is important to appreciate that such internal change is ordinarily correlative with external experiences. Over the course of every human life two, interrelated processes are at work: (1) internal impetus to growth, and (2) external reaction to the impetus. We shall not judge whether it is the social expectation or the internal drive which is determinative. Both are necessary. Where there is no impetus, I doubt that external exhortation will evoke much growth. No impetus will flourish healthily if repeatedly discouraged by society. It is desirable, therefore, that those who provide the primary encouragements to others' internal initiatives be reasonably in touch with the many ingredients of their own identities. In this matter of being a confirmer of others, few things are clearer than that one cannot give what one lacks. To encounter terrifying behavior in a child assures a suppressive reaction. This is not to suggest that parents, or parent-substitutes, must encourage or even tolerate all internally prompted behavior. Such permissiveness is probably as damaging as are the efforts of parents, unacquainted with themselves, who try to suppress the child's every deviant behavior. Children seek information from those around them as to what to do with the many impetuses which arise within. All those who are important to the child may assist in the crucial search.

Since all parents have had but limited experience, and most are out of touch with some of the "characters" of their own story, it is important that children have access to a wider range of potentially confirming persons. This need, which is common to people of all ages, may be met in a number of environments. Chief among these for our present purposes is the church catholic. In its local composition it encompasses the broad spectrum of the life cycle of a particular culture. In its universality it includes men and women of other times and places who have found their identity in response to the divine initiative. In its Lord it sees the normative humanity of one fully identified with all humankind. That there might be no limits to the extent of that identification, the Creed insists that "he descended into hell."

In the liturgy and life of such a community, children of all ages are able to confirm and to be confirmed by each other *as they know themselves confirmed in Christ*. As a constant reminder of the range of human ages, the diverse membership is good in itself. Every arrangement which isolates age groups from opportunities for knowing people of other ages is a source of misinformation and prejudice. In addition to engendering harmful social attitudes, such isolation makes it unnecessarily difficult to recognize the presence of all ages within one's own life. Cut off from accurate reminders of their own youth, the elderly are left to fantasies rather than nourishing recollections of their own childhoods. Youth who lack meaningful contact with older people are deprived of opportunity to recognize by anticipation the prospect of their own aging.

For men and women of all ages to assist one another in the confirmations which all desire, it is necessary that they know themselves to be confirmed in Christ. For such persons it is not a matter of being a certain age nor of reluctantly acknowledging reality they would rather conceal but of embracing the present stage of their lives *as from God*. It is this ability to be what one is, with but a minimum of pretense, which enables one to confirm others. Such men and women have kept their cast of internal characters alive while their major and minor roles changed with the passage of time. They have been open to instruction from God through the opportunities and limitations peculiar to the present stage of life: the vast, often unfocused energies of youth, the confining obligations and unique rewards of being the parents of small children, the single person's need to transform loneliness into the ability to be alone, the reservoir of experience and the sense of life's brevity of the elderly. In such people, others perceive something of the divine initiative and are part of that catholic company to whom we point as the communion of saints. They claim no particular achievements, but they are gladly open to the present as a gift from God. Through them, others are able to be more intentional about their lives without obscuring either memories or future hopes.

It is by such confirming experiences that one begins to appreciate the rewards of belief in the church catholic. Having been enabled to embrace the variety of selves within one's own life, one affirms kinship with ever more of humanity. It is not a matter of being just like them, which cultural differences make impossible, but of knowing that behind all dissimilarities there is the affinity of those who understand their humanity as a great gift, who affirm the successive life stages as God's ordinary means of self-acquaintance and of learning to relate to others, whose identity in Christ has freed them to get about the business peculiar to their time of life and place. Thus it is, in the great diversity of its membership and through confirming association with those members who are intentional about the stages of their lives, that the church catholic is a community of support and defiance.

Priests and *Prophets*

Of the many biblical forms of ministry, two predominate. It is with reference to the persistent tensions between priest and prophet that we may both conclude the present discussion. As was often the case in history, it will be useful to set in sharp contrast those offices which must ultimately be held together.

Inherent to a priestly ministry is the maintenance of continuity. There is the repeated rhythm of the seasons—both natural and ecclesiastical—and there are rhythms in lives. In the daily and seasonal patterns of institutions and of individuals, profound support may be found. By such continuities we are helped to relate to ourselves and to others; they assure us by repetition. Progress through the life cycle presupposes, in part, a cyclical sense of human experience. This is an important aspect of the support which many find in the holy community. The rhythms of my life are akin to those of all other lives; many have been where I today find myself. The biological bases of a priestly ministry are both obvious and good. Planting and cultivation and harvesting are undeniable *and* necessary ingredients of life. In fact, such continuities are *a* way of understanding life. The rhythms of life are a continuing source of support.

The problem is that a part seeks to become the whole. The undeniable continuities are forever suggesting, or insisting, that they *are* reality rather than but one aspect of an endless tension. Those who see chaos as the alternative to continuity are probably the privileged who are determined to resist every threat to their status. The present rhythms may yield limited rewards but they often seem preferable to any imaginable alternative. Those dying of boredom, which has many faces, may prefer that death to the remote possibility of rebirth.

Enter the prophet!

If it is the tendency of the priestly ministry to stress life's continuities, the prophet is captive to discontinuity. If a cyclical metaphor describes priestliness, the prophetic may be represented only by a linear model. If biology is the ultimate source of continuity, history is the prime source of the imperative to change. If the priest is primarily supportive, the prophet is inherently defiant. If life's continuities prompt us to arrest progress through the life stages in order to avoid the peril of uncertainty, it is the appreciation of discontinuity which impels one to risk for the sake of the yet to be. If the one is disposed to quiescent gratitude, the other is marked by impatient disapproval of the status quo. If chaos is for one the enemy, for the other it is resignation.

Both of these powerful models, which clearly correspond to central aspects of human experience, are central to the self-understanding of the community of support and defiance. One or the other may predominate at any time in individual lives; each enjoys periods of dominance in the institution. The crucial matter is for the holy community not to lose sight of the fact that both are necessary for its ordinary work of assisting men and women to persist in the cyclical *and* linear tasks of the life stages.

VII. | *Self-hate, Self-love, Self-denial*

Somebody has said that, "The poet must bear the full burden of consciousness." As a description of the artist's vocation, the statement is both true and misleading. It is true that, much more than most people, the artist is one who is unable to insulate her or himself against the alienating forces of the times. Whereas most people have a variety of devices behind which to hide, the artist is both exposed to destructiveness afoot and may have some sense of the direction from which more hopeful possibilities are emerging. On this understanding artists are both involuntarily sensitive to negative factors in their society and, by combining assent to this vulnerability with skill in some artistic form, willing exposers of social evil and evokers of qualities of life otherwise hidden. As such they function much as did the Hebrew prophets: calling attention compellingly to inhumanity ignored by many and beckoning their audience to more humane life and organization. A society without such pained and paining heralds is in grave danger.

Despite my great respect for persons called to such important work, and because I intend to apply the original statement to Christians, it is at least misleading—and could be presumptuous—to claim that the artist alone must bear the full burden of human consciousness. Often perhaps a tragic hero, the artist is not the Messiah. Inasmuch as he or she assumes the burden of consciousness, it is in order that all others may themselves undertake greater consciousness of their own experience. It is only thus that we both assume our God-given, human responsibility and, thereby, realize our kinship with all humankind.

Further, as a Christian I am committed to the belief that the full burden/glory of human consciousness has, once and for all, been borne by him who is called the Christ. It was this conviction which prompted the authors of The Apostles' Creed to insist on Jesus' birth, death, and descent into hell. In these affirmations the fathers of the church claimed Christ's kinship with all sorts and conditions of men and women. There is no level of consciousness—no blackest despair nor euphoric fantasy, no self-hatred nor creative yearning—with which the Christ is unfamiliar. Every potential of the human consciousness, which is to say every latency of our God-createdness, has been embraced as possible means for love of both God and neighbor. Nothing human is inherently to be demeaned.

Freed for Ourselves

This radical assertion is both terrifying and liberating. It may also be quite unfamiliar. Indeed this unfamiliarity probably underlies both the terror and the liberation one feels upon being told that there is nothing in our widest experience which may not be a vehicle for expressing love for each other and for God. We are so accustomed to assuming that since only aspects of ourselves are acceptable to others, only parts of who we are are acceptable to God. At best we have been taught to be *selectively* self-loving.

Possibly more hopeful is the need to see, *in our attitudes towards ourselves,* the source of our inhumanity: we are incapable of the self-love to which Jesus' summary of Hebraic law exhorts us. It is hard to believe that it is with our actual, incomplete, broken resources that we are to give evidence in our behavior of the love of God. We largely believe that it will only be when we have become something other than we now are that we will be capable of such life-giving deeds. For all of our mighty professions of faith in God and all our heroic efforts to

be the good neighbor, our professions and efforts are doomed
for as long as we are wrapped in self-hatred. This is the sin
against the Holy Ghost from which we need rescue; for, in our
alienation from ourselves, we both dishonor and decline whatever modest good we might have done and are blinded to our
kinship with all human life. By self-hatred we express our
scorn for God.

My assertion that nothing human is inherently to be demeaned is unsettling enough when applied to others. It is the
most radical surgery when we realize its equal, and necessarily
prior, applicability to ourselves. In our tormented present condition and with our chaotic history and our tangled network of
relationships, God has said "Yes!" Even we are loved! Grasped
by and grasping this almost unbelievable assurance, who are
we to hate that which God has so loved? Jesus gave his life in
order that we might be brought to our senses. Is it not by his
willing identification with the full range of human consciousness that we are freed to undertake the loving work of self-
acquaintance?

Is it not by the experience of growing familiarity with ourselves (depths and heights, and the potential for more of both)
that we recognize our sinews of kinship with all others? It is
not first *from* ourselves but simply *for* ourselves that we are
freed. Since those becoming familiar with themselves gradually
relinquish the pretenses behind which they conceal their self-
hatred, it is by self-acquaintance that we are at liberty to act
anew toward our neighbor. Self-indulgence is the peril on the
far side of self-hatred. Self-denial is what becomes possible in
consequence of a loving acquaintance with one's self. Knowing
and valuing my brokenness and my potential for some good is
the basis for the sense of kinship with others. Their rejoicing is
no occasion for resentment; their grieving no occasion for re-
moving myself. Far or near we are of one blood, one origin, one
destiny. Self-denial thus becomes an expression of felt kinship
rather than the attempt to suppress the self's desire to serve
only itself. Love for the neighbor is positively motivated by
acknowledged kinship rather than by the negative effort to sup-

press the selfishness which arises from self-hatred. The ordinary exhortation to self-denial is meaningless except as the self, however imperfect, is positively valued. The first work for those victimized by self-hatred is not self-denial. They must first learn to affirm their particular imperfection. Then the appeal to self-sacrifice implies a real struggle. That the outcome may be neighborly is the result of acknowledged common imperfection which self-hatred is always concealing.

There remains an enduring tension between the claims of the self and of others. There is no formula for how much and when I am to yield my desires to the needs of another. Those situations always involve judgments as to what action, or inaction, promises the better result. For example, a parent does not always do what may be requested by a child who must learn to take risks in the interest of growth. When to assist and to desist is simply not describable for every imaginable situation.

My point is to emphasize that, however one acts in such situations, it must be from self-love rather than from self-hatred. It is only as the believer is able to assent to the limited givens of his or her life that life-giving self-denial is possible. Deeds motivated by self-hatred cannot benefit others. Prompted by resentment or condescension, such deeds fail to see and honor the neighbor as she or he is seen by God. Only as we so see do we appreciate both our kinship with the other and the neighbor's God-given nobility.

The ordinary error is to limit life's struggle to the conflict between self-love and self-hate. This is the primary conflict which is overcome by the awareness that we have no warrant for hating that which God loves. It is in faith that we are able to say "yes" to our particulars which, with their unavoidable limits, are just like those of our neighbor. Able to assent to these uneven particulars, we become capable of Christian self-denial. The tension between the claims of the self and the other are not automatically or permanently resolved. Sin is too enduring for such reassurances to be possible. What is possible, however, is twofold: (1) in a given context, I (the believer) will see that the needs of the other are of greater value than my own, and (2) I have *some* resources to share.

In the midst of his farewell discourses in the Fourth Gospel, Jesus characterizes that self-denial which is self-love motivated: the good shepherd behaves differently from the hired man. There is a loving sense of self which is capable of self-sacrifice (John 10:11–18). In chapter 15 we find the description of that capacity toward which Christian life lures us: ". . . greater love has no man than this, that a man lay down his life for his friends" (vs. 13).

Everything depends on the inclusiveness of our understanding of friendship and on the depths of the self-love by which we know our kinship with all humankind. The alternative is a life progressively distanced from those whom we do not recognize as our neighbors.

Illustrations from Life and Literature

While there is no doubt about the importance of self-denial in the believer's life, many Christians are unaware of the self which is to be denied. Actually, most people affirm a blatant contradiction: belief that the creation is good and that self-denial is the prescribed response in *all* situations. While I affirm the doctrine of human sin and am all too aware of my bondage to it, I refuse the simplistic exhortation to constant self-denial. Not only does this emphasis contradict my experience, self-denial is often a means of avoiding a situation demanding action.

Equally serious is the fact that it assumes that the self which I deny is the self which needs to be denied. We are more complex beings than is recognized in the simple prohibition of self-expression. The purpose of the present book has been to suggest both how difficult and how crucial it is to identify the self which needs to be denied. I do not assume that the accomplishment of this difficult task of identification assures that the appropriate self will then be denied. We are too gifted at avoiding the good to permit any such confidence. Until the self to be denied has been identified, however, we will continue congratulating our success in addressing the wrong issues rather than struggling with the real issues of Christian life.

In order that the obligation to self-denial be properly understood, we must affirm two difficult things. First, that no matter the extent of our conscious alienation from God, it is in God's image that we all are made. In every human life, no matter how diminished, there is the arousable capacity to love. No compromise is possible with this elemental conviction, which is the ultimate source of hope for improvement. Second, that because of the difficulty of affirming God's presence as the key to one's identity, varieties of ways have been proposed to curtail human selfhood. For example, there are what Reinhold Niebuhr referred to as angelic and animalistic fallacies. Rather than affirming the God-given tensions inherent in human lives, we retreat from such dizzying freedom into either the angelic assumption that all will be right by getting rid of one's body or, less frequently espoused by Christians, that all will be right by simply giving in to one's body. Because we are both self-transcending and grounded in the world of nature, neither of these alternatives for denying human freedom is acceptable. It will not do to reduce self-denial to either the rejection of one's body, which is the common assignment, or the insistence that there is nothing more to one than her or his body. Both are patently false.

Clearly, these are tricky matters. We are called by God to be some kind of a self and are called to some form of self-denial. Every self-obliteration is the attempt to deny an essential aspect of the image of God in us. Each self-inflation is the attempt to obscure contingencies from which there is no escape in the world. Neither alternative takes seriously the commandment to love the broken self of yet limitless potential for whose sin, we insist, Christ died.

Clearly also, these are matters with which men and women have long struggled. I do not pretend to have grasped how these complementary ingredients of our createdness should be related. My hope is much more modest than that. I suggest that by paying closer attention to our actual experience over the course of life's stages, we may more willingly recognize the conflicts which have persisted: the life-long tension between our capacity for faith and the inescapability of doubt, the ability to love and the enduring power to hate, the continuing experience of joy and a persistent sadness. By these I mean only to suggest enduring tensions in all lives. Thus, that which we have denied because we have been told to do so, or because we could not imagine how our conflictedness could benefit us or others, we must learn to affirm. This is not the last step in the process of our Christian maturation, but it is clearly the often-neglected first step.

There is more than enough crucial material to understand as we try to take that first faltering move toward more accurate self-understanding. Whether or not we will be capable of self-denial once we have become clearer about ourselves may be more a matter of grace than of will. What I am convinced of about this process of self-clarification is two-fold: (1) that we will move beyond that self-righteousness which results from self-denial for which we now have the will, and (2) that the God who fashioned our initial complexity will be gracefully present to us as we struggle to affirm both our capacity for self-transcendence and the constraints of our contingent lives.

I am increasingly persuaded that there are times of life when one is better able to begin this work of self-clarification. That is, there are periods during which we are more inclined to remove the masks with which we have pretended there was nothing more to us than they suggested. A conversation late in Ingmar Bergman's film, *Fanny and Alexander*, suggests both the difficulty and the urgency of their removal. Bishop Edvard Vergérus has married the actress and widow, Emilie. Partly as the result of the contrast between their styles of life, but especially because of his harsh discipline of her son, Alexander, who had been generously indulged in his parental home, Edvard finds himself hated both by the boy and by Emilie. Having lived a righteous and ascetic life—". . . wise, broad-minded, and fair"—he is unprepared to discover that anyone could hate him. In sharp opposition to Emilie, who played so many stage roles that she finally did not know who she was, the Bishop has been single-minded.

> "... I have only one mask. But it is branded into my flesh. If I try to tear it off—" (Ingmar Bergman, *Fanny and Alexander*, New York: Pantheon Books, 1982, p. 188).

Because he truly loves her, he may wish he could remove the branded mask. That he is unable to do so illustrates the truth of what Norman Mailer calls the law of life: "... one must grow or else pay more for remaining the same." (Norman Mailer, *The Deer Park*, New York: Putnam, 1955, p. 346).

The middle years of life are for many a period in which one's masks are at least recognizable. Some things happen unavoidably during these years which may heighten one's instructability. Like Bergman's Bishop, however, there is no assurance that one will be able to discard, or even significantly modify outmoded ways. The opportunity is there, but many are terrified by their nakedness without familiar masks and unsure that anything more adequate can be fashioned, and they determine to deny change. This is the most common form of self-denial in the middle years. Beauty parlors and other profitable agencies which promise to conceal the effects of time are predicated on the widespread pretense of such denial. Does this not suggest that, for Christians, there is first something to be affirmed, some mask(s) to be acknowledged, before the proper work of self-denial may be discovered?

Those who prove teachable during these years may initially have to pay a heavy price. Many of our masks have become attached to our flesh. The precondition of the promise of new life, appropriate to one's age and stage, is the painful removal of those pretenses with which we have become comfortable. Nobody casually relinquishes the self-understanding and ways of self-presentation at which all gradually arrive. It would be insane to do so.

Fortunately, whether or not change will occur is not just a matter of mere will or of sheer willfullness. A double process of instruction is at work during the middle years. From *within* there is the gradual awareness both of diminishing satisfactions from many of the activities previously considered important and of the desire to give expression to aspects of one's self long neglected. From *without* a variety of things once important to one's sense of well-being are taken from us. It is this combination of inner and outer changes which I have come to recognize as part of God's pedagogy for us at mid-life. It is not for nothing that we grow older. There are at least two comparably traumatic stages in lives—adolescence and advanced aging—but neither of these combines the inner and outer promptings which are so potentially instructive. The middle years will be God's last dramatic opportunity to call us to greater wholeness. God does this by recalling us to ourselves.

Let me illustrate this from the private journal which Dag Hammarskjöld kept during most of his adult life. At age forty-seven, a few months prior to his election as General Secretary of the United Nations, he wrote: "Never, 'for the sake of peace and quiet,' deny your own experience or convictions" (Dag Hammarskjöld, *Markings*, trans. Leif Sjöberg and W. H. Auden, New York: Alfred A. Knopf, 1967, p. 84).

Out of context his exhortation is seemingly unexceptionable. (As I shall suggest momentarily, however, there is much more to it than is immediately evident. Indeed, perhaps without realizing it, Hammarskjöld has combined, as though they were similar, the very realities which come under siege in mid-life.) While his sentence stands by itself in the published journal, it appears in the midst of several entries about his profound loneliness. Both prior to and after the exhortation not to deny one's experience and convictions are questions and laments which arise from his personal isolation.

> Is your disgust at your emptiness to be the only life with which you fill it?
> What makes loneliness an anguish
> Is not that I have no one to share my burden,
> But this:
> I have only my own burden to bear. (*Ibid.*, p. 83, 85.)

I find these entries moving and revealing. Since this journal was, by Hammarskjöld's specific instruction in his will, only to be published posthumously, we may assume that nobody was aware of his inner life. On the surface he was an eminently successful figure and socially popular bachelor. The contrast between a person's public appearance and private feelings is rarely as clearly revealed as was made possible by the publication of reflections which he had kept scrupulously private. Those who knew him best must have been at least surprised to discover what underlay his calm appearance.

These might be interesting disclosures to many readers. In the context of what I am trying to say, they are of momentous importance for two reasons. First, because Hammarskjöld indicates that it was with his inability to have satisfying relationships, especially with women, that he struggled. That reality, on which he had not previously reflected in his journal, became of paramount importance in mid-life. At the time of his greatest public achievement, in which he demonstrated to a family world-distinguished for its public service that he was a true and deserving son, he records the profoundest sense of inadequacy and yearning. Two entries from that same period reveal both a brief glimmer of hope that his experience might yet be richer and the reason why it would not be.

> ... When the worries over your work loosen their grip, then this experience of light, warmth, and power. From without—a sustaining element, like air to the glider or water to the swimmer. An intellectual hesitation which demands proof and logical demonstration prevents me from "believing"—in this, too.
>
> Incapable of being blinded by desire,
> Feeling I have no right to intrude upon another,
> Afraid of exposing my own nakedness,
> Demanding complete accord as a condition for a life together:
> How could things have gone otherwise? (*Ibid.*, p. 84, 85.)

Apparently he experienced a momentary sense of the possibility of a more satisfying life: "... this experience of light, warmth, and power. From without. . . ." But because of his convictions—"An intellectual hesitation . . ."—he had to be re-

signed to the fact that, for him, things could not have gone
otherwise. How else can we see this than as a great man's tragic
resignation to the challenges of mid-life? One of his last entries
for 1952 suggests the depths of his despair: "Now at the age of
forty-seven, I am ridiculous because my knowledge of exactly
what I am putting down on paper does not stop me from doing so."

For the second reason why these disclosures are presently
very important let me repeat my original excerpt from *Markings*: "Never, 'for the sake of peace and quiet,' deny your own
experience and convictions." As I suggested parenthetically
then, there is much more to this statement than immediately
meets the eye. On superficial reading one might equate experience and convictions. That would be a grievous error, which
Hammarskjöld himself may have made. In this, if true, he erred
in a way which it is crucial both for us to be aware of and to
learn to avoid. Experience and convictions are utterly dissimilar realities. It is to this that the onset of mid-life is attempting
to alert us.

Ideally over the course of one's life, there will be regular
interplay between one's experiences and one's convictions. Our
problems at mid-life, which I contend are evidence of God's
gracious presence, arise from the fact that, in this society, the
interplay is minimal and discouraged. As the result of multiple
factors (the churches being one), we have elevated convictions
over experiences. For us it is by convictions that experience is
to be understood and controlled. As I see it, experience has no
rights of its own. It is to be sought, inasmuch as we are so
encouraged, by criteria derived from our convictions; and,
worse yet, experience is evaluated exclusively by these criteria.
We are required to account from our experiences to our convictions. Such experience as may be inexplicable is deemed at
least inferior if not positively harmful.

In this preference for convictions, we find both the source
of the peculiar dynamism of our society, and especially of our
economy, and of what is often referred to as the malaise of mid-
life. The very words we use to characterize these years—

malaise, trauma, or predicament rather than opportunity or opening or last chance—reveals our bias for order and control. For us, control is what life is all about, and the ability to control is seen and rewarded in those who prove themselves able to get accredited, to set and achieve goals, to maintain orderly lives. Those whom we honor are those who manage to contain experience—to confine its randomness, to rein in its enthusiasm, to classify its novelty, to suppress its passions. Is it really surprising that a purposefully controlled, eminently successful, Swedish world diplomat, would, in mid-life, ask himself the following questions:

> Is the bleakness of this world of mine a reflection of my poverty or my honesty, a symptom of weakness or of strength, an indication that I have strayed from my path, or that I am following it?—Will despair provide the answer? (*Ibid.*, p. 86.)

However Hammarskjöld answered his questions, and the answer seems evident to me, I take his struggles to be those of a profoundly religious man. Many have identified him as an important "modern mystic." He wanted supremely to believe that, with all of his brokenness, he had a calling from God. He was able to acknowledge that he would never be able to be, as others were, a complete man; but he was unwilling thereby to be anything less than he might be. For what he was able to be as a public person, the world is permanently indebted to him. In what he could not reveal while alive, we have his posthumous gift. That he so intended, or at least hoped, is clear from the next to last entry for the year from which we have quoted so extensively.

> How ridiculous, this need of yours to communicate! Why should it mean so much to you that at least one person has seen the inside of your life? Why should you write down all this, for yourself, to be sure—*perhaps*, though, for others as well? (*Ibid.*, p. 87.)

Perhaps Dag Hammarskjöld's middle years illustrate God's last dramatic opportunity to call us by recalling us to ourselves. By such unsettling experiences of grace, if we are able to allow them to occur and to acknowledge their transforming power, we may see again, though in a new way, who really is in control.

Human Consciousness: Burden and Glory

With these illustrations in mind of bondaged lives, we may return to the suggestion made at the outset of this chapter that it is the Christian's responsibility to bear ever more of the burden/glory of human consciousness. To do this two things are required: (1) to assent to the rewards which accompany the burden of consciousness, and (2) to identify self-hatred as the initial and enduring resistance to the enlargement of consciousness. Both clarifications are crucial.

It is incomplete to insist on human consciousness only as a burden. T. S. Eliot was not wrong to observe that humans can tolerate only a limited amount of reality—cf. "Burnt Norton" (*Four Quartets*, New York: Harcourt, Brace & World, 1943, p. 3). There is evidence everywhere of the preference for old wives' tales over truth, parochial prejudice over appreciation of the larger picture, for emphasis on my interests over those of anybody else. In varying ways we are all so trapped: "My mind is made up. Don't bother me with the facts!" For everybody the invitation to enlarge one's consciousness of the range of human experience is probably initially resisted. We are creatures of habit as much in our thinking as in our behavior. I often find myself impatient with students for the ease with which they assume that new ideas can be embraced. What they fail to realize is there is a world of difference between ideas in the mind and the need to act anew in consequence of the presence of such new ideas. Undergraduate work is often just playing with ideas with no intention to commit oneself to their consequences, refusing to struggle with the mundane but important conflicts and resources in every significant relationship.

Some students move beyond philandering. Some in the academy get caught up in their learning and are never again the same. Not long ago an alumna of 25 years past wrote to me thus: "My four years at Carleton irrevocably changed my life. I thank whatever providence brought me there . . ." Such are probably but a small portion of the undergraduate population, though one must be cautious in identifying those so transformed. While one might wish their numbers were larger, the fact is that some are lured to deeper human consciousness by what is not for them just a burden. It always involves lots of hard work, and it is burdensome to have internalized new truth. But it is never just that. Were that the case one could only assume perverse, self-hurtful motivation. There is also the excitement of sustained curiosity, at times almost euphoria, in the search for greater understanding of a problem. While the materials in question may be dramatically dissimilar, I have seen this experience in those pursuing the physical sciences as often as in students of literature. There is a glory as well as a burden in the enlarged consciousness. Both are intrinsic to the reality of being a human person ever more fully aware of the contingencies of both natural and historical existence. Both the rewards and the burden of such consciousness are latent in our creativeness. They are from God. It is evidence of human sinfulness to wish to separate them or to prefer one to the other.

At this point we must proceed with greater cautiousness. For what I wish to suggest, which is little more than a hunch, is that the deterrent to the enlargement of consciousness, which I believe to be God's will for us, is self-hatred. By this I mean to identify both that tendency, marked in contemporary life, to wish that one were other than one is and the reluctance to assent to one's limitations. These are very close to being the same thing. By the former, however, I identify the tendency to envy those who are necessarily different from oneself. By the latter I mean the spirit of resentment that one is subject to certain natural and historical contingencies. The former is seemingly blind to the fact that those envied may also be wishing that their lives were other than they are. The spirit of resentment seems blind to the universal fact of human contingency. Whatever its form or cause, it is characteristic of self-hatred both to decline enlargement of consciousness and to refuse to do that limited good of which all lives are capable.

Key to the enlargement of consciousness is acceptance of the givens of one's life. Theologically this means assent to the fact of one's createdness. I did not bring myself into existence. I live by virtue of the love and lust of my parents. By this I intend no disrespect. All conception is at least thus complexly motivated. In that power to recreate we have evidence of God's gracious presence in our midst. Often misused, and not a universal obligation, the capacity to generate new lives is a vital gift from God. The fact that each person is the child of particular parents, born at a definite time and place, is undoubtedly the primary given of every life. Our birth could not have been other than it was. Only one sperm may fertilize the egg. By that fact each of us has certain gifts and certain limitations. This is true for same-sex children of the same parents. To resent these facts, to wish that they might have been otherwise, may be unavoidable during the self-consciousness and uncertainty of adolescence. Such resentment is perilous as a lifelong attitude. It precludes both the capacity for self-acquaintance and the willingness to do such good as one can with such limited gifts as each of us possesses. While she or he remains endlessly self-preoccupied, the victim of self-hatred cannot undertake the work of self-acquaintance. The love which is its precondition is lacking.

Such resentment against the givens of one's life, which is resentment against God, results in both loveless self-denial and the refusal of love for the neighbor. Resentment against the peculiar contingencies of my life results in niggardliness out of fear that anything of my undervalued self which I give up will diminish me. By contrast, the ability to assent to the particular strengths and weaknesses of my own life, which is how I understand self-love, is what makes self-denial possible. Only as I have embraced my distinctive contingencies have I begun to appreciate my kinship with all humankind, which is comparably contingent. Assent to my own strengths and weaknesses, which could not have been otherwise, yields a generosity toward the neighbor because I appreciate both our kinship in frailty and realize that, in many situations, even I can do some good. In this understanding self-denial, about the ease of which I am not sanguine, begins to make sense: there is a valued self which, in certain circumstances, I am called on to deny in the name of a wider love.

He Who Saw Life Whole

Throughout this book I have argued that the progressive work of the life stages is an inescapable obligation/opportunity for those who profess Christian faith. Finally, let us look again at this work in light of what we have immediately been saying about assenting to the particular givens of one's life as the key to the enlargement of consciousness. The direction in which our lives should be growing can be stated simply: we are to try to see life ever more fully in its entirety. Our resources for this task are, for reasons of our varied contingencies, not identical. The realities with which we must grapple over the course of life's stages are, however, the same.

Without attempting here to summarize the specific tasks at the various stages through which lives pass, I would suggest two important ingredients of the desire to see life whole. First, one must embrace the unhaltable demand for change. Second, we must possess resources which enable us to affirm the ongoing conflicts within each life and between lives. The first is clearly from God: nothing remains static. The second, which we wrongly tend to think of as remediable imperfection, is, I suggest, also part of our God-givenness. William Blake concurs:

> Without contraries is no progression. Attraction and repulsion, reason and energy, love and hate, are necessary to human existence. (William Blake, *The Marriage of Heaven and Hell*, London, New York: Oxford University Press, 1975, Plate 3.)

About the first little needs to be said. At the heart of the biblical religion is the affirmation of both God and time as dynamic. It is that simple. Despite every effort to immobilize God, thereby to gain the impression that humankind is in control, God breaks through again and again with the reminder, "Behold, I make all things new . . ." (Rev. 21:5). Nothing in all human experience, at whatever level of consciousness, is static. From the most obscure individual life to the most celebrated of the world powers, all come and go. They have their day; they do not endure.

Without our willing them—indeed! despite all our efforts to

arrest or deny them—changes occur. The human task is to recognize gladly the instruction from God which inheres in this brute fact of change. It is the function of our life in history to remind us of both the inescapability of change and of our own transiency. This is the burden and glory of human consciousness which we must affirm as Christians.

With reference to the desire to see life whole, we spoke of two ingredients: (1) the inevitability of change and (2) the need to affirm the inescapable tensions over the course of a life. The second is peculiarly difficult for Western people who have been persuaded that single-mindedness is the norm to be sought. The success of this persuasion results largely from our reverence for the efficiency which single-mindedness makes possible. The success to which we aspire is, we believe, ever better assured by living efficiently. Distractions are, at all costs, to be shunned.

The trouble is that there is no way thoroughly to put down those ambivalences which, as we say, distract. They are intrinsic to who we are. We want both solitude and conviviality; we want both responsibility and to be free of it; we want both to be admired and to be ignored; we want both life and we want death; we both love and we hate. The task is to refuse any longer to consider these wantings and not wantings as distractions. They are the material of our lives and have great potential for our instruction. Perhaps nobody has put the task as forcefully—because few have paid the price as completely—as has Ralph Ellison in the last pages of *Invisible Man*. While the American Black experience is not universal, it has more similarity to other lives than is ordinarily recognized. Most people who will read this book have believed, as "Invisible" was led to do, that the system of the predominant group will reward those who are faithful to it. Few are as frequently disabused of this belief as was he, as blatantly used and misused, but in the middle years many discover that they were at least oversold. Having been driven to irresponsibility and hiding, the invisible man—who, as he says, may be invisible but not blind—realizes that he must reemerge. It is the *spirit* of his reemergence to

which I would call attention because he has come to the realization *on his own, from his actual experience.*

> ... The very act of trying to put it all down has confused me and
> negated some of the anger and some of the bitterness. So it is that
> now I denounce and defend, or feel prepared to defend. I condemn
> and affirm, say no and say yes, say yes and say no. I denounce
> because though implicated and partially responsible, I have been
> hurt to the point of abysmal pain, hurt to the point of invisibility.
> And I defend because in spite of all I find that I love. In order to
> get some of it down I *have* to love. I sell you no phony forgiveness,
> I'm a desperate man—but too much of your life will be lost, unless
> you approach it as much through love as through hate. So I ap-
> proach it through division. So I denounce and I defend and I hate
> and I love. (Ralph Ellison, *Invisible Man*, New York: Random
> House, 1972, p. 566 ff.)

Those comparative few who have been discouraged from recognizing or expressing negative feelings will have to be helped
to acknowledge their capacity for hate as well as for love. The
great majority of all colors must attend carefully to Ellison's
warning of how much is at stake in overcoming self-hatred: ". . .
too much of your life will be lost, its meaning lost, unless you
approach it as much through love as through hate." What most
of us have to learn is our own equivalent of "Black is beautiful!"

This is the burden and glory of human consciousness; this
is the whole life which we both want and do not want to see.
In this ineradicable ambivalence, which we are able to acknowledge only as we are disenchanted with the pursuit of
success and fatigued by its necessary efficiency, lie potentials
for the enrichment of lives. In no instance is the enrichment
cost free nor can we be sure that we possess it permanently.
Pressures from the society discourage such affirmation and societal lures endlessly tempt us to believe that we can be satisfied by something less than our full, complex selves. We are not
told by Ellison that the invisible man retained the convictions
with which he emerged from hiding.

Ultimately, we are saved by the irrepressible need to be more
fully conscious of our own experience. Nothing less will do.
And even this awareness—this irrepressible desire to affirm the

full potential of our God-given lives—will sustain us only if we recognize the need for it as part of God's gifts to us. It is not waywardness which so prompts us; we are prompted to greater self-awareness by means within which reflect the strange wisdom of the Creator. Otherwise the glory of it would be crushed by the burden of realizing what is involved in being human. We are saved by the realization that, at heart, we are but children of God. In this there is sufficient glory and burden for all.

In this light we know why Greek statuary is not our model for the truly human. Their artists desired perfection of physical form, and they fashioned many beautiful things. A better model for Christians is the paintings of Matthias Grünewald. To be repulsed by his broken, diseased Christ reflects the desire to obscure our own sickness, to pretend a health (wholeness) which we lack. In the Grünewald pieces, which were prepared for the hospital chapel at Isenheim, Christ was so depicted that every patient was able to see the kinship between his brokenness and that of the crucified Messiah. From that ability to identify with Christ grows the hope which is the precondition of any recovery. It was not the well but the sick for whom Jesus came. Ultimately, those who considered themselves healthy were unreachable. If we are content with our present, concealing lives, that and only that will be our reward.

At all times it is absolutely necessary that we recognize Jesus' kinship with ourselves. Whatever more he is, he was one like us. Whatever else his healing may mean to a believer, it involves the hope that it is our particular, limited but God-given resources which may be liberated for doing good. None of us has exceptional abilities: in this lies our universality. All of us have some particular gifts through which we may learn to do good; in this lies our uniqueness. It was by entering the depths of God-given humanity in the events of his death that Jesus manifested his universality. This is normative self-love: capable, for the sake of a greater good, of the ultimate self-denial. No circumstance was alien to him; no one hopelessly lost. In him we see most clearly the burden and the glory of God-given humanity. In his Spirit we become able to affirm the burden and glory of our particular God-givenness. The cross *is* God's strangely good language. By entering into the last hours of Jesus' life, which seemed progressively to isolate him from all human associations, we may know our connectedness—with our own life, with our neighbor, and to God—in the midst of seeming utter disconnection.

In the midst of Jesus' farewell addresses in the Fourth Gospel, he provided the disciples an amazing reassurance: "I tell you, whoever believes in me will do such things as I do, and things greater yet, because I am going to the Father" (John 14:12, Goodspeed translation). As the Artist who bore and revealed the glory and the burden of whole human consciousness, he assures his followers that, in the Holy Spirit, they share his vocation. In our time and with reference to the distinctive forces which now discourage us from seeing life whole, it is we who are to do yet greater things. Our first, tentative steps will be tiny. They will, however, be in the direction of that self-love which alone makes self-denial possible. So help us, God.